Contents

For Bernie and Sadie

Foreword

I write this foreword in the wake of the presidential election of 2016, a year of reckoning with who we are and who we want to be as a nation. Our country chose a president who was endorsed by the Ku Klux Klan, and we are witnessing the rise of vile symbols of hate such as the swastika and the Confederate flag as well as the permission for deep-seated oppression to rear its ugly head. The United States of America is anything but united, and we face an uncertain and scary road ahead. So many people have recently asked me, "What do we say to our children?"

As the musician Common said in the theme song from the movie *Glory*: "Justice for all just ain't specific enough." We have savage inequalities in our country . . . many are based on race and zip code. We are increasingly faced with huge gaps in income, achievement, privilege, health, and so much more. We struggle to figure out how to deal with complex challenges about identity, inclusivity, oppression, and how to bridge the divides in our nation.

America has come a long way since the ratification of the 13th Amendment in 1865, which outlawed slavery in our country, but we have a long way to go to be a truly inclusive "land of the free and home of the brave." This is as deeply entrenched as any issue facing our society today. As someone who has dedicated my entire adult life to building bridges across divides of race, class, age, gender, geography, sexuality, ability, and promoting harmony for all, I am inspired by the courage, authenticity, and passion of this book. No matter who you are or where you view these issues from, this book will challenge you to think about the world and your experiences within it in new ways.

Consider this book a new lens or a new prescription for your old lens.

Dr. Max Klau's vivid journey of discovery which you are about to read is a thoughtfully articulated and timely voyage filled with compelling insights, deep curiosity, and powerful personal vulnerability. The intriguing combination of personal soul searching, rigorous empirical research, and careful analysis as well as a poignant exploration of real-world implications result in a timely and important contribution to the conversation about equity, race, and social change in America.

Dr. Klau's expertise in adaptive leadership and his grounding in complex systems thinking are essential to understanding the variety of challenges contained in the work. Those fundamental underpinnings combined with his many years of grassroots work in the youth development and national service sectors make for a book that should be read by anyone who cares about equality, community development, and the future of race relations in our nation.

This book itself is a learning journey and a jewel for all of those folks seeking to build community, bring diverse and different people together for a common goal, and anyone who craves unity and harmony in our divided and challenged world. Dr. Max Klau presents a personal and a national call to action that needs to be heard.

Charlie Rose
Senior vice president and dean, City Year

"Justice is never given; it is exacted and the struggle must be continuous for freedom is never a final fact, but a continuing evolving process to higher and higher levels of human, social, economic, political and religious relationship."

A. Philip Randolph

"[C]onsciousness precedes being, and not the other way around . . . For this reason, the salvation of this human world lies nowhere else than in the human heart, in the human power to reflect, in human meekness and in human responsibility. Without a global revolution in the sphere of human consciousness, nothing will change for the better . . . and the catastrophe toward which this world is headed—be it ecological, social, demographic or a general breakdown of civilization—will be unavoidable.

VACLAV HAVEL

"*I would not have you descend into your own dream.
I would have you be a conscious citizen of this terrible
and beautiful world.*"
Ta-Nahisi Coates, Between the World and Me

Introduction

W*hat's true about race and social change?*

It's a seemingly simple question, but what's at stake in the search for an answer is nothing less than the soul of a nation.

America came into being in a manner that was laced with paradox and hypocrisy. On the one hand, the choice to launch a revolution against the monarchy in England was inspired by the most noble and advanced ideas of the Enlightenment. The founding fathers decided to take up arms against the mightiest empire in the world out of a commitment to the following ideals:

> "We hold these truths to be self-evident: that all men are created equal; that they are endowed by their Creator with certain inalienable rights; that among these are life, liberty, and the pursuit of happiness."

These words represented a revolutionary and enlightened notion in the eighteenth century, and they articulate an ideal that continues to inspire America and much of the world today.

1

However, at the same exact moment that the founding fathers were writing the Declaration of Independence, one could find an advertisement in the local newspaper with the following copy:

TO BE SOLD on board the Ship *Bance-Yland*, on tuefday the 6th of *May* next, at *Afhley-Ferry* ; a choice cargo of about 250 fine healthy

NEGROES,

juft arrived from the Windward & Rice Coaft. —The utmoft care has already been taken, and fhall be continued, to keep them free from the leaft danger of being infected with the SMALL-POX, no boat having been on board, and all other communication with people from *Charles-Town* prevented.

Aufin, Laurens, & *Appleby.*

N. B. Full one Half of the above Negroes have had the SMALL-POX in their own Country.

This is the inescapable truth of the founding of the United States: The most noble of humanistic ideals coexisted with the cruel reality of one of the most unjust and dehumanizing institutions in human history.

As the American experiment in democracy has unfolded, the struggle to narrow the gap between the brutal reality of racism and the inspiring aspirations of our espoused values has played out at the center of our civic life. Race relations often seemed stuck in some unjust, unchanging—and seemingly unchangeable—status quo that would endure for decades, until the nation found itself rocked by spasms of dramatic and rapid change. The institution of slavery endured from before the Revolutionary War through the founding of the nation in 1776 and on through another century, until the slowly accumulating tensions around the issue finally erupted into a Civil War that convulsed the nation. When the dust cleared and the hundreds of thousands of dead were buried, the Union prevailed and slavery officially ended.

What followed was another hundred years of the scarcely improved status quo of "Jim Crow" segregation, in which Black people continued to endure vicious discrimination. Examples of mistreatment in this era included frequent lynchings and murders with no consequences for the killers; policies such as redlining, which kept people of color segregated and impoverished; and deeply unethical medical practices such as the Tuskegee syphilis experiment. This was the American reality for nearly another century, until the nation once again found itself rocked by waves of protest and activism in the 1960s that wrought significant social change. Myriad racial injustices that had endured for decades were transformed in just a matter of years.

All that was not so long ago, and in the decades since the civil rights movement of the 1960s, the issues of race and social change have remained—as ever—central to American civic life. In 2008, America elected its first Black president, and whatever you think of his politics, there can be no denying that for a nation in which Black people were once owned as slaves and legally declared to be less than human, his election was a historic moment in American history. A man who just a generation ago would have been unable to drink from the same water fountains as Whites in many states had been elected to the highest office in the land. It was an undeniable sign that some meaningful degree of social change had occurred in America.

And yet.

Today's news reports are filled with stories of unarmed Black people—mostly men—shot and killed by police: Michael Brown, Eric Garner, Tamir Rice, Freddie Gray, Dontre Hamilton, Tanisha Hamilton, Akai Gurley, Eric Harris, Alton Sterling, Philando Castile . . . sadly, the list could go on and on. On June 17, 2015, a twisted White supremacist joined a prayer study group at the historic Emanuel African Methodist Episcopal Church in Charleston, South Carolina, and then shot nine Black congregants dead. It was an act of cold, vicious racial hatred that could have been ripped from the headlines of the darkest, ugliest days of Jim Crow.

During the 2016 election season, we watched Black and Brown Americans get physically assaulted at multiple political rallies for the leading candidate of one of America's major political parties.

It is apparent that each of these race-related incidents functions as a real-life Rorschach test: Different people look at the same images and facts and arrive at dramatically different understandings of what it all means. Some see indisputable proof of the persistence of a vast system of racial oppression and discrimination that has endured since the nation's founding. Others see something quite different: the regrettable consequences of a flawed mental health system perhaps, incidences of excessive use of force by the police, or a lack of individual responsibility among people of color—all dynamics that are understood to be unfolding in a nation that is so color-blind and post-racial that it has twice elected a Black president. There is, it seems, no solid ground on which to stand; only the idiosyncrasies of personal experience, the shifting sands of public opinion, and the void of moral relativism.

What's true about race and social change? It's a vital question. Any answer we arrive at is sure to inform our understanding of why we find ourselves in this difficult, polarized place and how we might heal our racial wounds, live up to our highest aspirations, and step together into a brighter, more promising future.

This question has burned in my soul for decades, and it has animated a lifelong quest for insights. My search began in the nearly all-White middle class suburb of Connecticut where I grew up, where my inquiries into matters of race and social change unfolded among family and peers in classrooms, living rooms, and at kitchen tables populated by people who looked much like me. In my mid-twenties, I experienced a life-changing adventure with a group of Black and Jewish adolescents on a month-long civil rights tour across the United States that took us through the secluded back roads of Philadelphia, Mississippi; the churches of Birmingham, Alabama; the classrooms of Central High School in Little Rock, Arkansas; and across the Edmund Pettus Bridge in

Selma. As I explain in Chapter 1, it was on that trip that the veils of blindness first began to fall away.

My quest led eventually to the classrooms of Harvard University, where my personal journey evolved into a rigorous empirical inquiry. In the early years of my doctoral studies in human development and psychology at the Harvard Graduate School of Education, I stumbled on the exercise that forms the heart of this book. I was investigating the topic of youth leadership and was conducting field research involving the observation of youth leadership programs. I wanted to know how these programs understood leadership, and then taught it to participants. It was in the course of that research that I visited a program called Camp Anytown, run by an organization now called the National Conference for Community and Justice (NCCJ). What I encountered on that visit changed the course of my life.

Camp Anytown is a week-long residential youth leadership experience that focuses on teaching young people about diversity and social justice. It occurs in multiple states across the country each year, and each Camp Anytown program brings together an extremely diverse group of 30 to 50 high school students who live together for 5 days immersed in intense experiential programming. Over the course of the week, participants engage in deep conversations about "isms" such as racism, sexism, ageism, and more in activities and sessions led by experienced educators.

On the last morning of the program, participants were separated into groups—Whites, Asians, Jews, LGBTQ, Latinos, Blacks—and told not to talk to or make eye contact with members of other groups.*

---

* At this early moment in the book, I'd like to offer a word of explanation about the choice to capitalize the names of all different races. In the writing process, I learned that some of these words—such as *Latino* or *Jewish* are nearly always capitalized, and others—such as *black* or *white*—are not always capitalized. Early drafts featuring some races with capitalization and others without seemed inappropriate, as though groups with capitalized names were more worthy of respect than groups without. I have chosen, therefore, to capitalize the names of all races. It reflects an intention to refer to all these different groups with a shared and equivalent sense of respect.

The program directors then created and enforced an unjust, segregated, hierarchical social system in which the White kids experienced tremendous privilege and opportunity and the darker-skinned kids experienced discrimination and oppression. They called it the Separation Exercise, and it was designed to simulate a Jim Crow–style social system in which participants would have a chance to practice challenging these unjust norms. Challenge them they did, and over the course of just a few hours events unfolded that were at times stunningly similar to what occurred during the real-life civil rights movement.

Watching the events of that morning, I realized that Camp Anytown's Separation Exercise was essentially a simulated civil rights movement. Here, at a rustic New England summer camp, I had stumbled on an opportunity to study the process of social change in something as close to replicable research conditions as I could imagine. I wondered: *What might we learn by carefully observing multiple civil rights movements in a petri dish?*

The next 3 years of my life were spent developing a rigorous research methodology, observing three more of these Separation Exercises, and then analyzing the findings that emerged from across the multiple observations. I spent the next decade of my life refining my understanding of the meaning and implications of this research into the ideas presented here.

As you'll see, this analysis of these provocative exercises led to several important insights. Here are just a few that emerged from this research that you'll encounter in the pages ahead:

- Dynamics of obedience and conformity play a powerful role in preserving the status quo of unjust systems. The unwillingness to question a troublesome status quo— even in the face of strong personal feelings that something is not right—is the major force in preserving current conditions. Equally important, these individual decisions contribute directly to the emergence of vast, system-wide patterns and structures in ways that most of us scarcely comprehend.

- Individuals at the top of systems of privilege and oppression have very limited insight into the nature of those systems. This system blindness need not result from intentional racism or malice, but it has the effect of making it maddeningly difficult for individuals immersed in these systems to achieve a shared understanding of the reality of what's actually going on.

- Individuals immersed in these systems tell stories to understand their experiences, and some of these stories hew closer to reality than others. Exploring the relation-ship between how individuals understand their experi-ence and how events actually unfolded in these exercises provides important insights into matters of race and social change.

- In complex social systems, some groups get enormous amounts of attention, and other groups remain completely ignored. With a higher consciousness concerning how that happens, we develop our ability to compensate for that dynamic and attain a deeper and more comprehensive understanding of the truth of these systems.

- Achieving higher consciousness about what is true about race and social change can only occur through an experience that can best be described as a journey of awakening. This is not a process of internalizing facts and data; it is about discovering that much of what one believes to be reality is in fact an illusion. This experience of awakening unfolds for White people and people of color in ways that are distinct and different, yet also complementary and related.

- Social change is nonlinear, meaning that seemingly minor events have the potential to trigger waves of dramatic transformation. This nonlinearity contributes to the emergence of "tipping points"—moments of sudden, major change that follow long periods that appear to be stuck in a state of unchanging stasis.

- Social change is fractal, meaning that underneath the complexity of phenomena as diverse as feminism, civil rights, the emergence of "flat" organizations, democratic revolutions, and recent shifts in global geopolitics lies a remarkably simple and elegant process of evolutionary change. Once we learn to look for it, we see this process everywhere, unfolding with unmistakable symmetry at every scale of analysis from the interpersonal to the geopolitical.

- Current-day experiences of discrimination and oppression can and often do evoke powerful memories of historical traumas. An understanding of how and why this happens reveals the fractal nature of race and social change in surprising ways. It is clear that in the absence of a clear understanding of this dynamic, we are certain to find ourselves stuck in an endless, repetitive cycle of pain and misunderstanding.

- The outer-world systems and structures in which we are immersed are actually a manifestation of our innermost ways of being. In other words, inner change and outer change are not simply parallel processes; they are deeply interconnected. We do not simply live in the world; we are each actively calling forth and cocreating the world in which we are immersed, and the day-to-day world we encounter right now needs be understood as a reflection of our current state of consciousness. When we undertake the inner work required to awaken to a higher

consciousness about the nature of the self and the system
in which we are immersed, we will begin calling forth
and cocreating transformations in the systems and
structures that exist beyond the self.

In the pages ahead, I'll be demonstrating that these findings
are not abstract philosophy: They are insights that emerged from
empirical research and careful analysis of the data gathered
from Camp Anytown Separation Exercises. This book was written
to explain these insights in detail.

Here, then, is what you'll find in the pages ahead:

Chapter 1 presents a brief narrative of my own personal quest for
insights regarding the workings of race and social change. It's an
effort to be transparent—and a bit vulnerable—about the journey
that I've had to undertake from the perspective of my personal
background. I describe my own experience of awakening to a higher
consciousness regarding the existence of a reality in which I have
always been immersed but had not always perceived. I explain how it
came to be that this personal quest led to the scientific inquiry at the
heart of this book.

Chapter 2 presents an overview of a long tradition of classic social
psychology experiments such as those of Stanley Milgram, Solomon
Asch, Philip Zimbardo, and others. This body of research has
illuminated some of the darkest shadows of human behavior in
productive and compelling ways, and the Separation Exercise presented here clearly represents an extension of this tradition. A review
of these past experiments provides invaluable context for understanding why this research represents a meaningful contribution to
this provocative line of inquiry.

Chapter 3 presents part one of an introduction to a level of
analysis that is central to this research: the whole system. Here, we
encounter and explore systems dynamics such as nonlinearity,
interdependence, self-organization, and the meaning of complexity
itself. We also learn about fractals, a phenomenon in which the same

structures or patterns appear across dramatically different scales of analysis.

Chapter 4 presents part two of this introduction to systems. Here, we learn how relatively simple human social systems develop over time into more complex social systems. And we discover that when we combine the two concepts of development toward complexity and fractals, we discover a hidden process underlying and driving social change across myriad seemingly unrelated dimensions throughout all of human history.

In Chapter 5, we encounter the detailed narratives from the three Separation Exercises at the heart of this research. We learn how the activity was run, what it was intended to achieve, and how it was studied, and how all three of these exercises unfolded. This is our chance to view these three exercises through the bird's-eye view of the team of researchers who observed and documented the three separate activities.

Chapter 6 presents the findings that emerged from the Separation Exercise research related to the first two levels of analysis that were explored in this study. At the *interpersonal* level, how did participants understand their experiences? How did they feel about being a member of their particular group? What were their reasons for challenging—or not challenging—the unjust norms of the system? In addition, at *the intergroup* level, what did participants think about the other groups in the system? What groups received attention in the system, and which were ignored? Why?

In Chapter 7, we take a look at lessons learned at the third and highest level of analysis: the whole system. First, we'll explore what patterns appeared across all three exercises and what shared narrative of social change emerged across all three exercises. Then, we'll dive into what turns out to be a far more complex question: Why did each exercise unfold so differently? We'll investigate some seemingly paradoxical insights that explain dynamics unfolding at this highest level of analysis.

Chapters 8 and 9 explore the real-world implications of this research. In Chapter 8, I discuss the foundational need to recognize the existence of a system of racial privilege and oppression in the real world and deepen our understanding of how to think about that system. I also discuss the process of awakening that we must undergo to arrive at a higher consciousness regarding these systems and share some important moments in my own ongoing journey of awakening. In Chapter 9, we explore questions of power and control: Who designed the system? Who is in charge? And what are the implications of the finding that there is a connection between our inner ways of being and the outer-world systems in which we are immersed?

The book will conclude with Chapter 10, in which I present a dual call to action on an individual and a national dimension based on the insights presented in this book.

Before wrapping up this introduction, I'll offer a few more thoughts intended to orient you, the reader, to the journey ahead. First, who am I? Second, who did I write this book for? And third, how do I understand the purpose of this book? Once these questions are answered, we'll be ready to set off on this journey together.

First, who am I?

I am a White, middle class, Jewish, straight, cisgendered male. I'm married and I live with my wife and kids in a Boston suburb. The path I have walked in my journey has been that of awakening from a place of privilege, with the inevitable result being that I have had to learn a great deal about race and social change through dialogue with people of color as opposed to lessons learned through direct personal experience.

I have completed a doctorate of education (EdD) that involved a dual focus on developmental psychology and leadership—specifically, the adaptive leadership model developed by Ronald Heifetz. Because both of these disciplines inform the ideas presented in the pages ahead in foundational ways, they merit some brief explanation.

As a developmental psychologist, I've been trained to view life as an ongoing developmental process unfolding over the course of time.

This process flows generally from a state of relative simplicity toward a transformed state of greater complexity. The developmental process is rarely a simple, linear progression, however. Development often happens in fits and starts; metaphorically speaking, life takes two steps forward and one step back. Long periods may go by with little development occurring to be followed by rapid spurts of change. Also, development is not inevitable. Under the right conditions, it may advance rapidly; under the wrong conditions, it may be delayed, arrested, or reversed. This professional training to view all of life as undergoing a constantly unfolding process of developmental change is foundational to the ideas presented in the pages ahead.

My training in adaptive leadership results in two key theoretical distinctions that inform the way I understand the world. First, I have learned to make a distinction between two types of challenges: *technical* and *adaptive*. *Technical* challenges are defined by the fact that we understand the problem and already have in our repertoire a set of responses that enable us to effectively address the problem. *Adaptive* challenges are different. With an adaptive challenge, the nature of the problem itself is often not at all clear, and whatever technical solutions we've already mastered are insufficient or ineffective at addressing the challenge. I have come to view matters of race and social change as adaptive challenges: There is no clear agreement on the nature of challenges embedded in these matters, there are no simple technical solutions that will quickly transform race relations in this nation, and any meaningful change will involve transforming some long-standing beliefs, values, and norms at work in our civic life.

The second theoretical distinction that I have learned to make involves differentiating between *authority* and *leadership*. Although we often conflate the two terms and use them interchangeably, that is problematic—especially when trying to understand matters of race and social change. According to this model, *authority* is a formal position of power in a community or organization. It is the president, CEO, principal, teacher . . . whoever is in the box at the top of the

hierarchy on the organizational chart. *Leadership* is something different: It is an activity that can be undertaken by anyone in the system
intended to mobilize a group to address an adaptive challenge. An
individual in a position of authority may try to exercise leadership . . .
but that individual may also use authority to preserve a problematic
status quo. And one need not be in that position of formal authority
to attempt to exercise leadership. With this theoretical distinction, we
have a powerful way of understanding the process of social change
throughout history. After all, individuals such as Gandhi, Rosa Parks,
and Malala Yousafzai did not have positions of formal authority, yet
they exercised tremendous leadership.

Over the course of conducting the research presented here, I've
had to engage deeply with some other subject areas as well. As you'll
see, this research is grounded in the fields of social psychology and
complex systems, and I've sought to digest enough of those literatures
for this work to represent a contribution to those fields. I've worked
hard to weave together insights gleaned from fields such as critical
race theory, organizational development, personal transformation,
and studying the lives of towering figures such as Nelson Mandela
and Malcolm X.

I am keenly aware of the fact that the terrain explored in this book
relates to a great many other disciplines that focus on matters of race
and social change. The Separation Exercises at the center of this
book would provide a rich source of exploration for scholars of
critical race theory; racial identity development; gender studies;
queer studies; group psychology; the history, psychology, and soci-
ology of social movements; adolescent and adult development; and
much, much more. On many occasions, I make passing references to
bodies of literature with which I have some familiarity and are
relevant to the matter at hand, but those references are undeniably
cursory and the attempt to reference related fields is incomplete.

I understand this to be the inevitable result of grounding this
research in the fields of leadership and complex systems: The
opportunity inherent in these interdisciplinary approaches is

the chance to explore dynamics that transcend traditional boundaries in ways that provide important new perspectives. The risk is that
anyone working in these fields opens themselves up to the critique by
scholars in dozens of related fields that they are uninformed dilet-
tantes because they do not know and say more about disciplines that
are undeniably directly relevant to the matter at hand.

So be it. If I have learned anything from this quest, it is that we
live our lives immersed in a web of relationships so vast, complex,
interconnected, and interdependent that it can never be described or
revealed in its totality. As with all mysteries that transcend the limits
of human understanding, these matters can only be encountered
properly through the cultivation of humility. Given that understanding of the deepest nature of these phenomena, my intention
here is to make a contribution, albeit in some small and inescapably
limited way. I am the first to declare that there is a great deal more
to learn about all of this, and I look forward to continuing my own
learning journey in the years ahead.

In my professional life, I have spent the last 10 years working for
City Year, a national service organization that engages young adults
(ages 17–24) in a demanding year of full-time service focused on
keeping students in high needs schools on track to graduate from
high school. I've spent the last decade working with the thousands of
diverse, idealistic young adults—and the remarkable staff members
who support them—serving in urban schools across the nation in a
pragmatic, collaborative, and data-driven effort to positively transform the nation's high school drop-out crisis. Currently, I'm involved
in a non-partisan effort to recruit and support alumni of service
programs (both military veterans and alumni of civilian service
programs like AmeriCorps and Peace Corps) to run for political
office. This focus on developing leaders through service is the theme
that runs throughout my career.

Regarding the question of who I wrote this book for, I've kept
an image of a particular audience in mind throughout the writing
process. Although I know that this book will be read, most likely,

by individual readers, the audience I've been writing for in my mind has not been a solitary individual but a small, highly diverse group of thoughtful, engaged, concerned citizens. They might be university students discussing course work in a classroom, activists connecting across communities in a local coffee shop, employees connecting across silos in a meeting room, congregants gathering in fellowship in the basement of their place of worship, engaged citizens gathered for an evening in a local school cafeteria, and elected officials coming together in a town hall or state capitol. The key detail is that the group is, in some infinitely variable way, a microcosm of the whole that is the United States: individuals of different races, creeds, backgrounds, sexual orientations, and beliefs sitting together in a circle with a desire to inquire, learn, and connect in a manner that happens far too rarely in our civic life today.

These readers feel called to engage with this topic out of a deep sense of pain at the discord, coarseness, violence, and suffering so prevalent in our civic life today, mixed with a deep pride in this country and an unshakeable idealism regarding the values and ideals it stands for. They dream of creating something better for themselves and for their children, despite the sense that the path out of all this darkness, strife, and confusion is not at all clear. Although they may not understand themselves in these terms, they are, in essence, a fractal microcosm of a society yearning for wholeness amidst the pain of disconnection. They are the incomplete parts of a living whole system that simply does not know itself fully yet and whose capacity to heal and thrive depends on achieving a deeper awareness and higher consciousness of the reality of that wholeness. It is my hope that if this group were to come together to share their reactions and responses to the ideas in the pages ahead, they might take a few meaningful steps toward not only understanding that wholeness but also actually experiencing it.

As a final thought and to answer the third question about the purpose of this book, I'll state that the process that led to this book was most eloquently illuminated by the Bohemian-Austrian mystical poet Rainer Maria Rilke (2013), who shared the following advice with a fellow poet in 1903:

> I would like to beg you, dear Sir, as well as I can, to have patience with everything unresolved in your heart and to try to love the questions themselves as if they were locked rooms or books written in a very foreign language. Don't search for the answers, which could not be given to you now, because you would not be able to live them. And the point is, to live everything. Live the questions now. Perhaps then, someday far in the future, you will gradually, without even noticing it, live your way into the answer.

After decades of living the question of *what's true about race and social change?* I feel that I have—at long last—lived into an answer that feels thorough and complete enough to merit sharing with the world. The insights presented here are offered in a spirit of humility, with a keen awareness that there is much about race and social change that I do not yet understand and have yet to learn. Still, it is my hope that this collection of insights gained over the course of a decades-long journey of awakening might represent a productive contribution to a dialogue about a matter of central importance to the past, present, and future of our nation.

1

A Personal Quest

I can't tell you precisely when the quest began, but I can share a moment when the first of a great many veils of blindness and ignorance fell from my vision, illuminating the first small slivers of insight.

It was in the basement of a college dorm in Virginia. I was working as a group leader for an organization called Operating Understanding DC—more often known by its acronym, OUDC—and we were 3 days into a month-long bus journey across the United States. Our travels would take us through some of the most important sites in the history of America's civil rights struggle: Birmingham and Montgomery, Alabama; Little Rock, Arkansas; and Philadelphia, Mississippi. OUDC brought together a group of 30 teens from the greater Washington, DC, area; half of them were Jewish, half of them were Black, and one or two were both. Together, we would encounter these historic sites and meet some of the courageous individuals who made these towns so significant. As a group, we would engage in an intense, honest, searching dialogue about race and social change that would unfold in an essentially unbroken stream for the entire 30 days.

We were just a couple days into the trip and still early in the process of evolving our group dynamic. The program this evening was a "fishbowl" activity that would be led by OUDC's remarkable founder, an endlessly colorful and energetic woman named Karen Kalish. She was Jewish, with a soul that burned for racial equality and social justice. It was thanks to her that we were all gathered that evening in the basement lounge of a college dorm in Virginia.

For this fishbowl activity, a group of six Black participants (three young men and three young women) were seated in an inner circle, with the rest of the group arranged in a larger circle surrounding them. Those of us in the outer circle were told to just listen; all the talking would be done by the six Black teens in the inner circle, who were invited to discuss their experiences growing up Black in Washington, DC.

The conversation began with a tone that was light and casual, but it didn't stay that way for long. In just a few minutes, the conversation entered terrain that I have since come to recognize as a space of sacred truth: a place where one can feel—in one's innermost heart—that truth is being spoken and that defenses are being lowered as people risk levels of honesty and vulnerability that are almost never revealed in day-to-day life. In that space, real tears began to flow, along with the sort of utterly genuine laughter and joy that emerges spontaneously in moments of authentic human connection. I had explored race in an intellectual way many, many times in the past via books, documentaries, and discussions with others who shared my own background. But it was in this space that I first had a significant, genuine, fully human experience with the "other" and had a flesh-and-blood encounter with all the bitter, painful, difficult truths and all the awe-inspiring resilience and spiritual strength that animated the inner lives of this group of young Black Americans.

The young people told stories of walking into stores and being stopped by store employees who suspected them of shoplifting. There was no ignoring the fact that if they walked into the store with White friends, the White friends were never stopped and questioned. They had stories of being pulled over while driving, even though they were certain they were going no faster than the speed limit to avoid exactly this outcome. They talked about struggling to get the sort of entry-level jobs in retail or restaurants that White friends seemed to land with minimal effort. They shared stories of parents struggling to pay the rent and of how the adults in their lives so often found their opportunities limited and constrained in a thousand small but significant ways.

In time, the deeper complexities of their experiences began to surface. A light-skinned Black girl noted that she was rarely stopped by store employees, even when she was with darker-skinned Black friends who were stopped. Part of her felt lucky to be able to "pass"— to move through the world enjoying the privileges that come with people simply assuming that she was trustworthy. But that privilege and relative ease of movement came with some heavy baggage. She struggled with guilt every time her darker-skinned friends had to endure some injustice that she had been spared, and she had to deal with Black friends regularly making comments suggesting that she wasn't "really" Black. To be light-skinned, I learned, was a blessing and a curse in the life of young woman of color.

The fishbowl lasted for at least 2 hours, and as I listened, a whole world of complexity, pain, resilience, and emotional truth about the lived experience of young people of color in America was revealed to me for the first time. And what I remember most about night was the thought that kept running through my head again and again as the discussion unfolded: *I had no idea.*

I had no idea how frequently people of color encountered discrimination and barriers to opportunity in their lives. I had no idea how much pain these incidents caused. I had no idea that differences in skin color created such social complexities in the lives of kids of color. I had no idea how much strength and wisdom and humor was required to stay healthy and resilient in the face of these relentless challenges. I had no idea how any of this felt, or how any of this worked, or what any of this demanded of these kids, because I had never really had to worry about any of it. I had no idea.

And I was the group leader.

I felt—and I still feel—that I was hired with good reason. Similar to Karen Kalish, I was a Jew with a burning passion for social justice and a deep desire to promote racial equality. I was appalled by America's history of slavery and viewed leading figures of the civil rights movement such as Rosa Parks and Martin Luther King Jr. as personal heroes. I had worked extensively with communities of color while participating in a year-long service program in Israel, and later I managed young adults engaged in similar service as a group leader. I even had a remarkable job that allowed me to spend 4 months traveling around America with an Ethiopian Israeli colleague and friend; together, we gave speeches and raised money to support the Ethiopian community in Israel. On my résumé, at least, I was no stranger to matters of race. At the age of 27, I could honestly claim years of involvement in service, youth development, and social justice education. Karen Kalish had every reason to hire me for that job. And yet still: *I had no idea.*

That night, my hunger to learn more was piqued, and the weeks that followed provided a treasure trove of opportunities for learning, dialogue, and understanding. We had amazing experiences, such as meeting the mother of civil rights worker Andrew Goodman, one of the three young organizers who was killed in 1968 while advocating for voting rights for people of color in Philadelphia, Mississippi. That night, we stayed overnight in the homes of Black residents of Philadelphia who had agreed to host our group. Our host offered to take us on a tour of how it all happened, so we got into his car in the pitch-black Mississippi night and he drove us around: *Here was the jail where the three young men were being held, and where they were pulled out of their cell by a White mob; here was spot where they were pulled from the car, beaten, and killed; here was the spot where their bodies were buried.* Driving through the thick woods on the darkened back roads of rural Mississippi, it was impossible to not feel a small dose of the terror those three young men must have felt that night, and I was left struggling mightily with the question of how a group of ordinary White people with jobs and families could transform into that kind of rageful, hateful, murderous mob.

While on the bus, we watched Spike Lee's powerful documentary *Four Little Girls* about the four Black girls killed in the bombing of the 16th Street Baptist Church in Birmingham, Alabama. The movie ended just as the bus pulled to a stop . . . in the parking lot of the 16th Street Baptist Church. We walked inside and immediately participated in a panel discussion with community members, including a parent of one of the little girls. Days later we walked across the Edmund Pettis Bridge in Selma, Alabama, Blacks and Jews holding hands, singing "We Shall Overcome."

It was a remarkable, month-long, encounter with something I can only call the civic sacred. Every day, we met seemingly ordinary men and women who had summoned levels of courage, creativity, and commitment that literally transformed a nation and inspired the world. In confronting some of America's darkest shadows of hate and intolerance, they had elevated everyday civic spaces—bridges, buses, roads, coffee counters—into sites that properly can be called sacred. Despite—actually because of—all the emotional complexity evoked by confronting this history, it was a wonder to encounter it all and a blessing to experience it as a member of this diverse group of young people.

The conversations begun that night with the fishbowl continued all month long as together we processed each day's experiences and learned more and more about how we all saw and experienced the world. Despite all my interest in these matters over the years, I realized that I had reached the age of 27 without ever having had the chance to have these kinds of deep, authentic discussions about race with people of color. I remember feeling waves of gratitude at finally having the chance to explore all this with people who didn't look just like me. It was a peak life experience, and to this day I remain amazed at how rare it is to encounter these spaces of authentic connection and deep dialogue about race with "the other" and how essential they are to achieving a genuine understanding of what is true about race and social change in American civic life today.

I have said that my OUDC experience was not the moment the quest began; I had been passionate about matters of race and social change for years before that remarkable experience. But it was beyond a doubt a pivotal moment in my journey. It was the time when I saw clearly just how blind I was to how race and social change actually worked. And it was the experience that crystallized the questions that would burn in my soul and animate much of the next decade of my life:

How does this whole thing **work?** *What's really true about race and social change in America?*

Just a few months after completing OUDC, I started graduate school at the Harvard Graduate School of Education. Harvard was a remarkable experience. I took classes with titles such as "Education for Social Change," "Promoting Morality in Children and Adolescents," "Exercising Leadership, Mobilizing Group Resources," and "Moral Development." I was immersed in topics I yearned to learn more about and was privileged to explore it all as part of an extremely diverse student body. Harvard is surely an elite institution, and I have no doubt that a great many students and professors could make compelling arguments about all the ways the school does not adequately confront the realities of issues such as race, gender, sexual orientation, socioeconomic status, and more. All I can say is that in my experience, I was pushed, challenged, and transformed by encounters with diverse peers on a nearly daily basis. My studies were so engaging that I knew almost instantly that a one-year master's program would not be enough; I applied to the doctoral program in human development and psychology and was thrilled when I heard the news that I had been accepted. I now had at least five more years to seek answers to the questions at the heart of my quest.

In those first years of my doctoral studies, the learning was intense and exciting. The professors were experts in their fields, and I was surrounded by hard-working, passionate, inspiring peers eager to dive into debate and dialogue. Despite all I was learning, though, something felt incomplete. In hindsight I realize that I felt a lot like the blind men in the well-known parable of the elephant, although I wasn't really conscious of the metaphor at the moment.

In that story, one individual touches the animal's leg and declares that the elephant is like a pillar, another touches the ear and declares the animal to be like a hand fan, another touches the tail and declares the animal to be like a rope. The blind men descend into a bitter argument about who is right, until a wise man appears and illuminates the truth: They are all correct, but they have all encountered different, limited aspects of what it is in fact a cohesive, larger truth.

So it was with my studies of race and social change. I listened to professors and peers share different insights and perspectives every day, and I realized quickly that it made no sense to assert that their experience was "wrong"; it was their experience, as true to them as my own experience was to myself. But how did all these perspectives on truth fit together?

I knew from personal experience that when it came to matters of race and social change, as a White male I arrived at adulthood blind to how things worked in profound and surprising ways, despite my good intensions and passion for these issues. I knew from many meaningful encounters with people of color that for them, blindness to race was impossible. Race was something they could never escape; they confronted discrimination and felt their "otherness" on a near daily basis. Every day brought a new lesson in the complexity of how race and social change was experienced; Asians, Latinos, Blacks, LGBTQ students, students of mixed ethnicity, as well as atheists and students deeply committed to their faiths all had distinctive stories to share.

I quickly learned that trying to absorb more about any of these issues inevitably opened up entirely new frontiers of complexity. Consider, for example, the effort to gain a deeper understanding of the Asian experience of race and social change in America. It didn't take long to encounter that there is no single monolithic "Asian" experience; individuals from Japan, China, Vietnam, Cambodia, and other Asian nations have their own identities, their own histories, and their own truths to share. The same goes for Latinos and Blacks; to inquire more deeply into any of these groups is to encounter a vast landscape of subgroups, each with their own experiences, histories, and traditions. It soon became obvious that it was quite simply impossible to truly understand all of this complexity; the full diversity of humanity is too vast for any one person to grasp. But I could certainly learn to expect that complexity and resist the tendency to think and talk about individuals as representing monolithic groups that have never really existed.

In addition, when I turned my attention from listening to personal narratives to examining the broad sweep of history, a whole new set of questions appeared. Day after day, I heard stories of discrimination and oppression met with resistance, resilience, and a deep commitment to working to create positive change. And it was clear that positive change could and did happen, in dramatic and sudden ways. After decades of Jim Crow segregation in the United States, a powerful civic rights movement emerged and in a few short years created transformational change in America. Similar stories could be found in other nations, such as the movements for Indian independence from Britain and the anti-apartheid movement in South Africa, both of which unfolded in a similar fashion: Decades of grinding oppression and stagnation followed by the rapid coalescing of movements that created transformational change in a relative blink of an eye. How did that happen? What is the connection between myriad experiences of individuals in the system and these large-scale patterns of sudden change? And how should we understand the next stage of the work to be done in these systems *after* those sudden, dramatic waves of transformation? Once the lunch counters have been desegregated, the lynchings declared illegal, the separate water fountains dismantled, the right to vote secured . . . *what's next?*

With each passing semester, I kept encountering powerful truths about something enormous, whole, and interconnected, but no matter how much I learned or how hard I tried, I couldn't see the full picture. There *had* to be a way that everything I had every learned about race and social change fit together, but I couldn't see it, and I had no idea how to figure it out.

That all changed in summer 2002, when I encountered an activity that would alter the course of my doctoral studies and my life in ways I could hardly imagine. I was in my second year of doctoral studies and I was conducting research exploring the theory and practice of youth leadership. I had identified several programs that focused on youth leadership education and was engaged in field research to better understand how those programs conceptualized the work of youth leadership and what tools and methods they used to teach it. At that time I visited a program called Camp Anytown, run by an organization called the National Conference for Community and Justice (NCCJ). There, I encountered the exercise that is at the heart of this book.

As explained in the introduction, Camp Anytown is a week-long youth leadership experience that focuses on teaching young people about diversity and social justice. It occurs in multiple states across the country each year, and each program brings together an extremely diverse group of 30 to 50 high school students for 5 days of intense residential programming. Over the course of the week, participants engage in deep conversations about "isms" such as *racism, sexism, ageism,* and more in activities and sessions led by experienced educators.

Although the whole program is powerful, it was an activity often run on the last day that stopped me in my tracks, transformed the focus of my academic studies, and led ultimately to this book. Here's what I encountered:

It was Friday morning, and the day began—as had every other day—with participants gathering in a circle outside the dining hall before breakfast. Usually, the circle involved a brief check-in to see how everyone was feeling, a few cheers to get everyone's energy flowing and then some announcements about the day's agenda before the group moved into the dining hall for some breakfast.

This morning, though, something different happened. Instead of announcements, the program staff members instructed participants to separate into groups: Whites, Asians, Jews, LGBTQ, Latinos,

Blacks. This arrangement was not meant to merely put individuals into similar groups, separated from others who are not like them; it was also very intentionally a hierarchical system in which the White group was granted considerable privilege and opportunity, and each group lower on the hierarchy encountered fewer opportunities and greater discrimination. Within moments, the unified circle was transformed into a cluster of small groups representing a segregated, hierarchical, and deeply unjust system with a social architecture that looked like this:

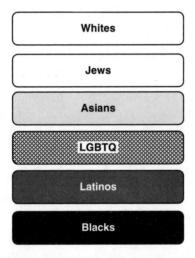

To everyone's surprise, the staff members then handed out a set of arm bands to each group, each with a different symbol clearly identifying every individual as a member of a particular group. The staff members then issued a chilling set of commands:

You must stay with your group. You are not to talk to members of other groups. You are not to make eye contact with members of other groups.

Then, the staff members explained that it was time for breakfast. The White group was invited into the dining hall first, and they were allowed to eat whatever they wanted, go back for seconds, and sit comfortably at a large table at the front of the hall. One by one, the next lower group in the hierarchy was sent in, and each was provided with fewer food options and less comfortable seating arrangements. The Black group was last to enter, and they got one meager serving of food and no table at all; they spent breakfast conspicuously sitting on the floor in the back of the hall.

Despite the awkward discomfort of the obviously unfair circumstances, breakfast concluded without incident and the groups were then sent to different activities. The White kids got to go to an air-conditioned room to watch TV and play video games, the Asians were given a math assignment to complete, the LGBTQ group was told to literally stand in a broom closet, the Latino group was required to wash the dishes from breakfast, and the Black group was tasked with sweeping and mopping the dining hall.

At Camp Anytown, this was called the "Separation Exercise." Coming at the conclusion of an intense week of exploring various isms, it was a provocative attempt to simulate a rigidly segregated, hierarchical, unjust social system. The true purpose of the exercise, however, was to give participants a chance to challenge these unjust norms and transform this social system.

And over the course of the next 3 hours, that was exactly what happened. After more than 90 minutes of stasis and calm, participants began to challenge the status quo; eventually, some seemingly minor act of disobedience triggered a massive wave of change that transformed the entire system in just a few moments. In a process that was clearly not being directed or controlled by any staff member, a subset of participants self-organized into a nonviolent protest movement that set out to engage and unite the other participants. After stepping back and allowing events to unfold with minimal involvement for nearly another hour, the staff members finally ended the exercise at lunchtime. Participants grabbed some food and then gathered together for a long, emotional, and cathartic debrief of the experience.

In my role as researcher, I observed the events of this simulation with amazement. Although the Separation Exercise lasted only about 3 hours, it simulated a dramatic transformation process. Somewhere between breakfast and lunch, this segregated social system transformed into something very different, and the process unfolded in ways that were at times stunningly similar to real-life events of the civil rights era.

Watching the activity that morning, I realized that Camp Anytown's Separation Exercise was essentially a civil rights movement in a petri dish. Here, amidst the buildings and fields of a rustic New England summer camp, I had stumbled on an opportunity to get a glimpse of the whole elephant: the blindness of the privileged, the anger of the oppressed, the impersonal unfairness of an unjust system, the frustration of individuals with complex identities forced to conform to simple, stereotypical social roles, the long period of seemingly inalterable stasis, the intense pressures to merely obey and conform, the courage of resisters, and the sudden, remarkable wave of transformational change unleashed by a seemingly insignificant act.

All of this—*all of it*—was present in an activity that was observable, replicable, and researchable. I was struck—*gobsmacked* is a better term—by the opportunity inherent in this exercise. What if we could explore what was true about race and social change using the methods of social science? What if we could investigate these matters that so bitterly divide our nation with rigorous empirical research? What lessons might we learn? What perspectives might we gain? What higher levels of consciousness about these matters might we achieve?

I recognized immediately that the potential to learn from this exercise was enormous, but the endeavor raised troubling ethical questions. As we will learn in Chapter 2, this exercise extends a long line of classic social psychology experiments, such as the obedience experiments of Stanley Milgram and the Stanford Prison Experiment by Philip Zimbardo. Although these experiments have become widely known, this type of research essentially never occurs anymore because of very appropriate concerns about the ethics of causing this much emotional distress and discomfort for participants.

There is no way that a grad student studying at any university today would have been able to get approval to design and implement this kind of provocative research activity. In this case, I was able to make the completely honest claim that in researching these exercises at Camp Anytown, we would not be asking the participants to do anything that they would not already be doing as participants in the program. We were just going to observe events as they happened and distribute a brief survey that merely added a few minutes to the extensive reflection time that always followed the activity. The Harvard Institutional Review Board (IRB) found this argument compelling and gave me the green light to go ahead with the research.

Of course, the deeper ethical issues here were not resolved through attaining IRB approval. This exercise involves taking adolescents who are at a developmentally sensitive stage of life and immersing them in a simulation the re-creates some of the most painful and unjust dynamics of the real world. There is every reason to believe that some of these participants have already been traumatized in the real world in some way by discrimination based on their race, gender, sexual orientation, ethnicity, or some other aspect of their identity, and this exercise has a very real potential to traumatize those kids further. Could any learning be worth the risk of causing this kind of emotional distress in young adult participants?

It's a very real question that I sought to keep in my consciousness at every point in this research. Clearly, the fact that I chose to move forward with the research and this book demonstrates where I landed on this issue. It is my belief that the answer is yes; the benefits of this activity outweigh the risks, and I arrived at this decision through two distinct ways of thinking about these ethical issues.

First, the NCCJ and Camp Anytown have been around for more than 50 years. After decades of programming that has engaged tens of thousands of participants, criticism of the experience by program alumni is so minimal as to be essentially nonexistent. These programs are run by experienced and compassionate educators, and they engage young adults who have proactively enrolled in a program designed to address issues of social justice and social change. I saw with my own eyes how the emotionally distressing Separation Activity was followed by a long (often 2 hours or more), cathartic processing session. In those discussions, I watched as participants were able to make meaning of their experiences, gain empathy for the experiences of peers, achieve important insights into the nature of these kinds of systems of privilege and oppression, and arrive at a place of insight, healing, empowerment, and genuine community. I have no doubt that for the vast majority of participants, the experience of this activity developed them into stronger and more empowered citizens possessed with a deeper understanding and higher consciousness of matters that are absolutely central to the future of American democracy.

Now here is a second—and more challenging—response to the question of whether the benefits of this exercise outweigh the ethical concerns: Quite simply, I recognize that there is no way that I can fully address or minimize the ethical concerns evoked by this exercise. Can I provide rigorous evidence that none of the participants in these activities were damaged or wounded by the experience? Unfortunately, I cannot. Am I troubled by the ethics of causing this degree of emotional distress in young people for an educational exercise? Yes, I am. Do I encourage other educators or activists to go out and replicate this activity because of the powerful learning it has the potential to produce? I definitely do not.

And yet, I know this: The simple truth is that the reason this exercise triggers ethical concerns is that it so directly simulates dynamics of privilege and oppression in the real world. NCCJ and Camp Anytown did not invent systemic racism; the organization aspires to transform it by educating kids to truly understand it out of a belief that we cannot effectively change systems that we do not fully understand, so they have designed and implemented an activity to help participants understand how these systems work. And in my heart of hearts, I could not construct any argument as valid to convince myself that I could avert my gaze from the discomfort evoked by this simulated microcosm while still witnessing fully, honestly, and courageously the full truth of these systems in the real world. Readers may encounter these facts and arrive at a different decision, but this line of thinking led me to a place where I felt not just willing, but compelled to move forward with this research.

By the time I had watched the emotional 2-hour debrief that followed the exercise, I had decided to make this activity the focus of my doctoral research. For years, I had been on a personal quest to understand what is true about race and social change in America; suddenly and unexpectedly, I had stumbled on an opportunity to explore my deepest questions using the tools and methods of social science. The next 3 years of my life were spent developing a rigorous research methodology, observing three more of these Separation Exercises, and then analyzing the findings that emerged from across the multiple observations. In that time, the scientific inquiry and my own personal quest blended into one integrated and all-consuming endeavor.

Because we were able to study multiple Separation Exercises using a comprehensive research methodology involving observation of the whole system and questionnaires for every individual in the system, this research enabled us to bring a high level of empirical rigor to the effort to understand the complex phenomenon of social change. Essentially, we could *zoom in* to investigate the inner lives and experiences of individuals immersed in these systems while simultaneously *zooming out* to obtain a bird's-eye perspective on the large-scale change process occurring at the level of the whole system. It was an intellectual and an emotional challenge to confront everything happening at the macro and micro levels of the system, but this was the ultimate goal and promise of researching the whole elephant. The result is an expansive perspective—intimately personal and vastly large-scale—that illuminates the phenomena of race and social change in surprising and important ways.

I discovered that it is not really possible to fully understand the dynamics that unfolded in those Separation Exercises without engaging with the relatively new science of complex systems, so I immersed myself in the study of interdependence, nonlinearity, development toward complexity, and fractals. Although scholars in fields such as economics, biology, environmental science, and finance had been exploring these matters for years, empirical research into how these dynamics related to matters of race and social change was scarce. But the effort to bridge these fields proved to be valuable: After years of being overwhelmed by the complexity of all that went into matters of race and social change, an elegant simplicity hidden underneath it popped sharply into focus.

When I finally finished my doctorate in 2005, I felt as though I had completed my quest: I had found a way to explore race and social change in a rigorous and empirical way, and as a result I had arrived at a much deeper level of personal understanding about how all of this works in a comprehensive, integrated manner. I would never claim that with this research I had *figured it all out*, but I did and still do believe this project represents a meaningful contribution to our national dialogue about these matters that is grounded in empiricism, data, and research. If my quest was driven by a need to understand what is true about race and social change, I could surely look in the mirror and tell myself honestly that I had explored those questions with depth, rigor, and sustained commitment, and I had arrived at useful, meaningful insights.

After years spent on research, reading, and writing, it was clear to me that I wanted to go beyond thinking about these topics. Fortunately, it didn't take long after graduation before an opportunity appeared to engage in a practical and constructive effort to advance the causes of racial equality, harmony, and positive social change in real-world ways. In what was surely one of the most fortuitous events in my life, I had brief informational interview at a Boston-based organization called City Year, and soon after that I found myself with a job there. City Year is an organization that engages young adults of all backgrounds in a year of full-time national service. It was founded by Michael Brown and Alan Khazei, two remarkable social entrepreneurs who met as freshman roommates at Harvard. By the time I began working there the organization was 18 years old and had already grown and expanded in remarkable ways. It was just in the earliest stages of pivoting to its current ambitious focus on leveraging young adults engaged in national service to address America's high school drop-out crisis.

Since its founding, City Year has believed that national service could complete the civil rights movement. In his book *Big Citizenship*, City Year cofounder Alan Khazei (2010) states:

> National service would help complete America's mission written into our Constitution—"to form a more perfect union." It would bind the country together, hand-in-hand with military service, around the idea of service to the nation. It could help heal America's racial and class divides by uniting people from diverse backgrounds for a cause larger than themselves. The Civil Rights movement of the 1960s changed the laws of America, but it did not entirely change people's hearts and minds. That best happens through shared service experiences, working together for the common good, and voluntary comprehensive national service is perhaps the best way to complete the Civil Rights movement in our country; a country that by 2050 will have no majority race. (p. 34)

My encounter with City Year and the idea of national service have quite simply changed my life. My years with this organization have only deepened my belief in the unique power that national service has to promote racial equality and to heal and strengthen the civic life of our nation. For that reason, this book will end with a call to action to make a year of national service a ubiquitous experience in the passage to adulthood for all Americans. I'll have a lot more to say about this in the final chapter of this book, because the institution of national service provides powerful answers to a whole host of questions raised by this inquiry into what is true about race and social change. After years spent studying these matters, it was a remarkable blessing to become part of an organization that is working on such a powerful, practical, constructive, and large-scale effort to strategically promote social change, racial equality, and civic engagement.

Over the course of the last decade of my life spent working at City Year, all that thinking and research I did about race and social change for my dissertation has informed my work on a daily basis. But the substance and full breadth of this research has for the most part gone unshared. In recent months, I have decided that needs to change as a series of shocking and deeply troubling events have brought the pain, anger, and injustice of race to the forefront of our national consciousness once again.

As a nation, we have witnessed the killing of Trevon Martin, an unarmed 17-year-old Black in Florida. Eric Garner, an unarmed 43-year-old Black and father of six died after being suffocated by police in an incident captured clearly on video. Michael Brown, an unarmed 18-year-old Black died after being shot 12 times by a police officer in Ferguson, Missouri. Tamir Rice, a 12-year-old Black was shot and killed in Cleveland, Ohio, by a police officer who thought that the toy gun Tamir was playing with was real. We've witnessed the emergence of Black Lives Matter, a modern movement for racial justice that has gained strength and urgency with every killing and every announcement that the police officers involved in these shootings would not be indicted.

And still the headlines keep coming. In South Carolina, 50-year-old Black man Walter Scott was shot in the back by a police officer as he tried to run away. Video of the incident made it clear that police officer shot and killed an unarmed Black man with no provocation. Also in South Carolina, nine congregants at the historic Emanuel African Methodist Episcopal Church in Charleston were gunned down by a twisted White supremacist in the middle of a bible study group. Over the course of the 2016 presidential election season, we have seen multiple cases of Black and Brown citizens being beaten and harassed at political rallies for Donald Trump, who as of this writing is our president-elect. On July 5, 2016, 37-year-old father of five Alton Sterling was shot and killed by two White police officers; video of the incident made it clear that Sterling was already pinned to the ground and was unable to resist at the time he was shot. The very next day, another video surfaced of the moment when 32-year-old Philando Castile was killed by police officers in St. Paul, Minnesota, when he was clearly complying with police requests to raise his arms over his head. The day after that, a Black man named Micah Javier Johnson killed five police officers and wounded nine others in an act of revenge at the end of what had been an otherwise peaceful Black Lives Matter protest.

Individually, any one of these incidents would be painful to confront and should rightfully challenge us all to think deeply about the work yet to be done to advance the cause of racial justice and equality in this nation. Taken as a whole, this long list of events surely represents a wake-up call for America.

As I have watched these events unfold, I have felt an overwhelming mix of pain, fear, and sadness. I love this country, and seeing so clearly that we are still so very far away from living up to our own espoused ideal of providing liberty and justice for all of our citizens breaks my heart. But I have also found that these events have evoked in me a firm resolve to try to contribute in some meaningful way to creating positive change. In this moment that is so heavy with sorrow and so ripe with possibility, I refuse to be a bystander. This is why I have now—10 years after graduating—decided to publish these insights as a book in the hopes that it finds an audience and contributes to our national discussion of these important matters in productive and meaningful ways.

2

Introduction to Classic Social Psychology Experiments

Although more than 50 years have passed since it first appeared, the grainy, black-and-white footage remains as compelling as the day that it was filmed:

> A middle aged White male is sitting at a desk on which we see a microphone and some sort of electrical contraption featuring a long horizontal line of switches. Speaking into the microphone, the man at the desk asks some sort of test question: "*Cloud: Forest, Rock, House.* Answer?" Someone off-screen responds, and the man at the desk looks devastated. "Incorrect," he says. "150 volts. Answer: *Forest.*" Reluctantly, he reaches out and flips a switch on the box in front of him. We hear a brief mechanical buzz and then frantic screams from a man off screen:
>
> AAAARGH! GET ME OUT OF HERE! GET ME OUT OF HERE! YOU HAVE NO RIGHT TO KEEP ME HERE! MY HEART IS BOTHERING ME! LET ME OUT OF HERE!
>
> The man at the desk is clearly intensely disturbed by this response. He turns around to look at a figure behind him just off-screen and gives a pleading, anguished look. A male with a confident and commanding voice responds immediately: "Please continue. The experiment requires that you continue." The man turns back to the machine

and asks the next question. Again, the wrong response is given and the man flips the next higher switch on the machine. Again, we hear anguished screams and pleading from the unseen figure. The man at the machine turns around to protest to the authority figure behind him. "This is awful! Who is going to take responsibility for this man if he gets hurt?!?"

The experimenter responds quickly and decisively. "I'll take responsibility. It is absolutely essential that you continue."

Despite his obvious misgivings, the man continues to ask questions and deliver shocks to the increasingly agitated man off-screen. Eventually, the screams and protests stop, and the shocks bring no response. For all we know, the man off-screen is now either unconscious or dead. But the experimenter continues to insist that the man must continue, and so he does . . . all the way to the last, highest-voltage switch on the machine.

The Individual Level of Analysis: Obedience and Conformity

The scene is from a famous (or more accurately, infamous) series of experiments conducted at Yale University in the 1950s by social psychologist Stanley Milgram. The details of the experimental design are explained in the next section, but for now the important point to note is that Milgram's authority experiments were among the first in a series of provocative social psychology experiments that have become classics in the field. Many of these studies have become widely known far beyond the boundaries of social psychology researchers because they compel us to confront the darker shadows of some of the most basic and universal dimensions of human behavior. Because the Separation Exercise that is the focus of this book builds on and extends this tradition in important ways, a review of these classic experiments provides an invaluable context for the insights and perspective that we'll encounter in the pages ahead.

Milgram's Obedience Experiments

Social psychologist Stanley Milgram conducted his famous experiments exploring obedience to authority at Yale University in the 1950s. Deeply disturbed by the Nazi genocide of Jews during the recently completed Second World War, Milgram (1974) wanted to understand how ordinary individuals could participate in mass cruelty and violence:

> The Nazi extermination of European Jews is the most extreme instance of abhorrent immoral acts carried out by thousands of people in the name of obedience. Yet in lesser degree this type of thing is constantly recurring: ordinary citizens are ordered to destroy other people, and they do so because they consider it their duty to obey orders. Thus obedience to authority, long praised as a virtue, takes on a new aspect when it serves a malevolent cause; far from appearing as a virtue, it is transformed into a heinous sin. Or is it? (p. 2)

In an effort to explore this question, Milgram designed the provocative experiment described at the start of this chapter. For this study, a volunteer subject was brought in to serve as a "teacher" who would administer electric shocks to a "learner" who would—by design—consistently fail to provide the "correct" response to a prefabricated series of opaque and ambiguous test questions. Unaware that the learner was really a collaborator in the experiment and was not actually being harmed, the subjects were ordered to continually increase the intensity of the shock on a machine that clearly noted that the voltage levels began at "mild" and progressed all the way up to and beyond "lethal." The experimenter—a middle-aged White male wearing a formal white lab coat—would stand behind the teacher and insist that the experiment had to continue, even though the teacher believed that the learner was experiencing an increasing level of pain and distress. Milgram wanted to know how far people would go in this experiment before they chose to disobey the commands of a perceived authority figure.

As part of his exploration of this phenomenon, Milgram asked a large number of laypeople and professionals to predict the outcome of this experiment. He presented groups of psychiatrists, college students, and middle-class adults with the design of the experiment and asked them to predict how many subjects would obey all the way through the highest level of electric shock. All groups predicted that "virtually all subjects will refuse to obey the experimenter; only a pathological fringe, not exceeding one or two percent, was expected to proceed to the end of the shockboard" (p. 31).

The actual results were quite different. It turns out that 65% of subjects continued through the end of the experiment, despite the belief they were causing extreme pain and possibly lethal harm to the learner (p. 35). In the videos (which you can find on YouTube), you can see teachers in obvious moral anguish about their actions. They give pleading looks to the authority, they protest verbally, they clearly feel horrible about what they are being asked to do . . . but can't bring themselves to actually disobey the commands of a perceived authority figure. It's those images and the surprisingly high level of obedience that have made this experiment so infamous.

Milgram conducted numerous additional experiments involving alterations in the experimental design, and these variations inevitably yielded different results. For example, he changed factors such as closeness to victim and found that it matters if the teacher was seated right next to the learner or was in another room and out of sight. He tweaked the level of involvement in flipping the switch and found different outcomes when teachers had to actually flip the switch that administered electric shocks or whether they just read the questions and another individual was present to flip the switches. He explored variations in the perceived legitimacy of the authority figure by having some experiments involve a laboratory professional in a white lab coat and others involve an ordinary individual with no special clothes and no perceived expertise. Each of these tweaks to the design of the experiment resulted in reduced levels of obedience.

In the years since these original experiments, subsequent research has expanded on these findings and raised questions and concerns about the validity of the research. The ethics of the experiment continue to inspire debates today, fueled by follow-up interviews that revealed that some participants in the study remain deeply troubled by the experience even after the passage of decades (see Gina Perry's 2013 book *Behind the Shock Machine* for a comprehensive overview of these matters).

Still, the Milgram experiment endures as an infamous and iconic undertaking in the history of the social sciences. To this day, it challenges us to think deeply about our own tendencies to obey authorities even when confronted with demands that fly in the face of our own moral code and ethical standards.

Solomon Asch's Conformity Experiments

In the early 1950s, social psychologist Solomon Asch (1951) set out to explore the dynamics of conformity. Similar to Milgram, he felt compelled to understand the powerful ways that ordinary individuals are influenced by their interpersonal relationships—in this case, with peers:

> Our immediate object was to study the social and personal conditions that induce individuals to resist or yield to group pressures when the latter are perceived to be *contrary to fact*. The issues which this problem raises are of obvious consequence for society; it can be of decisive importance whether or not a group will, under certain conditions, submit to existing pressures. (p. 177)

In his experiment, Asch gathered a group of eight individuals and asked them to take a simple perceptual test. In this case, the task was to view flashcards presenting a series of lines; participants were asked to identify which of the last three lines of various lengths perfectly matched the length of the first line on each flashcard. The subject of the experiment was unaware, however, that all seven of the other individuals involved were actually collaborators who were part of the experiment. On multiple occasions, the seven individuals unanimously asserted that a line that was clearly too long or too short was the line that matched the length of the first line. The subject was then placed in the position of having to either deviate from the group by saying what he or she perceived to be the correct answer or make the choice to ignore the evidence of his or her own senses in order to conform to the group. In his original experiment, Asch found that more than 30% of participants chose to conform to the group, suggesting that roughly one out of every three people would make statements that they did not believe to be true rather than risk standing alone in their responses.

Similar to Milgram, Asch also varied the experimental design and found a variety of factors that dramatically reduced the level of conformity. For example, the presence of one "partner" who also deviated from the group made it much easier for subjects to resist the pressure to conform. Employing a smaller majority (for example, three collaborators as opposed to seven) resulted in lower levels of conformity.

Asch's experiment has been repeated numerous times in the decades since, enabling researchers to explore the role of gender, the impact of the culture, and—in meta-analyses—the change in levels of conformity over time (Bond & Smith, 1996). Again, however, these variations do not undermine the experiment's basic finding that a significant percentage of individuals will conform to group pressure, even when doing so requires disregarding the evidence of their own senses (Asch, 1951).

I present the Milgram and Asch experiments together because they explore the *interpersonal* level of human behavior. Both focus on the behavior of *individuals* relating to each other either vertically (in authority relationships) or horizontally (in peer relationships). Surely, a key reason why these two experiments have become so well-known is that these dynamics are felt every day in our own individual lives as we strive to manage relationships with peers, authorities, and subordinates. To some degree, each one of us encounters some level of social pressure to either obey or conform, and the experiments of Milgram and Asch compel us to recognize just how influential those forces are in our own daily lives. I hope, by shining a light on the power and influence of these forces, their work empowers us to operate with more insight, clarity, and courage regarding the choices we make in our own relationships.

The Intergroup Level of Analysis: Studies of Intergroup Group Conflict, Cooperation, Privilege, and Oppression

The next three classic studies explore dynamics at a higher level of analysis: the *intergroup* level. It is important to note that the intergroup level of analysis includes and transcends the interpersonal level. In the following experiments, we will still see individuals navigating the forces of obedience and conformity, but now we see an additional level of complexity in that these dynamics are playing out within two different groups that must simultaneously negotiate relations with each other. It's an additional dynamic that adds a whole new level of complexity to our understanding of human behavior and illuminates an additional set of dynamics that are integral to the Separation Exercise.

The Stanford Prison Experiment

In March 2003, the United States began its long and highly controversial war in Iraq. Just a few months after the war began, a scandal exploded regarding the treatment of Iraqi prisoners by American servicemen and -women. Photos appeared of American soldiers striking happy poses while they were in the act of humiliating prisoners. As more details emerged, it became clear that these photos were just the tip of the iceberg; a group of American soldiers at Abu Ghraib prison in Baghdad had engaged in horrifying acts of torture, mistreatment, and humiliation. The details were shocking and deeply disturbing, seriously corroding America's moral standing at home and abroad.

In the discussions generated by the scandal, many asked how it was possible that American soldiers could behave so inhumanely toward the prisoners in their charge. How could seemingly decent, ordinary individuals end up engaging in such outrageous acts of cruelty? It was an understandable response to the scandal. But to anyone who had ever heard of the infamous Stanford Prison Experiment, the power of institutions such as Abu Ghraib to warp individual behavior was hardly a surprise.

The Stanford Prison Experiment was conducted in the early 1970s at a moment when the United States was mired in the Vietnam War. The stated purpose of the study was to understand "emerging conformity pressures in 'total situations' in which the processes of deindividuation and dehumanization are institutionalized" (Zimbardo, Maslach, & Haney, 2000, p. 193). The method involved the creation of a simulated prison in the basement of the psychology department at Stanford. The subjects were all area college students, who had agreed to participate in an experiment scheduled to last for 2 weeks. The subjects were screened with a battery of psychological tests; 24 students rated to be the most average, healthy, and normal according to the screening process were selected to participate. They would receive $15 per day as payment for their participation.

At the start of the experiment, the students were randomly separated into a "guard" group and a "prisoner" group. The similarity of the subjects prior to the start of the experiment, combined with the thoroughly random inclusion in either group, made the ultimate outcome of the experiment all the more surprising.

The researchers took great care to create a "total environment." Guards were given military-style uniforms and assigned shifts to ensure the prisoners were watched 24 hours a day. Prisoners received simple jumpsuits with sewn-on prisoner numbers. Individuals were allowed to enter the basement area only in the context of the experiment.

The results were dramatic. Within a day, the participants in the simulated prison began to take on the characteristics of their assigned roles with frightening sincerity and commitment. The prison guards became aggressive, dictatorial, cruel, and malicious. They created daily regimens of forced exercise, woke prisoners up repeatedly at random intervals during the night, withheld rations because of perceived insubordination, and willingly used force to keep the prisoners obedient and subservient.

The prisoners quickly fell into a very different pattern of behavior. After an early and brief effort to revolt against the system was quickly struck down by the guards, the prisoners succumbed to despair and helplessness. The severity of the situation increased rapidly:

> Within 36 hours after being arrested, the first prisoner had to be released because of extreme stress reactions of crying, screaming, cursing, and irrational actions that seemed to be pathological. The guards were most sadistic in waking prisoners from their sleep several times a night for "counts," supposedly designed for prisoners to learn their identification numbers but actually to use the occasion to taunt them, punish them, and play games with them, or rather on them. (Zimbardo, Maslach, & Haney, 2000, p. 227)

Very early in the study, the researchers decided that the situation had become too violent, and the subjects' identification with their roles had become too complete. Although the experiment was designed to last for 2 weeks, it was called off after just 6 days.

Although this experiment was related to—and in some ways inspired by—the work of Milgram and Asch, it represented more complex levels of analysis. Milgram and Asch were interested in the way individuals negotiated relationships of obedience or conformity. Subjects participated in those experiments only for an hour or two before being debriefed and released. In the Stanford Prison Experiment, the focus was on the dynamics between two groups immersed in a complete environment. They participated in a situation that institutionalized a set of norms, rules, and relationships over the course of 6 days, and the results are a testament to the remarkable ability of institutional factors to overwhelm individual personalities and values. Again, the experiment demonstrated the surprising ease with which average, normal individuals can be compelled to take on roles that demand violence or aggression toward others.

The Robbers Cave Experiment

Another influential study of group social psychology is known as the Robbers Cave Experiment (Sherif, Harvey, White, Hood, & Sherif, 1961). The name is derived from the location where the experiment was conducted: Robbers Cave State Park in southeastern Oklahoma, where researchers brought together 22 boys for a 3-week experience at a rustic summer camp.

The experiment was designed to explore dynamics of group conflict and cooperation, and it was carefully designed to control for a number of variables. The boys were all White males about to enter sixth grade from very similar geographic and socioeconomic backgrounds. Potential subjects were given a battery of psychological tests, and once again only the most stable and well-adjusted boys were admitted to the study. None of the boys in the study were social isolates, poor or failing students, or came from unstable families. In addition, care was taken to ensure that none of the boys knew each other prior to the experiment. By creating a cohort of homogenous strangers, the researchers sought to limit the influence of preexisting social or psychological problems, preexisting friendship groups, and diversity of race, gender, or socioeconomic status.

Throughout the study, the researchers worked as participant observers by organizing events and activities and then carefully observing dynamics within and between the groups. The experimental design included three distinct stages. The first was focused on *experimental in-group formation*. In this stage, the boys were divided into two groups of 11. The groups were separated, given names—the "Eagles" and the "Rattlers"—and were repeatedly given tasks designed to foster a strong sense of group solidarity and in-group identity. The boys were asked to come up with group cheers and were encouraged to talk about all the positive attributes that made their own group so great.

The second stage of this exercise was called the *intergroup relations—friction phase*. In this stage, the two groups were brought together and given tasks designed to create competition and conflict between the two groups. The groups competed in activities such as a tug-of-war and foot races and were encouraged to engage in raids on the other group. Almost instantly, an intense animosity developed between the two groups, with both sides believing that their own group was good, noble, and superior while the other group was bad, flawed, and inferior. Boys who had just hours earlier been pleasant, polite, well-adjusted individuals had quickly transformed into something quite different. The Eagles and the Rattlers were soon calling each other names, and on multiple occasions staff members had to break up arguments and fights. It seems that when separated into an "us" and a "them," even the most homogenous and otherwise healthy boys become enthusiastic participants in a culture of intergroup violence and aggression.

Had the experiment ended here, the lessons from Robbers Cave would have been uniformly bleak. Fortunately, however, the experiment had a third and final stage that revealed lessons with clear relevance to the inquiry at the heart of this book, a stage called the *intergroup relations—integration phase*, and it involved deliberate attempts to foster cooperation and integration between the two groups. This was done through the introduction of what researchers called *superordinate goals*—tasks that would benefit both groups but that neither group could complete alone. For example, the boys were told that a truck carrying food for the boys had broken down on the road, and they would have to work together to push the truck into camp. Soon, the two groups were working side by side in a strenuous effort to push the truck a final few hundred yards. Before long, the Eagles and the Rattlers began to realize that perhaps the "others" weren't quite such terrible people after all.

Over the course of pursuing a series of these superordinate goals, the animosity, aggression, and sense of "us versus them" gradually faded, to be replaced by a renewed sense of cooperation and friendship between the Eagles and the Rattlers. Although traces of the earlier in-group loyalties remained, the experiment proved that two hostile groups are not destined to endure an eternity of aggression and animosity. The final lesson of the Robbers Cave Experiment is that it is possible to transform a pair of warring tribes into a more-or-less united whole, capable of once again treating each other with dignity and respect.

The Blue Eyes/Brown Eyes Exercise

In 1968, Jane Elliot was working as a third-grade teacher at an elementary school in the small town of Riceville, Iowa. On Thursday, April 4, she turned on her TV and was shocked to learn that the great civil rights leader Martin Luther King Jr. had been assassinated in Memphis. That night, she decided that she had to find a way to help her class of all-White students gain a genuine understanding of the oppression and discrimination endured by Black people in America. The next morning, she implemented for the first time an activity that has become famous around the world.

Elliot realized that simply asking a group of White 8- and 9-year-old students to reflect on topics such as racism, discrimination, and oppression was ineffective. Because it was their good fortune to have never really experienced those dynamics in their own lives, the result was, in her words, "just an exchange of ignorance." So she found a way to give her students a chance to actually feel the sting of those forces. All of her students were White, so she could not use skin color as a factor in her activity. Instead, she chose to focus on eye color. About half her class had brown eyes, and the other half had blue eyes. This unremarkable distinction had never really mattered to the students, but for the next few days it would become the most important aspect of their lives.

The next day, Elliot announced that the class would be divided between blue-eyed students and brown-eyed students. She explained that blue-eyed students were, quite simply, superior to brown-eyed students. They were smarter, kinder, and better behaved than brown-eyed students. Naturally, then, they would be granted extra privileges, such as having 5 extra minutes at recess, being able to get double servings at lunch, and being able to use the water fountain. The brown-eye students would get none of these things . . . and they were now required to wear conspicuous collars around their neck that marked them unmistakably from any distance as being brown-eyed. Elliot made it clear that brown-eyed students were unintelligent, slow, and in every way inferior to their blue-eyed peers. The two groups were forbidden to play together at recess.

As class continued that day, Elliot made use of every opportunity to praise the blue-eyed students and disparage the brown-eyed students. If a student with blue eyes gave a correct answer, she would say something like, "See—just like a blue-eyed student! They've always got the right answer!" If a brown-eyed student took just a few seconds too long to pull out her homework, Elliot would say, "That's always how it is with brown-eyed students. Always slower than everybody else. Brown-eyed students can't do anything right." The activity continued throughout the day, with blue-eyed students enjoying a stream of privileges and praise while brown-eyed students were given conspicuously less of everything than their peers while enduring shaming and discrimination.

The impact of this newly imposed system of privilege and oppression on the behavior of individual students was rapid and dramatic. Within hours, the behavior of a number of blue-eyed students became arrogant, dismissive, and cruel toward their brown-eyed peers. It did not take long for them to internalize the belief that they were indeed superior and that their brown-eyed peers were deserving of scorn. The brown-eyed students had the opposite experience. After briefly resisting the rules of the exercise, they soon became quiet, dejected, and subservient. At recess, they kept themselves isolated from the blue-eyed kids who were playing energetically on the playground. Based on their actions, it was apparent that they had rapidly internalized the message that they were inferior and not deserving of the same privileges as their blue-eyed peers.

The next Monday, things did not just go back to normal. Elliot had the brown-eyed kids put their collars back on, and kept the activity going for a while. Midway through the day, however, she announced that there would be a change. From then on, it was the *brown-eyed* students who were actually superior, and the *blue-eyed students* who were deficient in every way. All the privileges that had been enjoyed by the blue-eyed students—extra recess time, extra servings at lunch, use of the water fountain—would now be granted to the brown-eyed students and forbidden to the blue-eyed students. She then told all the brown-eyed students to stand up, take off their collars, and place them on the neck of a blue-eyed student. With obvious joy, the brown-eyed students quickly removed their collars and wrapped them around the neck of a blue-eyed peer.

In an instant, the whole system of privilege and oppression that had governed the classroom for the last day and a half was turned on its head. Suddenly, it was the brown-eyed students who could do no wrong, and the blue-eyed students who were constantly made to feel stupid, slow, and all-around inferior. Remarkably, the behavior of both groups almost instantly reversed. Brown-eyed kids who had been quiet and subservient that morning soon became arrogant and cruel toward their blue-eyed peers, and blue-eyed students who had been confident and outspoken quickly became quiet and dejected. It was now the blue-eyed kids who sat in isolated misery on the playground, having internalized almost instantly the message that they were now inferior and unworthy.

In an interview Elliot explained, "I saw kids who could be harmless, cooperative, wonderful, thoughtful children turn into nasty, vicious, discriminating third graders in the space of 15 minutes." The magnitude of the change was unmistakable and remarkable, and made all the more amazing by the fact that the behavior of individual students was instantly transformed when the structure of the system—which group was "superior" and which was "inferior"—was inverted.

At the end of the day on Tuesday, Elliot asked her class to reflect on how they thought it felt to be a Black person in America. It was no longer an abstract discussion, because everyone in the class had now enjoyed the confidence and pride evoked by unearned privilege and felt personally the sting of shame, doubt, and self-hatred of undeserved discrimination. When Elliot asked her students if they thought it was fair to judge other people just by the color of their eyes or the color of their skin, the students unanimously shouted "No!" When she stated that racism and discrimination are terrible things, the students nodded fervently in agreement. When she invited the blue-eyed students to finally remove their collars and throw them in the trash, the sense of joy and relief was palpable. For the first time in days, the class was able to once again join together as equals.

Within just a few years, Elliot and her work gained a wide audience. She was invited to talk on *The Tonight Show* with Johnny Carson, and the activity she designed became the focus of multiple TV documentaries (*Eye of the Storm* and *A Class Divided*; clips from both are accessible on YouTube). More recently, she has appeared on *Oprah* five times, including an episode in which the TV audience unexpectedly found themselves participating in the exercise. Today, Elliot remains a legend in the field of antiracism activism and education.

Beyond Intergroup Dynamics: The Unexplored Frontier

The Stanford Prison Experiment, the Robbers Cave Experiment, and the Blue Eyes/Brown Eyes Exercise powerfully illuminate dynamics that appear at the intergroup level of analysis. It is important to note once again the relationship between these intergroup experiments and the interpersonal experiments of Milgram and Asch. On the one hand, the intergroup level of analysis *includes* those interpersonal dynamics, because individuals within each group clearly had to negotiate authority and peer relationships throughout their experiences. On the other hand, the intergroup level simultaneously *transcends* those dynamics by including another level of events— the relationship between two groups—that was completely absent in the interpersonal level of analysis. In moving from the interpersonal to the intergroup level of analysis, we have essentially zoomed out from a close-up focus on interpersonal dynamics to a wider focus that includes a new and distinct set of dynamics.

The relevance of these intergroup experiments to real-world events is undeniable. The Abu Ghraib prison scandal in Iraq demonstrated beyond a doubt that the behaviors observed in the Stanford Prison Experiment can—under the right conditions— surface in horrifying ways in the real world. The patterns of conflict observed between the Eagles and the Rattlers in the Robbers Cave Experiment surely mirror real-life us-versus-them intergroup conflicts similar to gang violence in many cities, violence between the Hutus and Tutsis in Rwanda, and dynamics between the United States and Russia during the Cold War (and, as of this writing, right up to our current day). And it should be readily apparent to anyone who has followed the news over the last few years that despite undeniable progress on racial reconciliation over the years, systems of racism and discrimination remain all too real in America.

A key theme that emerges across all of these exercises is a challenge for many of us to accept. The West in general—and America in particular—is deeply invested in the notion of individual freedom, and we have always had a deep faith in the power we each have to control our own actions, make our own choices, and operate independently from any forces at work outside of ourselves. And yet again and again, these experiments show that systemic forces have a powerful and dramatic ability to warp individual behavior. When placed in a total institution such as a prison, even the most healthy and well-adjusted individuals can become cruel guards or despairing, disempowered prisoners. When divided into two groups, even the most homogenous individuals can easily fall into a heated us-versus-them dynamic in which "we" can do no wrong and "they" can do no right. When they find themselves immersed in a system that privileges one group while discriminating against another on the basis of utterly meaningless aspects of appearance, ordinary third graders quickly internalize systemic messages they receive regarding their "inherent" superiority or inferiority.

Again and again, we must confront the uncomfortable truth that none of us is really as free and independent as we would like to believe. Clearly, the systems in which we are immersed have a powerful ability to shape our perceptions of reality and influence our behaviors; in certain situations, those systems have an immense power to warp our common decency and diminish our own individual humanity. Given this reality, it is important that we strive to understand the power of these systemic forces and—with courage and persistence—engage and transform them through understanding, insight, and wise action.

This, surely, was the motivation of the researchers and educators who carried out these classic experiments. Without a doubt, the dimensions of human behavior illuminated by these efforts are dark and unpleasant. But it was their belief that through the direct confrontation with the reality of these dynamics, we might be empowered to confront, transcend—and eventually transform— the violent and dehumanizing forces unleashed in these intergroup encounters. And there is reason to believe that encounters with this research have this effect. Just as the Milgram and Asch experiments have compelled us all to grapple seriously with our own susceptibility to mindless obedience or conformity, the intergroup experiments presented here have generated powerful and productive dialogues related to intergroup conflict, cooperation, privilege, and oppression.

On the one hand, then, the contribution these classics experiments have made to our understanding of human behavior is invaluable. On the other hand, it is also true that these studies have some significant limitations. After all, in the real world, there are almost always more than just two groups interacting. Although most of us are immersed in institutions—school, work, family, houses of worship, and so on—most of us do not live out our lives in total institutions that constrain our every action, such as the simulated prison in which guards were empowered to control every aspect of daily life for prisoners. Rather, the vast majority of us live in social systems that are far more complex and that provide a far higher degree of freedom than those explored in any of these classic experiments. Our cities, towns, and nations are in fact diverse ecologies involving multiple groups coexisting amid complex patterns of interconnection and interdependence.

Equally important, the power structures and social norms of these communities are in no way static and unchanging. The underlying social architecture governing these communities has been undergoing a process of significant and ongoing change. In just the past few decades, rigid, highly segregated patterns of power, privilege, and opportunity have shifted toward norms that are dramatically more equal and fairer than before. An unmistakable recent example of this process of dramatic change is the transformation of the legal status of gay marriage in just a few years. Without a doubt, the real world is a remarkably alive place that is more complex, more dynamic, and allows for far more individual freedom than the situations that were simulated and explored through these classic social psychology experiments.

The fact is that if we want to truly understand about race and social change, then we need to zoom out even further, to a third and higher level of analysis that includes and transcends interpersonal *and* intergroup dynamics—while illuminating a whole new set of human dynamics that suddenly bring recent real-world events into vivid focus. It turns out that this additional, higher level of analysis is a very strange place, full of dynamics that—when properly understood—compel us to question some of the deepest assumptions we hold about how the world works and the very nature of the reality in which we are immersed.

It is to this third, additional level of analysis that we turn our attention to now. In the following two chapters, we'll take a deep dive into understanding systems. In Chapter 3, "Understanding Systems, Part I," we'll explore the dynamics that govern these systems. We'll engage with concepts such as nonlinearity, interdependence, self-organization, and fractals. In Chapter 4, "Understanding Systems, Part II," we'll discuss how dynamic systems develop toward complexity. We will also discover how bringing these two concepts together illuminates a simple, elegant process underlying and driving social change from the dawn of human history right up through today's headlines.

3

Understanding Systems, Part I: Dynamics of Complex Systems

In 1982, at the height of the Cold War, the United States and the Soviet Union were locked in an arms race with potentially catastrophic consequences. The question of how to address the issue of nuclear disarmament was on the minds of many when personal growth expert Ken Keyes Jr. published his powerfully influential small book called *The Hundredth Monkey* (1982).

The book begins with a story—allegedly true—about a group of monkeys living on a Japanese island. One of the monkeys discovered a novel approach to eating sweet potatoes that involve washing the food in a nearby stream before eating. As the monkey began teaching the method to family and friends, the number of monkeys practicing the new approach grew and grew. Eventually, something surprising happened:

> In the autumn of 1958, a certain number of Koshima monkeys were washing sweet potatoes—the exact number is not known. Let us suppose that when the sun rose one morning there were 99 monkeys on Koshima Island who had learned to wash their sweet potatoes. Let's further suppose that later that morning, the hundredth monkey learned to wash potatoes.
>
> THEN IT HAPPENED!
>
> By that evening almost everyone in the tribe was washing sweet potatoes before eating them. The added

energy of this hundredth monkey somehow created an ideological breakthrough!

But notice: A most surprising thing observed by these scientists was that the habit of washing sweet potatoes then jumped over the sea . . . Colonies of monkeys on other islands and the mainland troop of monkeys at Takasakiyama began washing their sweet potatoes.

Thus, when a certain critical number achieves an awareness, this new awareness may be communicated from mind to mind.

Keyes's book developed a devoted following. The notion that just one more supporter could catalyze a transformation of global consciousness inspired and sustained many activists seeking to address seemingly intractable challenges. It turns out, though, that the hundredth monkey phenomenon was bad science. It seems that Keyes misrepresented the monkey research; although it's true that most monkeys on the island did begin to wash their sweet potatoes, the spread of the new best practice was easily explained through social processes. Older monkeys who did not encounter the cleaning method at an early age never used the new method, and the observed leap of knowledge to monkeys around the world was not empirically observed. The whole notion of a more-or-less mystical leap of global consciousness was really an embellishment by Keyes that went beyond the facts.

Eighteen years later, in 2000, another author brought the same idea back. This time, however, it was not necessary to invent a modern myth grounded in an embellishment of obscure research. The phenomenon in question had become so commonplace that examples could be found nearly everywhere. In his best-selling book, *The Tipping Point*, Malcolm Gladwell presented numerous engaging examples of situations that clearly operated according to the principles of the "critical mass" concept. It turns out that moments of sudden, dramatic change appeared in contexts as disparate as sales of

Hush Puppy shoes, suicide epidemics, and the popularity of cell phones.[1]

Today—years after the publication of Gladwell's book—the term *tipping point* has become even more commonplace. We see the phenomenon it describes all around us: blog posts or tweets suddenly "go viral"; fashion trends suddenly sweep the nation; memes burst into the public sphere and are discussed everywhere for a few days until the next idea grabs our attention. When the events that became known as the Arab Spring began to unfold in 2010, we all understood exactly what they meant when the media referred to the self-immolation of a Tunisian fruit seller as a tipping point.

The scientific literature uses a different term to describe the tipping point concept. The word is *nonlinearity*, and it highlights the fact that the relationship between an action in a system and the outcome of that action has the potential to be wildly out-of-whack. To people accustomed to thinking that cause and effect have to be roughly equivalent, it's a deeply counterintuitive notion. But it's a phenomenon that's now been empirically observed in a remarkable array of contexts, and—as we'll see—it's a dynamic that is undeniably relevant to understanding social change efforts as well.

It's important to recognize, however, that nonlinearity is just one of many inherent properties of complex systems. Some of the other properties are perhaps less well-known and understood than the idea of tipping points, but the insights from this field advance our effort to understand matters of race and social change in important ways. For this reason, this chapter provides a brief overview and introduction to some key insights from the new field

---

[1] Given the subject of this book, it should be noted that Gladwell also highlights the "broken windows" theory of crime reduction in his book. It's a concept that has been hotly contested as a flawed approach to criminal justice that increased racial profiling without actually reducing crime. A detailed exploration of this topic is beyond the scope of this chapter, but interested readers can find an overview of the critique in Bellafante (2015).

of complex systems. These ideas represent an essential context for understanding events that unfold in the Separation Exercises we'll encounter in Chapter 5.

The field of complex systems attempts to understand a set of governing principles that seem to transcend the narrow focus of any single scientific discipline. Physicist Yaneer Bar-Yam (2001) introduces the subject as follows:

> "Complex Systems" is the new approach to science studying how relationships between parts give rise to the collective behaviors of a system, and how the system interacts and forms relationships with its environment. Social systems formed (in part) out of relationships between people, the brain formed out of relationships between neurons, molecules formed out of relationships between atoms, the weather formed out of relationships between air flows are all examples of complex systems. Studying complex systems cuts across all of science, as well as engineering, management, and medicine. . . . It focuses on certain questions about relationships and how they make parts into wholes. (p. 4)

The field is so interdisciplinary that it provides a challenge to authors seeking to provide a general overview of key ideas. Bar-Yam's (2001) textbook, for example, includes chapters on neural networks, protein folding, polymer dynamics, thermodynamics, and human civilization. It's important for readers to appreciate that the dynamics described in the following can be observed across all of these domains of inquiry. But because we are interested in understanding human behavior and social change, we will stay focused on disciplines, experiments, and examples with a clear relevance to our area of interest, even though the reader may feel at times that we are exploring matters that are far afield from our focus on race and social change.

With that in mind, here's what we'll explore in the pages ahead: first, we'll go a bit deeper into our understanding of nonlinearity. Then, we'll explore the concepts of interdependence, self-organization, and fractals. We'll end with a discussion of the concept of complexity itself. Then, in Chapter 4, we'll explore how all of this informs our understanding of the sort of human social change that is the primary focus of this book.

Nonlinear Dynamics

Perhaps the best-known example of the concept of nonlinearity is the butterfly effect. In her book *Leadership and the New Science*, leadership scholar Margaret Wheatley (1999) explains the phenomenon like this:

> Edward Lorenz, a meteorologist, first drew public attention to this with his now famous "butterfly effect." Does the flap of a butterfly wing in Tokyo, Lorenz queried, affect a tornado in Texas (or a thunderstorm in New York)? Though unfortunate for the future of accurate weather prediction, his answer was "yes." (p. 142)

The phenomenon can be demonstrated through a variety of examples. Wheatley (1999) describes attempts to explore the impact of infinitesimally small differences on mathematical models as follows:

> Hypothetically, were we to create a difference in values as small as rounding them off to the thirty-first decimal place (calculating numbers this large requires astronomical computing power), after only one hundred iterations the whole calculation would go askew. The two systems would have diverged from each other in unpredictable

ways. This behavior demonstrates that even infinitesimal differences can be far from inconsequential. (p. 121)

Later, she states,

Many organizations have learned that events occurring in a relatively minor part of their business suddenly grow to threaten their overall viability. Before disaster struck in Union Carbide's plant in Bhopal, India, the plant contributed a mere 4% to corporate profits. However, this horrific tragedy led to a major restructuring of the entire company and a serious decrease in its overall evaluation. (p. 142)

Wheatley presents the Union Carbide example to demonstrate that nonlinearity is a property that matters in the real world, not just in abstract math computations. We all need to understand the principle that seemingly minor events can have undeniably major consequences.

Once you know to look for them, similar examples of nonlinearity appear everywhere. The perspective of complex systems provides us with a language with which we may describe and explain this dynamic.

Interdependence

The field of complex systems emerged out of a recognition that, in many disciplines, scientists had reached the limits of their ability to reduce the world to ever smaller component pieces. Physics provides the clearest example of this reductionist approach to understanding the world around us. The discovery that matter is composed of components called *molecules* was eventually followed by the discovery that molecules are composed of atoms; which are themselves composed of neutrons, protons, and electrons; which are themselves composed of quarks. At a cost of tens of millions of dollars, the global scientific community built the Large Hadron Collider, which just recently enabled us to empirically confirm the existence of the Higgs Boson, an infinitesimal particle that physicists have been seeking to confirm experimentally for years. With each passing decade, we seem to grow closer to understanding the most basic building blocks of the physical world.

Eventually, however, this effort to reduce the world to its smallest component parts reaches its limits: as scientists get close to finding the smallest, most basic components of the phenomenon in question, it becomes very clear that even a robust understanding of the individual parts provides limited insight into its actual working dynamics. For example, we can achieve a detailed understanding of the molecular structure of DNA, the functions of mitochondria, and the chemical makeup of cell walls. . . . and still not really understand how a living cell *works*.

Essentially, there comes a time when the field must zoom out from its laser-like focus on component parts and begin viewing systems as a whole. From this perspective, scientists must begin to refocus not just on the pieces but also on the interactions and relationships among all the pieces. The field of complex systems provides a focus on this interdependence, a language with which to understand it, and a new level of clarity about the dynamics that govern the workings of whole systems.

Bar-Yam's overview of interdependence invites us to consider three different types of systems and imagine what happens when a piece of the system is removed:

> The first example is a material such as a piece of metal or a glass of water. In these instances, it is possible to remove a component of the system (by cutting off a corner of the metal sheet or removing a spoonful of water from the glass) without significantly changing the system. The removed component and the larger part of the material remain more-or-less unchanged.

A second example of a more interdependent system is a plant or tree. Imagine what happens when you cut some roots or branches from a tree: although the tree as a whole may continue to grow, it will surely be affected by the loss of the part. And the part itself will be profoundly affected (it will die) because of the removal.

We see an even higher level of interdependence when we look at a more complex system such as an animal. Remove a leg or a lung, and the animal and the part are—to put it mildly—strongly affected. Unlike a tree, the attempt to separate almost any component part from the whole in a living animal is sure to have a major impact on the whole animal and the part that was removed.

Bar-Yam (2001) states:

> These three examples show very different kinds of interdependence. Recognizing that these different behaviors exist is an important part of characterizing all of the systems we are interested in. Consider the family or organization you are a part of. How strong are the dependencies between the parts? . . . These are key questions for understanding the system and how we might affect it by our actions. Just asking these questions when we think about our world is an important part of understanding relationships. (p. 8)

This underlying interdependence—which may vary in degree or intensity—is another key component of complex systems. It is relevant to note that as the level of interdependence increases, it becomes increasingly problematic to try to understand the system in question through reductionism. It may be helpful, for example, to understand the molecular structure of a piece of metal or a spoonful of water: this focus on parts actually does go a long way toward helping us understand the entire sheet of metal or glass of water. When we shift our focus to the animal, however, reductionism doesn't work as well. It is surely helpful to understand the molecular structure of, say, olfactory nerves that contribute to the remarkable sense of smell that dogs have, but it would be a mistake to believe that a deep understanding of one component part of the dog gives us any truly meaningful understanding of the whole living animal. At some point, we have to recognize the fundamental limitations of focusing on component parts and begin to study the workings of the system as a whole to accurately understand how that dog actually exists and functions in the world.

Self-Organization

Complex systems frequently exhibit complicated and intricate patterns. Consider, for example, the flowing lines that appear in desert sands or on sandy ocean floors or the striking patterns of stripes on tropical fish or on zebras and leopards. A key insight of complex systems is that these orderly and sophisticated patterns emerge through a process of self-organization. When each individual unit in a system follows some very simple rules, some remarkably sophisticated patterns can emerge at the level of the system as a whole. Bar-Yam (2001) explains:

> When people make something, like a car, they put each part in a particular place to make a specific structure that will do a specific task. When someone paints a picture, they place each patch of paint in a particular place to make the picture. In nature we notice that there are patterns that form without someone putting each part in a particular place. The pattern seems to simply happen by itself. It *self-organizes*. (p. 9)

We now know that the natural world abounds with examples in which remarkably sophisticated levels of structure, order, and stability are achieved through self-organization that emerges from within the system. Consider, for example, the work of researchers in the late 1980s who set out to explore the phenomenon of self-organization using a computer simulation. The purpose was to "capture the essence of flocking behaviors in birds, or herding behavior in sheep, or schooling behavior in fish" (Waldrop, 1992, p. 241). In the simulation, a large number of bird-like agents were placed in an on-screen environment full of obstacles. Each individual agent was programmed to follow three simple rules:

1. Keep a minimum distance from other objects in the environment, including other "birds."
2. Match the velocity of the other "birds" in its neighborhood.
3. Try to move towards the perceived center of mass of "birds" in its neighborhood. (Waldrop, 1992, p. 241)

When each simulated agent followed these simple rules, the results were dramatic. Flocks of bird always formed, and these flocks were able to navigate the environment with fluidity and agility. Flocks headed for a wall would suddenly part and then reform on the other side of the obstacle; whole flocks would seem to change direction almost in unison. Although each individual bird was following those three simple rules, some incredibly complicated and sophisticated behaviors emerged at the system level. There was no single alpha bird telling all the other birds when to turn; the stunningly well-organized and highly synchronized collective behavior emerged without any leader at all.

The phenomenon is illuminated powerfully through a computer simulation tool called *cellular automata*. Similar to the flocking simulation, this tool demonstrates system-wide pattern formation that occurs as a result of individual behaviors. It presents a perspective that is relevant to our focus on social change.

In a classic example, the cellular automata tool is used to present a model of panic in a crowd. In this model, individuals are represented by individual squares (cells) on a vast grid. The model breaks this large grid down into 3 × 3 "box-of-nine" subsections, and it assumes that individuals in the crowd will be influenced by the eight other individuals in their given subsection. Given these assumptions, it is possible to create mathematical rules about how individuals will behave. For example, we might create a rule stating that an individual will panic if four other people in the box-of-nine panic; if fewer than four other people are panicking, then the individual will remain—or become—calm.

The possible outcomes of this rule are presented in Figure 3.1. In these diagrams, panicky individuals appear as black squares, and calm individuals appear as white squares. As you can see, different ratios within a given box-of-nine subsection will dictate the status of the middle square (if four or more squares are black, the middle square turns black; if three or fewer squares are black, the middle square turns white).

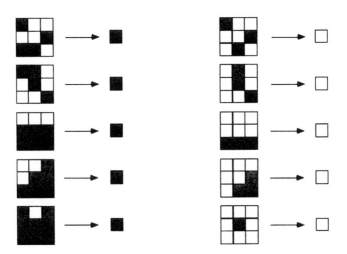

Figure 3.1 Possible Outcomes in the Cellular Automata Model of Panic in a Crowd

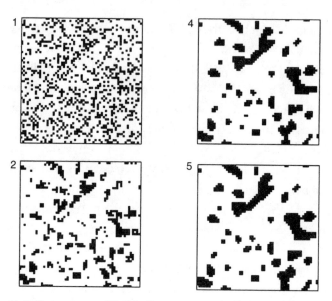

Figure 3.2 Emergence of Stable Patterns in a Cellular Automata Simulation: Iterations 1, 2, 4, and 5

Of course, each of these subsections is just a small piece of a larger system. By zooming out to view the system as a whole, it becomes possible to view the global patterns that emerge over time as individuals continue to react to changes in their local environments.

The diagrams presented in Figures 3.2 and 3.3 demonstrate how these patterns emerge and change over the course of time. Be sure to look for the small numbers next to the upper left corner of each image; they indicate the number of times the system was updated using the described rule. So the first image in the top left of Figure 3.2 is the initial state; this is how the system looked at the very beginning. Right below it is iteration 2; this presents how the system looked once the rule governing the change in the states of individual cells was implemented once. The top right box in Figure 3.2 shows the fourth iteration, and below that is the fifth. Then, the four boxes in Figure 3.3 show the state of the system after the tenth, twentieth, fortieth, and fiftieth times that those rules were applied. What we see is the emergence of some large-scale and stable patterns emerging

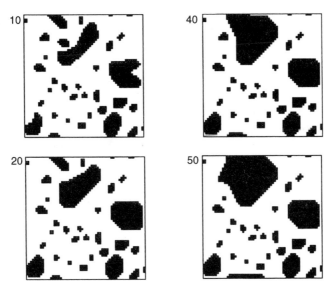

Figure 3.3 Iterations 10, 20, 40, and 50 of the Cellular Automata Simulation

from rules governing dynamics at the level of individual cellular behavior.

Bar-Yam (2001) states:

> Over the first few updates, the random arrangement of dots resolves into areas of panic. Isolated panickers calm down and regions of higher-density become the areas of panic. Then over a longer time, the panicking areas grow and reach a stable configuration. We can try this from a different initial arrangement of panickers. In some cases the panicking areas grow until they combine and fill the entire space. For this panic rule, in this size space, starting from more than a quarter of the people panicked (Black), the panic will grow to cover the space, while for less than this the panic will stay isolated. We can think about this more generally as a model of fads, mobs, and hysteria. (p. 14)

As with the flocking simulation, this computer model enables us to explore the connection between individual behaviors and larger systemic patterns that emerge from those behaviors. Again, the crucial point is that these sophisticated patterns in complex systems are *not* created through the direction of some agent with the power to dictate the outcome; rather, the system self-organizes by following simple rules at a local level, and these simple rules generate complex patterns that emerge at the higher level.

The cellular automata research illuminates some key insights about the nature of complex systems. For example, researchers found that changes in the initial state of the system have major impacts on the patterns that ultimately form. For example, starting this system with slightly less than 25% of the individuals in a panicked state generates a stable pattern of black-and-white zones; starting the system with more than 25% of the individuals in a panicked state results in a dramatically different outcome. Similarly, even small changes to the rules governing the system result in dramatically different outcomes. When we alter the rules to state that an individual will panic when three—not four—other individuals in a subsection panic, an entirely different outcome emerges.

As it may seem that we are exploring terrain that is far removed from our interest in race and social change, let's take a moment to unpack the connection between this cellular automata concept and the social psychology experiments presented back in Chapter 1. As you will recall, the Milgram and Asch experiments explored the level of individual behavior; essentially, individuals in those experiments were faced with fairly simple choices: *obey the authority/don't obey the authority* or *conform with peers/don't conform with peers*. In a meaningful sense, they were like individual cells whose state was powerfully influenced by relationships with the other cells immediately above and below themselves (authority relationships) and on either side of themselves (peer relationships).

Zooming out a bit, the Stanford Prison Experiment, the Robbers Cave Experiment, and the Blue Eyes/Brown Eyes Exercise focused on a different level of analysis: intergroup behaviors. In the cellular automata context, those experiments could be represented by two boxes-of-nine, either side-by-side (as in the Robbers Cave experiment) or one on top of the other (as in the Stanford Prison Experiment and the Blue Eyes/Brown Eyes Exercise). Either way, we can now imagine ourselves simultaneously observing the interpersonal dynamics occurring within each box-of-nine as well as the intergroup dynamics occurring between both sets of boxes.

As Figures 3.2 and 3.3 make clear, however, the whole-system perspective compels us to zoom out—way out—to observe an even higher level of analysis. All those local individual and intergroup dynamics generate some remarkable patterns that can only be observed when taking a global view of the whole system. If we were to conduct a little thought experiment and imagine ourselves to be one of the cells in that matrix, it's easy to imagine being completely focused on the calm or panicking individuals in our immediate vicinity. How would we handle things if our boss (or parent or president) began to panic? How about if our direct reports (or children or constituents) began to panic? How about if our friends (or colleagues or siblings) began to panic?

Although we were immersed in the stress and chaos of these hyper-local events in our part of the system, we may well be surprised to learn that our individual actions contribute to the emergence of some remarkably sophisticated, orderly, and stable patterns that only become clearly visible at the global level. From the perspective of any individual cell in the matrix, it's an understandable challenge to recognize that those global patterns even exist. Attaining some level of insight into how those patterns develop and how our individual actions play a small but integral role is an even greater challenge. But this is exactly the leap of consciousness that we are invited to embrace when we zoom out to observe this third, higher level of analysis.

The jump to this higher level of consciousness regarding the connection between individual choices and the emergence of global patterns provides a vital dimension to explore matters of race and social change. However, it's not enough. Another group of research-ers took the cellular automata idea beyond dynamics of self-organi-zation when they set out to find a way to model concepts such as adaptation, evolution, and creativity. It turns out that their insights will play a key role in our efforts to understand the workings of the Separation Exercises.

The "Game of Life" and Complexity in Social Systems

Mitchell Waldrop's (1992) book *Complexity* is an engaging overview of the process by which the study of complexity has broken down traditional boundaries in the way established disciplines understand the world. It is also an introduction to the many new findings and insights that illuminate the rules that govern complex systems.

Waldrop's "Game of Life" plays an important role in achieving a greater understanding of complex systems because it is an attempt to use computers to model a complex living system. Although it is based on the previously presented concept of cellular automata, it is considerably more complex than the simple panic–don't panic model. In this simulation, individual cells can move to a wide range of possible states, depending on conditions in their immediate neighborhood. Waldrop (1992) describes the rules of the simulation as follows:

> Imagine a programmable universe. "Time" in this uni-verse would be defined as the ticking of a cosmic clock, and "space" would be defined to be a discrete lattice of cells, with each cell occupied by a very simple, abstractly defined computer—a finite automaton. At any given time and in any given cell, the automaton could be in only one of a finite number of states, which could be thought of as *red, white, blue, green, and yellow,* or *1,2,3,4* or *living and dead,* or whatever. At each tick of the clock,

moreover, the automaton would make a transition to a new state, which would be determined by its own current state and the current state of its neighbors. (p. 219)

In designing this simulation, researchers were seeking to go beyond the focus of the cellular automata in previously described experiments, which sought to understand how patterns might emerge through self-organization. Instead, their goal was to create a system that exhibited some of the key qualities of life itself. Was it possible to create a computerized universe that didn't just eventually settle into stable patterns but instead possessed a capacity to constantly evolve and adapt over time? Was it possible to do this for long periods of time . . . perhaps even indefinitely? In the end, it took years to make it happen, but the researchers succeeded. Along the way, they discovered something surprising and important about the nature of complexity itself.

After designing and testing hundreds of variations of the Game of Life simulations, researchers found that the systems that emerged according to different sets of rules fit into four different categories:

> Category I systems "contained what you might call *doomsday rules:* no matter what pattern of living or dead cells you started out with, everything would just die within one or two time steps. The grid on the computer would go monochrome" (Waldrop, 1992, p. 224). In other words, the system would immediately settle into a very simple, inactive, unchanging state.

> Category II systems were a bit more interesting. They would quickly settle into a slightly more complex pattern (such as the panic model presented previously) and then remain unchanging in that fairly simple state.

> Category III systems demonstrated the exact opposite tendency: they were too active and were eternally changing in ways that had no discernible order or structure. In these

systems, "nothing was stable and nothing was predictable: structures would break up almost as soon as they formed" (Waldrop, 1992, p. 226). If categories I and II were characterized by static simplicity, category III systems were characterized by constant chaos.

Category IV systems, however, were different. They produced "coherent structures that propagated, grew, split apart, and recombined in a wonderfully complex way. They essentially never settled down" (Waldrop, 1992, p. 226). In other words, these relatively rare systems appeared to simulate dynamics found everywhere in the natural world: an ability to self-organize in complex ways, a remarkable balance between order and creativity, and an ability to continue changing and evolving without end.

A key insight grew out of researchers' attempts to understand why certain rules generated these different types of systems. After much experimentation, it was found that a key variable in these systems assessed the probability that any given cell would be alive in the next generation. When this variable (called by the Greek letter *lambda*) was set too low, the result was category I or II systems. When it was set too high, the result was category III systems. Set this variable within a small window somewhere in between the two extremes, and the result is a category IV system.

Waldrop (1992) explains:

At very low values around 0.0 he found nothing but dead, frozen Class I rules. As he increased the values a little bit, he started finding periodic Class II rules. As he increased the values a little more, he noticed that the Class II rules took longer and longer to settle down. Then if he jumped all the way to 0.50, he found himself in the total chaos of Class III . . . But right there in between Classes II and III, clustered tightly around his magic "critical" value of lambda (about 0.273) he found whole thickets of complex Class IV rules . . . Somehow, this simpleminded lambda parameter had put the . . . classes into exactly the kind of sequence he'd wanted—and had found a place for the Class IV rules to boot, right at the transition point:

I & II –> IV –> III

Moreover, the sequence suggested an equally provocative transition in dynamical systems:

Order –> Complexity –> Chaos

Where "complexity" referred to the kind of eternally surprising dynamical behavior shown by the Class IV automata. (p. 228)

These computer simulations are an attempt to use technology and mathematics to model the dynamics that characterize living systems: self-organization, pattern formation, evolution, and complexity itself. The Game of Life suggests that complex systems are eternally walking a razor's edge between order and chaos. Systems that find this balance demonstrate a remarkable capacity for eternal renewal, creativity, stability, and transformation. As we'll see later, this is an insight with a surprising degree of relevance to our exploration of race and social change.

Introduction to Fractals

According to *Wikipedia*,[2] a fractal is "a natural phenomenon or a mathematical set that exhibits a repeating pattern that displays at every scale." Perhaps the easiest way to clarify what this

---

[2] It's relevant to note that *Wikipedia* is a manifestation of the complex system dynamics we are exploring here. It harnesses the power of self-organization that becomes possible when the level of interconnection of a network reaches a high level of complexity. Launched in 2001, *Wikipedia* is now the largest online compilation of knowledge on the planet.

means is to provide a basic example. Consider the following black triangle:

Now, imagine drawing an upside down white triangle within that first triangle, so that it looks like this:

Then, repeat the process within the three black triangles that now appear in this pattern, as follows:

And then, do it again . . .

And again . . .

This is what it means to "exhibit a repeating pattern that appears at every scale." Although we would quickly reach the limits of the resolution that we are able to display on this page, it's easy to imagine that we could repeat this process endlessly, moving toward either infinitesimally small or incomprehensibly large scales. No matter how far in or out we zoom, we encounter the same pattern repeated over and over.

Once you learn to look for it, it's a phenomenon that appears everywhere in the natural world around us. For example, the shape of rivers is fractal: a single large waterway branches off into two or three smaller tributaries, which branch off into two or three even smaller tributaries, creating the following form:

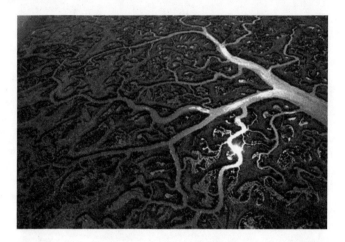

The same pattern appears in trees, in which a main trunk splits into smaller branches, which split into even smaller branches, which eventually split into twigs:

And on those twigs we encounter leaves . . .

which take in carbon dioxide and release oxygen, which we humans then breathe in and absorb into our bodies via the alveoli in our lungs:

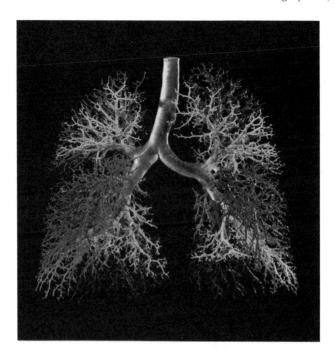

. . . and then distribute throughout our body via a vast network of veins and arteries:

Once we go looking for them, it quickly becomes apparent that these fractal patterns are ubiquitous in the natural world around—and within—us. Clearly, many of the complex systems found in the natural world are designed via the principles of fractals, with fairly simple patterns appearing at different scales to produce the remarkably complex and highly functional structures we see everywhere. As we'll see in the next chapter, it's a concept with important implications for understanding how the process of social change has unfolded over time.

Complexity

Throughout this chapter, the term *complexity* has been used extensively. Given the centrality of this concept to this whole-system level of analysis, it is important that we achieve some clarity regarding the meaning and importance of this term. We'll bring this chapter to a close by unpacking a few ways that this term has been understood by the field of complex systems.

One way of understanding complexity is to think about the amount of information required to describe an item (or a system, process, etc.). A red dot is much easier to describe completely than an individual human being. It turns out that scientists have found it helpful to quantify the amount of information required to describe different systems and use that number as a metric that represents the complexity of a system. In many disciplines, it is possible to compute and compare levels of complexity by quantifying the amount of information involved in the description of the entity or phenomenon in question.

Another aspect of complexity involves understanding that the complexity of an object frequently changes depending on the scale at which it is observed. For example, a person viewed from several hundred yards away may look like little more than a speck on the horizon. Zoom in closer, and you can clearly see arms and legs. Zoom in even closer, and details of the person's face and clothes become clear. As we move along the scale from coarser to finer levels of observation, complexity tends to increase.

Scholars have also found it helpful to distinguish between the concepts of *complex* and *complicated*. Something is complicated it if has a lot of interconnected component parts that must work together in sophisticated ways. A car is an obvious example of a complicated system, because it has thousands of parts that are organized in multiple interdependent systems that all must work together for the car to function properly. It's important to note, however, that it is possible to predict with great certainty what would happen if parts of the system were to be removed or altered. Take out the carburetor or the brakes, for example, and a knowledgeable mechanic could tell you exactly what that would mean for the functioning of the car.

However, something is complex if it is not possible to predict how the system will react to changes to the component parts. Imagine removing all predators from a forest ecosystem or launching a new type of smartphone in the marketplace. We can make informed guesses about what might happen, but the only way to really know how a complex system will respond to a change is to actually go ahead and make the change. In these systems, the concepts we've been exploring here—such as nonlinearity, interdependence, and self-organization—all govern the behavior of the whole system. Because everything is connected, little actions can have potentially enormous effects, and small differences in systems can lead to dramatically different patterns that emerge through self-organization. It's just not possible to predict how specific actions will affect the whole system. Furthermore, we can expect that those unpredictable effects of our actions may appear in places or at times that are far removed from the initial causes.

It's worth noting that complex systems operate in ways that challenge some deeply held and long-standing assumptions about the world. For more than 300 years, we've been operating with a worldview powerfully influenced by the work of Isaac Newton. With his breakthrough insights into the workings of gravity and laws governing physical motion, Newton gave us a sense of living in a clockwork universe. He illuminated a world in which the planets orbit the sun with machine-like precision, forces such as velocity or friction can be calculated exactly, and objects at rest stay at rest until moved. It's a view that revolutionized our ability to understand and master our world.

Yet is important to understand that many of the assumptions that are so helpful in illuminating the workings of the physical world around us do not apply to complex systems. In these systems, outcomes cannot be predicted, never mind precisely calculated. Seemingly small events can produce enormous reactions. Organization and structure can result not only from the workings of universal laws but also through the aggregation of decisions made by vast numbers of individual agents. Although Newton's insights remain invaluable, it's clear that complex systems operate according to a different set of rules. And it turns out that because the social systems in which we are all immersed operate according to this different set of rules, we must understand them if we are to deepen our understanding of the process of social change.

It's relevant to note that there is an important philosophical implication embedded in the workings of complex systems. On some deep level, we often assume that it requires direction and control to produce order and structure. We believe that the world in which we live is constantly in the process of disintegrating into chaos, and it is only through the constant oversight by someone in charge that we are able to keep this chaos at bay. Given this understanding of reality, it is only natural that we feel a powerful compulsion to look for the few exceptional individuals out there with the strength and intelligence to tell us exactly what we must do to keep our world from falling apart.

By contrast, the complex systems perspective invites us accept that order and structure are normal and dependable states in the natural world. We need not live with a constant fear of encroaching chaos; rather, we can live with a deep trust that order and structure will eventually emerge from within the systems in which we are immersed. Instead of hoping and praying for a lone superhero to lead us away from darkness, we can spend our time being curious about the patterns and systems that we ourselves are immersed in. And we are invited to consider that we are not merely passive participants in these patterns and systems; rather, we are actively involved in producing, sustaining—and perhaps even transforming—these patterns through our own seemingly insignificant individual choices and behaviors.

With that, we come to the conclusion of this review of the dynamics of complex systems. We have gained some perspective that informs our understanding of race and social change in important ways. But our inquiry into the workings of these systems is not yet complete. It turns out that human systems undergo a process of development toward complexity that illuminates the process of social change in surprising and unexpected ways. Understanding this process is the next step on this learning journey, and we turn our attention to this topic now.

4

Understanding Systems, Part II: Development Toward Complexity and the Hidden Process Driving Social Change

In Chapter 3 we explored a variety of dynamics in complex systems. In this chapter we are going to explore the process through which relatively simple human social systems become ever more complex. The real world abounds with systems that naturally develop toward higher levels of complexity. Consider a relatively simple seed, which eventually develops into a far more complex tree, which continues to develop into an even more complex ecology of birds, insects, and other animals. A human infant—already an incredibly complex system—eventually develops into an intellectually and emotionally far more complex adult, able to negotiate a similarly complex cultural, linguistic, and relational environment. The small settlement of New Amsterdam, once a humble collection of homes, over the course of many decades developed into modern New York City— a place that is socially, technologically, architecturally, and economically bewildering in its complexity.

As with self-organization, it is clear that this process need not— and does not—proceed under the direction and control of some powerful agent guiding every action. Barring the experience of a crisis or disruption that permanently, irrevocably impedes the unfolding of this process, development toward complexity is something that happens naturally.

Given the focus of this book, it's appropriate to poise our attention to how the field has explored this concept in ways that are specifically related to the human social systems. It turns out that scholars have offered important insights on that front. Bar-Yam (2001) dedicates a whole chapter of his book to the subject of human civilization as a complex system, and the insights that he presents there are relevant to our own efforts to understand the workings of race and social change.

Development of Sociopolitical Systems

Bar-Yam suggests that development toward complexity is a powerful concept for understanding the progress of human civilization. Over the course of history, he states, human societies have evolved through increasingly complex ways of organizing themselves. It's worth noting that in this sense, we have clearly distinguished ourselves from gorillas, our closest genetic ancestors. Throughout history, gorillas have organized themselves into small groups led by a silverback—a dominant older male who is clearly in charge of the whole group. When a silverback gets old and weak, younger silverbacks begin to challenge the aging leader, and eventually one of them defeats the incumbent silverback. The younger silverback then becomes the recognized leader, and the group begins to look to the new boss to provide the same sort of direction and control provided by the old boss. This cycle unfolds among gorilla communities today in much the same way that it occurred millions of years ago.

The same cannot be said for humans. Way back at the dawn of human civilization, we surely organized ourselves into similar simple hierarchies. But over time, our more advanced capacities for thought and communication have enabled us to transform the ways that we have organized ourselves toward ever more interconnected and complex networks. In his book *Sapiens: A Brief History of Humankind*, Yuval Noah Harari (2015) illuminates this truth with a colorful anecdote:

> Consider a resident of Berlin, born in 1900 and living to the ripe old age of 100. She spent her childhood in the Hohenzollern Empire of Wilhelm II; her adult years in the Weimar Republic, the Nazi Third Reich and Communist East Germany; and she died a citizen of a democratic and reunified Germany. She had managed to be a part of five very different sociopolitical systems, though her DNA remained the same. (p. 38)

In this chapter, we'll take a careful look at this process and consider its implications for our effort to understand race and social change.

Looking at long-term trends in human civilization, Bar-Yam suggests that a central theme in the development of human social systems is the transition away from simple hierarchies and toward a fully networked model of organization. The series of graphic illustrations and stories presented in the next section walk us through the unfolding of this process. Note that this description is not meant to offer an accurate historical description of this process; rather, it presents a slightly tongue-in-cheek overview of the essence of each distinct stage.

Early History: Development of Hierarchies

In the earliest centuries of human history, we organized ourselves into simple hierarchies that were hardly more sophisticated and complex than those of our gorilla ancestors. As Figure 4.1 suggests, we lived in relatively small groups of hunter-gatherers with one individual (almost always a male) very clearly in charge. His

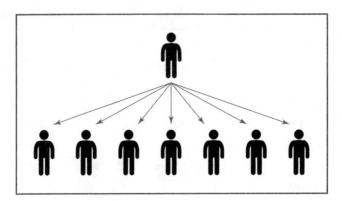

Figure 4.1 Simple Hierarchy

authority to provide direction and control was total and complete, and those under his command were required to obey his wishes. With the discovery of agriculture, human communities grew much larger and surely more complex, but the essence of this organizational structure remained in force. This was the era of the god-kings, pharaohs, and absolute rule by hereditary monarchies.

As time passed, it became apparent that this simple organizational structure was highly problematic in that it was ineffective at handling the full complexity of the system. Those individual leaders at the top of the hierarchy could handle only so much information and make only so many decisions, and the limitations of this organizational structure became increasingly apparent. In time, the structure in Figure 4.2 emerged, and it enabled authority to be distributed among a greater number of individuals in the system.

A story from ancient times provides an invaluable perspective on exactly how this transformation in organizational complexity unfolded. It is a personal favorite of mine because of the ways it highlights a key challenge in this process of developing toward higher levels of complexity. Challenging the status quo is only half the work of creating change; imagining a different—and more complex— alternative arrangement is equally important and an entirely different piece of work.

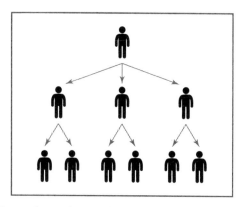

Figure 4.2 Hierarchy with Distributed Authority

We learn this lesson in the biblical story of Exodus through an exchange between Moses and his uncle by marriage, Yitro (Jethro in English). Moses, as we all know, played a key role in one of the best-known movements for social change in the mythology of Western civilization. In an unprecedented move—and with more than a bit of help from God—he freed the Jewish people from centuries of slavery under the cruel and absolute rule of pharaoh in Egypt. (Regardless of whether you accept this as historical fact or as mythology, there is no denying that this is a story that has been inspiring human societies to develop toward higher levels of complexity for millennia.)

The story of Yitro appears in Exodus Chapter 18, after the Israelites have escaped through the Red Sea and are now living as free people in the Sinai Desert. Moses may have led the Jews out of bondage in Egypt, but now that he has become the leader of his people, he and his followers have organized themselves according to the only social structure that they have ever known: with Moses as the lone leader at the top of the hierarchy. To be sure, he is no hard-hearted pharaoh; he exercises his authority with levels of compassion, empathy, and wisdom that were utterly lacking in the cruel Egyptian ruler they left behind. But given that he is tasked with managing a community of 600,000 people, it doesn't take long for someone to see that the situation is unsustainable.

Watching Moses struggle with the impossible burden of being responsible for everything all the time, Yitro has a few words of advice for his overwhelmed nephew-in-law:

> What is this thing that you are doing to the people? Why do you sit by yourself, while all the people stand before you from morning till evening? . . . The thing you are doing is not good. You will surely wear yourself out . . . for the matter is too heavy for you; you cannot do it alone. (Exodus 18:14–18)

Yitro suggests that Moses go out into the community, find men of good character, and empower them with some new responsibilities:

> You shall appoint over Israel leaders over thousands, leaders over hundreds, leaders over fifties, and leaders over tens. And they shall judge the people at all times, and it shall be that any major matter they shall bring to you, and they themselves shall judge every minor matter, thereby making it easier for you, and they shall bear [the burden] with you. (Exodus 18:21–22)

Moses sees the wisdom in this approach, and he agrees to give it a try. The result is an early and influential example of the evolution toward a more complex organizational structure for human societies. In creating this new hierarchy, the leader (Moses) relinquishes some of his power and influence, and a whole group of followers suddenly gain a degree of power, influence, and responsibility that they never had before. That is what happens as a network develops toward higher levels of complexity, and it's a trend that is relevant to our interest in understanding matters of race and social change.

There's another important lesson embedded in this story as well. The story does more than illuminate the practical implications of the development toward complexity. It is amazing that Moses and the

Jewish people took all those incredible risks to escape from bondage under the rule of pharaoh . . . and then the moment they achieved their freedom chose to organize themselves according to exactly the same simple hierarchy they lived with in Egypt. The story highlights the fact that the work of overthrowing the old, simple system and the work of envisioning and bringing into being a new and more complex system are two very distinct undertakings. Without some invaluable perspective from his uncle and a new level of effort and responsibility on the part of previously disempowered community members, Moses and the Jewish people might have continued to live in a simple hierarchy for many more years in the desert.

From the Social Contract to Networked Democracy

Although Moses's organizational restructuring of the Israelite community was surely a leap forward in many ways, it was still a situation in which power and control flowed exclusively downward, and those lower in the hierarchy had little choice but to obey the commands of those at the higher levels. It was an arrangement that endured for centuries and generations, but eventually the need for a transformation to a still higher level of complexity become apparent.

Many, many centuries after Moses and Yitro, the seeds of the next great advance in complexity were sown by Frenchman Jean-Jacques Rousseau in his 1762 treatise on the social contract. Seeing the miserable condition of so many of his countrymen and -women living as powerless and voiceless subjects of the state, he advanced the revolutionary notion that the only form of legitimate authority was authority granted with the consent of the governed. In an era when it was widely believed that monarchs were divinely ordained to rule, this was a radical notion. But it was an idea whose time had come, and the belief that members of a society should have a say in the matter of who governs them and the rules by which they govern developed a growing following. Before long, this notion catalyzed a democratic revolution that in many ways is still unfolding to this day.

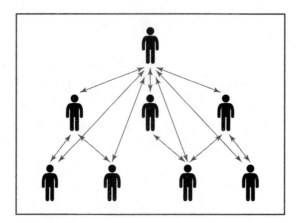

Figure 4.3 Hierarchy Constrained by "The Social Contract" Between Rulers and Ruled

It took centuries and was only accomplished with war and conflict that claimed the lives of millions, but in time human societies evolved toward the level of complexity represented by Figure 4.3. Note that here the lines between levels in the hierarchies have arrows going in *both* directions. Those in authority may still exercise power and control, but that power is constrained by a social contract in which ordinary citizens now have a level of power, voice, and choice that was entirely absent in earlier levels of development.

It would be difficult to overstate how significant and consequential that leap forward in complexity has been for humanity. These days the majority of humans live in democratic societies that reflect this level of development. Although there is surely a great deal of injustice and inequality in these networks, the fact that most of us enjoy rights and protections as citizens, can vote for our leaders, and can raise our voices to express either support or dissent is a quantum leap forward from the way things used to be. We should never lose sight of the freedoms and privileges we enjoy today that were quite literally unthinkable to those living for most of human history.

It is important to note, however, that the process of development does not end there. Here at the dawn of the 21st century we have

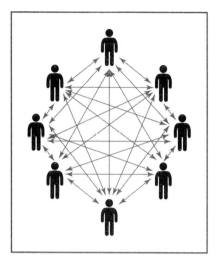

Figure 4.4 Complex Network

begun to experience dynamics that emerge only in a fully networked system in which the level of complexity makes the whole notion of hierarchy irrelevant. This is the level represented by Figure 4.4.

The implications of this level of development are captured clearly in a 2008 book called *The Starfish and the Spider: The Unstoppable Power of Leaderless Organizations* by Ori Brafman and Rod A. Beckstrom. They state:

> We look for hierarchy all around us. Whether we're looking at a Fortune 500 company, an army, or a community, our natural reaction is to ask, "Who's in charge?"
>
> This book is about what happens where there is no one in charge. It's about what happens where there's no hierarchy. You'd think there would be disorder, even chaos. But in many arenas, a lack of traditional leadership is giving rise to powerful groups that are turning industry and society upside down.
>
> In short, there's a revolution raging all around us. (p. 5)

One of the many engaging stories that Brafman and Beckstrom share focuses on the controversial online music-sharing program called *Napster*. Created in 1999 by Northeastern University undergraduate Shawn Fanning, Napster allowed anyone with an Internet connection to share music files for free by uploading tunes to a central server. Very quickly, Napster went viral; millions of users had downloaded the program and were using it to swap free music files. Not surprisingly, the record labels were not happy; before long, they estimated that the free—and clearly illegal—sharing of music was costing them a full 25% of their revenue. So they took a case all the way to the Supreme Court and succeeded in getting a ruling against Napster, which soon went bankrupt.

The only catch was that Napster was soon replaced by Kazaa, a program that allowed free music sharing without requiring that songs be uploaded to a central server. Now users could just swap songs right from their own hard drives. When the record labels succeeded in suing the creator of that program, a new option called Kazaa Lite soon appeared. Kazaa Lite was completely open-sourced software; it was created and maintained through the self-organized efforts of hundreds of anonymous coders. At this point, the record labels literally had nobody to sue; in the deepest sense, there was nobody in charge of Kazaa Lite. Brafman and Beckstrom state:

> Decentralization has been lying dormant for thousands of years. But the advent of the Internet has unleashed this force, knocking down traditional businesses, altering entire industries, affecting how we relate to each other, and influencing world politics. The absence of structure, leadership, and formal organization, once considered a weakness, has become a major asset. Seemingly chaotic groups have challenged and defeated established institutions. The rules of the game have changed. (p. 8)

Here, then, we see what happens when a network develops to this highest level of complexity. At some point, the level of inter-connection among individuals in the system becomes so great that the whole concept of hierarchical organization no longer applies. And the concepts that we have been exploring in this chapter—self-organization, nonlinearity, complexity, and inter-dependence—emerge as the primary governing dynamics at work in the system. In other words, the system starts to look a whole lot like the world we find ourselves immersed in today.

To be clear, these four diagrams are meant to represent a trans-formational process unfolding over time. They are not snapshots of four different systems operating at different levels of complexity; they represent the same social system that starts at a simple hierarchy and in time develops toward higher levels of complexity.

I find it helpful to imagine the process as a brief animated film in which the whole transformation occurs in perhaps a minute or two. Before our eyes, individuals from the bottom of the simple hierarchy rise up to form additional layers of leadership. Arrows that used to point only in one direction become multidirectional and lines representing new relationships among individuals at all levels begin to multiply until nearly everyone is connected with nearly everyone else (at some point in this process, it becomes possible to begin playing games such as "Six Degrees of Kevin Bacon"). Conceived of in this way, the process of development toward complexity in human social systems appears as a simple (as in "easy to understand"), elegant transformation in which complexity increases as the individuals within the system become more deeply connected to each other.

Complex Systems and the Dynamics of Social Transformations

It may have taken millennia, but it was this process that transformed the powerless, voiceless subjects in those early simple hierarchies into the empowered and emboldened citizens who are today able to vote, protest, swap music files—and do so much more—with a degree of freedom that we are still only beginning to fully comprehend.

Of course, there's an obvious question here: *What does any of this have to do with race and social change?*

Here's the answer: Imagine combining the concept of development toward complexity with the fractal structure of self-similarity appearing across different scales. For example, picture a simple hierarchy developing toward an increasingly interconnected network . . . and then imagine zooming in and finding that developmental process occurring at roughly the same time and same rate at every scale of analysis. With this mental image, we encounter a mechanism that explains a great deal about how social change has unfolded throughout history.

Consider the following example: In *The End of Leadership*, leadership scholar Barbara Kellerman offers a book-length argument that leadership is not what it used to be. She notes that over the course of centuries,

> Leadership and followership have continued to evolve . . . from what they were into something quite different. More nations now are democracies as opposed to autocracies. There is less respect for authority across the board—in government and business, in the academy and in the professions, even in religion. Power and influence have continued to devolve from the top down—those at the top having less power and influence; those in the middle and bottom having more. (pp. xvii–xix)

This is, of course, a spot-on description of the trend we first encountered in ancient times with Moses and Yitro. As the process of development toward complexity unfolds, the balance of power continually shifts toward greater equality between leaders (at the top of the hierarchy) and followers (those lower down). As we've discussed, leaders experience this transformation as a relative loss of power, and followers experience this as gaining new levels of power. Eventually—in a fully networked system—it's no longer even clear if there *is* a top of the hierarchy anymore.

In making her case about "the end of leadership," Kellerman hops nimbly across different scales of analysis. She begins by focusing on the most personal and intimate unit of social organization: the family. Her detailed explanation of the changes to the institution of marriage over the course of centuries is so relevant to our interests here that it is worth quoting at length:

> In mid-eighteenth century England, a woman's property and children belonged to her husband. Divorce was impossible and, if a wife dared leave home and hearth, she had to leave her children in the process. Moreover, marital rape was perfectly legal and probably frequent— though in 1782 a law finally was passed that forbade a husband to beat his wife with a stick wider than his thumb.
>
> A hundred years later, marriage was different, but only slightly. In 1848, at the Seneca Falls Convention, Elizabeth Cady Stanton charged that marital abuse still remained the norm . . . By the mid-twentieth century, marriage had changed yet again, particularly in the United States. By then Betty Friedan, author of *The Feminine Mystique*, . . . reveal[ed] a truth hiding in plain sight: that though there was nothing obvious for them to be unhappy about, many married women were, nevertheless, deeply unhappy, feeling stifled rather than liberated.
>
> Now, of course, another fifty years on, the institution of marriage has changed yet again. . . . In other words, in the last 150 years or so, American marriage has evolved from an arrangement in which wives were subservient to

one in which they are nearly, mostly, the equal of their husbands. (pp. xv–xvi)

These few paragraphs offer a quick survey of the way marriage has changed over the course of the last two centuries. Kellerman makes a compelling case that when we focus on this smallest unit of social organization (the family) we encounter a process of dramatic change from pure hierarchy (the man is totally dominant, the woman is totally subservient) to today's experience of near (but not complete) equality.

Zoom out to a slightly higher scale of analysis, however, and the exact same trend appears. Kellerman makes it clear that the same transformation that occurred in the family occurred simultaneously in the workplace:

> At the office the line between those lower down and those higher up was sharply drawn, the man being advised always to step "back to allow his superior to go first if the other is about to leave too, or, if there seems to be some delay, ask permission to go first."
>
> The workplace was, in fact, famously formal and famously, insufferably conforming . . .
>
> The literature on leadership and management back then was in keeping with the times—employers were at the top and employees in the middle or down below—which is why leadership scholarship focused on leadership traits. After all, no one else seemed much to matter . . .
>
> But, by the late 1950s, things began gradually to change. . . . The idea that leaders could simply command and control and their will would be done gave way to the slow, sober realization that times were changing. (pp. 27–28)

Just as with marriage, these trends continued as the years rolled by. Kellerman continues:

> By the turn of the century, no leadership course, text or consultant would dare to teach how to be a leader without referring, if only sparingly and obliquely, to the follower. [Warren] Bennis wrote about "getting people on your side," while words and terms such as *team, network, engagement, empowerment, cooperation, collaboration, participation,* and *flattened hierarchy* became touchstones in a time when power and authority were diminished, and influence necessarily was shared. (p. 32)

So the process that we observed in families has been unfolding in roughly the same ways in our workplaces, organizations, and institutions.

Remarkably, if we zoom out even further to observe events occurring on the national scale, we see the exact same transformational process unfolding over time. After millennia in which the vast majority of people lived as powerless subjects of monarchs who ruled with absolute power, transformational change began to appear in nations across the globe. Kellerman states:

> Let's go back to the late eighteenth century, to that time of upheaval when the ideas of the Enlightenment were beginning to be realized. Patterns of dominance and deference were changing in marriage and, simultaneously, they were changing in the body politic. The two most obvious examples are the American Revolution and the French Revolution. Both were transformation events in which followers came to the fore, while leaders came under attack. In Europe and America, life—political, economic, and social—was never again the same.

Nor was it coincidence that some fifty years later, as Stanton was penning her list of grievances by the power-less (women) against the powerful (men), Karl Marx and Friedrich Engels were penning their list of grievances by the powerless (the proletariat) against the powerful (bourgeoisie). Indeed, just as the year was precisely the same—both Stanton's "Declaration of Sentiments" and Marx and Engels *Communist Manifesto* were published in 1848—the point was precisely the same. A half century after the American and French revolutions large numbers of followers remained restive—eager to change their status as subordinates. (p. xvii)

Kellerman goes on to discuss the successful movement to end British colonialism in India as well as the successful effort to end apartheid in South Africa. The process continued with the collapse of the Soviet Union and the emergence of newly independent states such as Belarus and Kazakhstan, as well as the 1989 Velvet Revolution in Czechoslovakia and the 2004 Orange Revolution in Ukraine. All over the globe, at a national scale we observe networks that had long operated as relatively simple hierarchies transformed to a higher level of complexity and begin to function as independent democracies.

I cite Kellerman at length here because her book offers such a concise, informed, and easily accessible presentation of the history, literature, and ideas related to the various movements of social change that have unfolded over the course of the last two centuries. Her intention here is to be descriptive, and she makes a compelling case about the more-or-less universal historical trend toward less power for leaders and more power for followers, which has made leadership in the 21st century such a difficult task. What's missing in her argument, however, is *an underlying mechanism to explain why and how all these changes could be observed occurring simultaneously at so many different scales of analysis and across so many different contexts.*

It's worth highlighting the consistent appearance of symmetry in the changes unfolding at different scales. Kellerman noted that Elizabeth Cady Stanton's "Declaration of Sentiments" and Marx and Engel's *Communist Manifesto* were both published in 1848. Kellerman later notes that the seeds planted by these two revolutionary documents both bore fruit at almost exactly the same moment about 70 years later: Women received the right to vote in 1920 . . . and the Communist revolution in Russia began at almost exactly the same time, in 1917. In other words, whether you zoom all the way in to observe the process by which the feminist movement transformed the relationship between men and women or zoom way out to observe the process by which the Russian czars were overthrown by the Communists, the timing of key events unfolded with near perfect symmetry.

And this is hardly the only example of events unfolding in different contexts at almost exactly the same moment. As Kellerman also notes, Betty Friedan's *The Feminine Mystique* appeared in 1963—the same year that Martin Luther King Jr. published his seminal essay "Letter from Birmingham Jail." One year earlier, in 1962, Cesar Chavez and Delores Huerta founded United Farm Workers, a movement for greater justice and equality for Latinos. Just a few years later, in 1969, the Stonewall riots occurred in New York City, catalyzing a movement for LGBTQ equality that has begun to win major legal victories for gay rights in just the last few years, culminating in the decision by the Supreme Court in 2015 to declare gay marriage legal across the nation.

The key point here is that once we understand a few of the most important principles governing dynamics in complex systems, we can go beyond simply reminiscing about all that groovy cultural upheaval that unfolded in the sixties. We have a scientific framework for explaining *why* there was such symmetry in the timing of all these movements for change across so many different scales of analysis and social contexts.

Social systems—similar to so many other phenomena in the natural world—develop toward complexity and have a fractal structure, meaning that patterns that appear at one scale repeat themselves across every other scale of analysis. That's how things work in the world of complex systems, and it's an insight that is relevant to anyone seeking to understand what is true about race and social change.

Before moving on, I'll leave you with one more example to consider. Fareed Zakaria is among the most respected and insightful observers of global geopolitics working today. In 2008, he published a book entitled *The Post American World*, which offered his take on changes unfolding at the global level in the wake of the 2008 financial crises:

> The rise of the rest is at heart an economic phenomenon, but the transition we are witnessing is not just a matter of dollars and cents. It has political, military, and cultural consequences. As countries become stronger and richer, and as the United States struggles to earn back the world's faith, we're likely to see more challenges and greater assertiveness from rising nations. In one month this past summer, India was willing to frontally defy the United States at the Doha trade talks, Russia attacked and occupied parts of Georgia, and China hosted the most spectacular and expensive Olympic Games in history (which cost more than $40 billion). Ten years ago, not one of the three would have been powerful or confident enough to act as it did. Even if their growth rates decline, which they surely will, these countries will not quietly relinquish their new roles in the global system. (p. xxiii)

Once we learn to look for it, these trends appear at every scale of analysis of human dynamics. It's present at the interpersonal level, in the transformation in the relationship between husbands and wives; it's present at the organizational level, in the transformation in the relationship between bosses and subordinates; it's present at the societal level, in the transformation in the relationship between different social groups; it's present at the national level, in the transformation in the relationships between rulers and their subjects; and it's present at the global level, in the transformation in the relationship between the global superpower and "the rise of the rest." No matter how far in or out we zoom, we encounter a development toward complexity that is relevant for anyone seeking to understand how social change has unfolded over the fullness of time.

Final Thoughts on the Whole Systems Perspective

It was Kurt Lewin—the father of social psychology—who gave us the well-known claim that "there is nothing so practical as a good theory." If we are going to extend a long line of classic social psychology experiments to explore the as-yet-unexamined whole system level of analysis, we need to have at least a rudimentary way of thinking about the dynamics that govern events at that level. That's why we've made this effort to develop a theoretical model of how social change unfolds in a complex system; it provides a level of insight and clarity that empowers us to bring a whole new level of context to the activities that we'll encounter soon. But before we turn our attention to those activities, here are a few final thoughts about the whole systems level of analysis.

First, it's important to note that we are working with an approach intended to illuminate processes that transcend the boundaries of more established disciplines. There are surely dozens—perhaps hundreds—of perspectives that we could apply to deepen our understanding of the social change processes described here. Economists, political scientists, psychologists, sociologists, historians, lawyers, anthropologists, politicians, poets, and novelists could all offer insights that illuminate these events in substantive and important ways. But what we are striving for is an understanding of events that shatter the boundaries between these different disciplines.

Consider the implications, for example, of using a term instead of *network* to describe the processes we've discussed here. We could talk about families, but that would imply that these processes are not equally relevant to organizations and governments. We'd have the same problem if we used the term *organizations*; that would imply that these trends are not operating in our own personal lives while also appearing at the scale of geopolitics. So we've reached for a scientific term that evokes all of these scales and contexts while being firmly attached to none of them.

Our search for this underlying unity across so many scales and contexts raises another question as well. Are we really suggesting that all of these social change movements—feminism, civil rights, anti-colonialism, democratic revolutions, gay rights—are really exactly the same thing? Well, the answer to that is yes . . . and no. I do not want to dismiss the utterly unique experiences of all of these different movements and the individual identities of the people immersed in them. Rather, my intention here is to see through the bewildering complexity to discern the elegant simplicity that lies beneath it all.

In some very important ways, the Indian movement to end British colonialism was very different from the South African movement to end apartheid, which was very different from the Velvet Revolution in Czechoslovakia. Similarly, the experience of a feminist seeking to create change as a senior executive in Silicon Valley is different from the experience of a feminist in rural China, which is different from the experience of a feminist in Orthodox Judaism. The distinctions among these various experiences matter a great deal, and we can truly understand the nature of social change only if we open our hearts and minds to the profound uniqueness of each of those stories.

We do not face an either-or choice here. Remember the design principles that we encountered in our discussion of fractals: Every-where we look in the world around us, we see examples of *infinite complexity emerging from elegant simplicity*. Everywhere we look, the development of networks from simple hierarchies toward fully connected networks is unfolding with remarkable symmetry across every scale and context imaginable. It is, at heart, a very straightforward process to understand . . . and there is no contradiction in stating that this underlying simplicity generates the infinite complexity and diversity of experiences. Benoit Mandelbrot, a pioneer in the field of fractals, states it best: "Bottomless wonders spring from simple rules . . . repeated without end."

Another important thing to understand about the whole systems perspective is the paradoxical way that it illuminates our human experiences by compelling us to zoom out and assume a perspective far removed from our own individual humanity. I find it helpful to think about the whole systems perspective by comparing it to what happens when we view a city from the observation deck of a skyscraper. At ground level, the city is a riot of noise, smells, sites, commotion, and stimulation. We are assaulted with the experience of honking horns, homeless people, the smell of sewage and hot dog venders, the million individual human dramas unfolding in the lives of the strangers around us.

When we head up to the observation deck of a skyscraper in the same city, however, everything looks different. The noise and chaos becomes a distant murmur, and a whole world of order, structure, pattern, and organization suddenly comes into view. The millions of people now look like so many ants moving in a smooth and orderly fashion along sidewalks, progressing in neat lines into buildings or down into subway stations. An endless stream of cars move smoothly down streets, pausing momentary at traffic lights before turning left, right, or continuing straight ahead in a finely choreographed dance. Down on the street, one is struck by the overwhelming energy, intensity, and endless variety of the city. At the top of the skyscraper, one is struck by the remarkably elegant order and structure within which that chaotic and overwhelming stream of individual experience unfolds.

We must not make the mistake of believing that we face an either-or choice here. The fact is that both of these realities—the street and the observation deck, the micro and the macro—are real and 100% true, and they coexist at exactly the same time, always. Our ability to understand and influence the world around us depends on our ability to hold both of these perspectives in our heads and our hearts at the same moment.

As a student of complex systems, I have often experienced feelings of awe and wonder as I contemplated this remarkable story of the underlying simplicity and elegance generating the over-whelming complexity of our era. As I pursued these insights into the marvels of self-organization, fractals, and development toward complexity, I have often been moved to silence by a sense of reverence and awe for the wondrous nature of life. At times, the theoretical model of social change presented here has evoked for me a sense of watching one of those time-lapse films of a desert landscape in which we see weeks pass by in just a few moments—a mesmerizing flow of day and night, with clouds sailing swiftly by and constellations of stars swinging rapidly in their journey through the night sky. Or, perhaps more appropriately, I've imagined time-lapse films in which gardens grow from invisible seeds to lush vegetation in just moments. In real life, the process takes months, but in these films it only takes seconds for small shoots to appear in seemingly empty beds of soil and then blossom into fully grown plants and flowers, forming a complex ecology of radiant life in a place where just moments before there was only void, nothingness, and hidden, unrealized potential.

The truth is, however, that these feelings of awe and reverence are inevitably momentary and fleeting. As a student of social justice and social change, I have no illusions that the processes described here are all elegance, beauty, and serenity. There is no separating the dynamics from the full drama of the human experience. To focus our attention on these processes is to confront directly all of the darkest ugliness and violence of our own shadows as well as all of the awe-inspiring nobility and courage of the light that exists within each of us.

We must not let the scientific language of networks and development toward complexity obscure the truth of what we are talking about here. This story is in part a story of evil, such as the Nazis, whose hunger for dominance and control unleashed dark forces that destroyed the lives of millions. That was a situation in which Germany had dabbled briefly with the attempt to move toward a higher level of complexity, exemplified by the democratic Weimar Republic. Unfortunately, the chaos and uncertainty of the era was too much for the majority of Germans to tolerate. Rather than maintain responsibility for their nation and their collective destiny, Germans voted a despot into power and enthusiastically supported his decision to revert the nation back to a lower level of complexity, the simple hierarchy.

It was one of the darkest hours in human history, and the network perspective we encounter here compels us to zoom out from a morbid fascination with Adolph Hitler to recognize that in Nazi Germany, leaders and followers were joined together in a deeply interdependent web of relationships. The story of the Nazis is not only the story of one madman's unquenchable thirst for power, control, and dominance; it is simultaneously the story of vast numbers of ordinary citizens so unable to tolerate the uncertainty, doubt, and fear of their own existence that they gladly granted all power over their lives to a monster who asked of them only that they live in the simplicity of perfect obedience and conformity.

Once you know to look for it, this story of a network engaged in a collective refusal to grow and develop toward a higher level of complexity appears at every scale of analysis throughout history. It is the story of the Jonestown Massacre, in which a group of more than 900 Americans allowed a charismatic demagogue named Jim Jones to lead them to their deaths. It is also the story of China's Great Leap Forward, in which an entire nation obeyed the preposterous demands of a dictator named Mao Zedong, resulting in the deaths of tens of millions. A compelling case can be made that this collective hunger to regress backward toward a far more simple hierarchy is alive and well in the United States today, and it is manifesting in the surprising success of Donald Trump's presidential campaign. When faced with the challenge of accepting the levels of responsibility and awareness required to adapt to life in a more complex and interdependent network, history suggests that an egomaniacal individual and a large number of citizens craving simplicity may collude together to take a giant developmental step backward.

But the story we are telling here is not all cowardice, hatred, violence, despair, and abdication of responsibility; the darkness is matched equally by the light. We must remember that the process of the development toward complexity is also seen in the stories of Harriet Tubman, Gandhi, Martin Luther King Jr., Cesar Chavez, Nelson Mandela, and Malala Yousafzai. It is the story of America's founding fathers, who—despite their imperfections and hypocri-sies—ushered in a quantum leap forward in the development of networks at the scale of nations. And once again, we are compelled to zoom out from our narrow focus on a few great men and women of history. The perspective we encounter here demands that we bear witness to the stunning courage, bravery, and heroism of masses of ordinary citizens who chose responsibility instead of blind obedi-ence, hope instead of nihilistic despair, and who stepped fully into their own individual power to create a more just, fair, and equal world for us all.

We can choose to be either horrified or inspired by the choices made by those who have navigated this process before us, but the fact is that this developmental process is most definitely not finished. Each morning, every one of us awakens to a new moment in the unfolding of this process, and, without a doubt, the choices that we each make every day are creating the world that we will leave to our children and grandchildren. It is my hope that with a higher level of consciousness about the interdependent nature of our world and a fuller appreciation for the consequences of our choices, we may together cocreate a world of far more light than darkness in the years ahead.

And with that, we now turn our attention to the Separation Exercises at the heart of our inquiry into what is true about race and social change.

5

The Separation Exercises

A good theory is valuable in its own right, but the inquiry at the heart of this book aspires to present more than just a theory. We are seeking insights into how race and social change actually work by conducting empirical investigations into the matter. In other words, we're not here just to offer a theory but to test it as well. And that is why we turn our attention now to the Camp Anytown Separation Exercises.

As you'll recall from the Introduction and Chapter 1, the Separation Exercise is an attempt to simulate a segregated, hierarchical, unjust social system. The intentions and the design of the activity place it in the tradition of the provocative social science experiments that we explored in Chapter 2. What makes this activity important, however, is the way that it extends that tradition of experiments into new terrain by enabling us to observe how large-scale change unfolds from the whole systems perspective.

Although readers can surely understand and learn from these activities without an in-depth understanding of the organization that runs them, a brief overview of this background information is helpful to contextualize the events we'll explore in this chapter. Similarly, a basic overview of the methodology used in this research will provide a useful sense of the empirical rigor that went into crafting the narratives in this chapter. We briefly address both of those topics before diving into the narratives themselves.

The Separation Exercise in Context: The History and Philosophy of NCCJ and Camp Anytown

The National Conference for Jews and Christians (NCJC) was founded in 1927 by prominent members of the Christian and Jewish communities as a response to the rise in popularity of hate groups such as the Ku Klux Klan, and the increasingly strident voices of anti-Semitism and anti-Catholicism at the time. According to the website of the New England chapter of the organization:

> Its founders included prominent social activists such as Jane Addams and U.S. Supreme Court Justice Charles Evans Hughes who dedicated the organization to bringing diverse people together to address interfaith divisions. Several years later NCCJ expanded its work to include all issues of social justice including race, class, gender equity, sexual orientation and the rights of people with different abilities. In the 1990's, the name was changed to the National Conference for Community and Justice to better reflect the breadth and depth of its mission, the growing diversity of our country and our need to be more inclusive. (NCCJ, 2016a)

Today its mission reads as follows:

> The National Conference for Community and Justice (NCCJ) is a human relations organization that promotes inclusion and acceptance by providing education and advocacy while building communities that are respectful and just for all.
> *Celebrating the diversity of races, religions, cultures, genders, abilities & sexual orientations.* (NCCJ, 2016a)

The organization pursues its mission in a variety of ways, including initiatives focused on public policy, media and advertising, interfaith relations, economic opportunity, and education of adults and youth. Camp Anytown is one of several NCCJ's programs focused on youth education.

Within this wider context of youth education programming, Camp Anytown is the most intensive and comprehensive youth program run by the NCCJ. Because it is a 1-week residential program (usually occurring at a summer camp or similar facility), it enables a uniquely in-depth exploration of the issues that the NCCJ is committed to addressing. Relative to other NCCJ youth education programs, it requires a considerable commitment of time and emotional energy as participants explore a broad range of topics in a highly experiential manner.

According to one region's website, the purpose and history of the program is as follows:

> NCCJ ANYTOWN is a nationally recognized, award-winning leadership and social justice program for youth ages 14–18. Founded in 1957, NCCJ ANYTOWN is designed to educate, liberate, and empower youth participants (delegates) to become effective, responsible leaders and community builders. (NCCJ 2016b)

Research Methodology

The three Camp Anytown Separation Exercises presented here were all observed between the months of June and November 2004. On every site visit, I was accompanied by at least one (and sometimes two) other researchers who were individuals of color, ensuring that there was diversity within the research team observing these exercises. Together, we observed the staff planning meeting that occurred prior to every Separation Exercise (either the evening before or the morning of the activity), the activity itself, as well as the participant debrief session that immediately followed each activity.

Within 3 days of each site visit, each observer wrote up notes from the observation. I then reviewed all the notes and used them to compose a first draft of the narratives that you'll encounter in the pages ahead. All the researchers then reviewed the draft and provided feedback, and we continued to revise the description of events until all researchers agreed that it accurately reflected the events that they observed at each activity.

As you'll see, the narratives are written in the first-person voice ("I walked into the dining hall . . ."); this was a stylistic decision that was agreed on by all researchers, because early attempts to try present the viewpoints of two or three different researchers complicated the narratives considerably. We agreed to write the narratives as though there was only one observer, while using a review process that ensured that the perspectives of all researchers were accurately represented in the narrative.

In addition to in-person observation by multiple researchers, we also distributed a questionnaire that participants filled out at the conclusion of the debrief session following the exercise. The full text of the questionnaire can be found in Appendix B, and we'll have a lot more to say about the findings from those questionnaires in Chapter 6.

Note that the following narratives do not claim to present every detail of what occurred at each exercise. Rather, our goal was to craft a description that accurately captured the overall progression of events, the pedagogical decisions made by staff members, and the major incidents that influenced the outcome of the exercise.

In an effort to preserve the confidentiality of all staff members and participants, all names have been changed, and the locations where the exercises occurred are not revealed.

The Narratives

The time has come to turn to detailed accounts of the Separation Exercises we observed. We've reviewed the classic social psychology experiments, explored the dynamics of complex systems, and developed a theoretical model of large-scale social change. Now, you are invited to join us in stepping into a Camp Anytown experience and watch—three times in a row—as a Separation Exercise unfolds before our eyes.

Separation Exercise 1: Thomasina and Drake's System

The morning of the Separation Exercise, all the counselors report to a 7 AM staff meeting. They are gathered in the common room of a staff cabin, and a diverse crowd of approximately 20 teenaged and 20-something counselors are seated on the floor. Thomasina, the director of the program, is seated on one of the two couches in the room. She is a tall Asian woman with an army-style buzz-cut hairdo. Seated next to her is Drake, the program's assistant director, a White male in his late 20s, who is unshaven and looks like he is barely awake.

Thomasina explains how the exercise is going to work. She says that the delegates will be broken up by culture group. The rules of the exercise are simple: Don't talk to anyone outside of your group, don't make eye contact with anyone outside your group, and always stick together.

The list of groups (in hierarchal order, from bottom to top) includes the following:

1. Black Male
2. Black Female
3. Latino/a
4. LGBTQ
5. Jewish
6. Asian (Four staff members, no participants)
7. White female
8. White male

Thomasina advises the staff members to "participate as if you have no idea of what it is about. You are not to shift the dynamics. You are neutral. Filler. Sheep. It will be as if all the camp stops leading except for me and Drake."

She continues: "If a delegate asks you what is going on or tries to break the exercise, you can say some of the following things:

'I don't know what we are doing'

'This is a new exercise . . . we didn't do this when I was a delegate'

'Thomasina keeps changing things, so I don't know what we are doing . . . ' "

She explains that it ends when the exercise breaks and the delegates come together as some sort of community.

The hierarchy will be made apparent through some assigned tasks: The Black females will have to clean tables. The Latinos will sweep the floors after breakfast. The White men will have breakfast all laid out for them.

Finally, she explains that Tammy and Roger—two of the most outspoken individuals in the program—will be by themselves, without a group. This is done out of a belief that, with their strong personalities, these two delegates might end up breaking the exercise so early that the educational value of the experience is undermined.

Although the staff members go on to discuss their concerns about the morning and specific delegates, the conversation seems superficial. This is a controversial exercise, and its effect on the delegates, staff members, and the community as a whole are not given much weight. One staff person is obviously asleep during the conversation, and the assistant director, Drake, never says a word.

As a wrap-up, the director offers the following encouragement: "We want to see if folks can be incited to riot against authority," she states. "Let's do it; it'll be great!"

The delegates emerge from their cabins for morning circle, at 7:45 as always. Some look half-asleep, and others already seem full of energy. One delegate—a short Black boy with a backwards baseball cap and a "Sean Jean" sweatshirt—has found a bottle of bubble liquid and is running around blowing bubbles into the air.

Someone shouts out, "Lead us in song!"

Another yells, "It's my birthday in 2 days!"

Soon, many in the group are singing "Happy Birthday." When that is done, a counselor heads into the center of the circle and starts to sing a call-and-response cheer about a little green frog. Although some delegates are enthusiastic participants, not everyone is joining in. To the eyes of outside observers, it appears as though there is a curious lack of respect for authority among many delegates.

Following the cheer, Thomasina steps into the center of the circle.

"We are going to have an exercise this morning," she states. "Drake doesn't know a lot about it; I will explain it to you all at the bottom of the stairs" (on the way into the dining hall for breakfast). "But first, Drake is going to call your names out and put you in groups."

Drake begins calling out names; he begins with the White males. When they have gathered around him, he hands them each a patch to wear on their shirts. In this case, it is a White square made of felt. As the group of White males makes their way down toward to the dining hall, he begins calling out the names of White females. They receive a White circle to pin on their shirt. He continues down the list, and soon delegates still in the circle begin to realize that the groups are similar to the culture groups they have been working in for the previous two days (Blacks, Latinos, Asians, Jews, etc.).

It is not long before some of the delegates recognize the pattern.

"That's the Latino group!" says Tammy quite loudly.

Some of the Black and Latino delegates begin to get uncomfortable with having to wait so long. Latesha, a Black female, says "I hate this going last! I feel outcast!" Mark, surrounded by other Black males at this point, says, "I guess we're the niggers; why can't we be middle or first? Why we always last?"

Down at the entrance to the dining hall, Thomasina is explaining the rules of the exercise to each group as they arrive.

As the Black group arrives at the entrance, she repeats the directions she has already given to the other groups that are already inside the dining hall eating breakfast. "This is a chance to get to know each other better. No talking or eye contact with other groups. Everything you do, you need to do together." She goes on to state that this is just an exercise, and it won't last all day.

The delegates mutter comments to themselves. "Why is Roger out there instead of with all of us?" asks one of the delegates, upset that the ever-charismatic Roger has been placed alone, without a group.

"It's just for the exercise," states Thomasina. "Now head on in to breakfast."

Someone says they need to use the bathroom, and Thomasina explains that the group must stay together. "If one of you has to go to the bathroom, you all need to wait outside the door while that person is in there. And no interacting with delegates who are not in your group!"

Eventually, Roger—one of the isolates—makes his way down to the dining hall, walking alone. Thomasina explains, "You are not allowed to talk to, make eye contact with, or communicate with anyone else. I think you probably figured out that you are the only one with that patch, so don't talk to anyone else at all."

By 8:20, all the groups have made their way into the dining hall for breakfast. Inside the dining hall, the atmosphere is quiet and reserved. Groups sit at separate tables, talking softly among themselves.

At one point, the Black males appear to be making contact with Roger, who is sitting alone at a table. Quickly, Drake intervenes. "We told you not to talk to anyone outside your group! What do you think you're doing?!"

The Black males put up a halfhearted protest. "But he's our race! He should be with us!"

Drake shakes his head. "Follow the rules! Talk only to people in your group!"

Another Black male stands up to get some more food. Thomasina quickly confronts him: "Where do you think you are going? You can't go somewhere without your whole group!"

The delegate shakes his head. "Come on guys," he says to the rest of the Black males, who stand up and follow him to the food line. They are clearly frustrated.

After about 20 minutes, groups appear to be finishing their meals. Thomasina tells the Black females that it is their job to clear off everyone's tables. They begin even though some groups are still eating. Thomasina leads the Latino group to the broom closet and hands them all brooms. Soon they are all sweeping up the floor in the dining hall.

Some of the groups are sitting in near silence (the White females, the White males, the Asians, the LGBTQ group). Other groups are growing increasingly boisterous (the Black males and Black females are laughing loudly at the unfairness of the situation).

Thomasina sees Roger talking to a Latino delegate and immediately intervenes. "You are not to be talking to people not in your group! It's a simple rule! Everyone else is following it without a problem! Why can't you?!?"

Over the next 10 minutes, as groups finish eating and the cleanup of the room is completed, groups begin to head outside to the field. Thomasina and Drake point them to places where they are expected to stay. It is a beautiful, clear, day, and the groups all have more-or-less clear view of each other. It is approximately 8:50.

The White males are sent to a cabin porch at the top of the hill. They sit down in chairs and begin chatting and laughing quietly. The White women sit on a picnic table at the edge of the field. The Asians are at a picnic table behind one of the cabins, essentially out of sight. The two LGBTQ delegates simply stand on the field, as do the

Latinos and Black females. The three Jews sit on a set of stairs at the edge of the field, talking quietly to each other. The Black females, in particular, are growing angry about the situation.

"Damn! White people sitting up there in rocking chairs, and we gotta stand up all the way back here near the woods!" says one woman angrily.

"Fight for your rights!" shouts another.

Tammy, the Black female isolate, is alone in a chair on one of the cabin porches. She seems to be going to sleep.

Roger is alone on a different porch. His gaze keeps wandering toward the Black males, who are gathered near some picnic tables at the bottom of the hill. The Black women, on occasion, laugh loudly, or someone shouts out a half-joking, half-serious cry of resistance. "Fight for your rights!" yells one delegate. "Black is power!" shouts another. Despite the rhetoric, however, the group remains in its spot.

The Black males are talking quietly together. At around 9:15, Drake approaches the group and throws them a beach ball. "Here," he says, "You guys can play with the ball if you want."

A few delegates begin halfheartedly tossing the ball back and forth.

The system remains essentially static as the minutes slip by. Occasionally, a group walks to a cabin to use the bathroom; although the trip takes them in close proximately to some other groups along the way, nobody makes eye contact. After a few minutes in the cabin, the groups inevitably head right back out to where they were standing.

The Black females occasionally shout something out to nobody in particular: "OK! We get the point! Enough already."

At approximately 9:35, Roger leaves his porch and walks into the cafeteria (walking right past where the Black males are hanging out). Minutes later, he emerges holding a cup of coffee. He walks back to his porch and stands there staring toward the Black males for several minutes.

At 9:50, the Black females all head over to the porch of the discussion room. A few of them head inside and apparently turn on the radio. Soon loud music spills out onto the field for all to hear. Through the windows, it is clear that some of the women are dancing.

At this point, Roger is emboldened to leave his porch. He walks down toward the Black males and sits down on a picnic table next to them. A minute later, he breaks the rules and starts talking to them. He then heads up to the porch of the discussion room, where the Black females are sitting.

"Yo! What's the point of this?" he asks them. "I can stand 10 minutes of this, but I can't do all day!"

The Black females nod in agreement, but they seem content to hang out on the porch or inside with the radio. After three or four minutes of conversation, Roger heads back down to the Black male group.

Despite the fact that music is now blaring across the field, the other groups seem to not be moving at all. The White men chat quietly on a porch at the top of the hill; the White women sit quietly at their picnic table; the Jews, Latinos, LGBTQ group, and Asians are all stationed around the field. As before, a group will occasionally make its way to a cabin to use the bathroom and then quietly return to their spot. But the system of groups remains essentially as it had been arranged since leaving breakfast.

At 10:10, the Black males gather together as a group and start to head up the hill toward the porch where the Black females are sitting. They make it about half the distance to the porch and then stop. Although nobody confronts them for moving (actually, Thomasina and Drake have been inside a cabin for the last 30 minutes or so), they don't make it to join with the Black females at this point. After a brief hesitation, they all turn around and return to their spot.

At 10:25, there is another flurry of movement. One of the Black men seems to have had enough. "What is the point of this?" He asks to nobody in particular, "To waste time?" He heads back up toward the meeting room where the Black women are listening to music, and the group follows. This time, they make it all the way to the meeting room porch. Soon, they are all inside dancing and chatting with the Black women.

The minutes continue to tick by. Despite the festivities going on in the meeting room—and the unmistakable fact that the rules of the exercise have been broken with no immediate consequences—the other groups are making no moves.

At around 10:45, a group of Black men and women walk out on the porch and notice the Jews still sitting on a set of stairs just a few yards from the meeting room porch. "Y'all still sitting here baking in the sun?" asks one of the Black women. Although this could be taken as a chance to end their isolation, the Jewish group continues to avoid contact.

Soon after this exchange, two Latino men head over to the meeting room. After a minute or two, they emerge to invite the rest of their group to join. At this point, the Black women, Black men, the Latinos, and both isolates are comfortably hanging out in the meeting room or on the porch. The other groups (Whites males, White females, Asians, Jews, and LGBTQ) are all still seated at separate locations around the field. The loud music continues to echo across the field. As the minutes continue to tick past, the remaining groups sit quietly in their places.

At 11:12, Thomasina makes the decision to end the exercise. She emerges out onto the field, blows a loud air horn, and invites all the participants into the discussion room to debrief the experience. Slightly more than 3 hours have elapsed since the start of the morning circle.

Separation Exercise 2: Connie and Laurie's System

The evening before the Separation Exercise occurs, members of the staff gather for their regular evening meeting. Things are quiet; the participants have all gone to bed and everything feels calm and under control. The codirectors of the program, two White women named

Connie and Laurie, explain the rules of the exercise to the staff members.

Connie says that the participants will be separated into their culture groups, and members of each group will be given same-colored armbands to wear. The participants will be told to follow a simple set of rules:

1. Don't talk to anyone not wearing your same color armband.

2. Don't make eye contact with someone not wearing your same color armband.

3. Always stay together with everyone wearing your color armband.

Connie and Laurie make it clear that they will be in charge during this activity; however, they have a list of guidelines for the staff members to follow. Connie tells the staff members, "No lying. If someone asks you when it will end, say that you don't know." Also, no military-style tactics. Apparently, both directors have seen the exercise run in a very aggressive, militant style, and they do not want to emulate that here. They insist that there be no berating of participants or other sorts of staff activism. Essentially, the staff members are just to follow the rules obediently, making no effort to break the exercise or go beyond Connie and Laurie's efforts to enforce the rules.

Connie says that Malcolm will be the isolate. An outspoken and well-liked Black male, they think he would be most likely to break the exercise too quickly.

Laurie states that she will be wearing a scarf during the exercise. When she removes the scarf, it will be a sign to the staff members that they should stop offering any resistance to the groups coming together.

Finally, Connie tells the staff members that some participants may be upset by the exercise. She says that if one of the members of their group is really angry or disturbed, the staff member should try to have a one-on-one conversation with the participant to try to calm him or her down.

The staff members have very few questions. Everyone seems to understand the rules and is comfortable with what is going to happen. Conversation turns to a review of the events of the day and a discussion of how a few participants are feeling. After a few minutes of this process discussion, the meeting is over and staff members head off to bed.

The next morning, morning circle starts at 8:15. The forty participants begin to gather around the flagpole in the central square. By 8:22, everyone has arrived and the group begins doing roll call. After a few administrative announcements, Connie announces that the morning activity is going to start before breakfast today. She quickly and clearly explains the rules.

"You're going to be separated into your culture groups this morning. Each person will get a colored armband. You may not make contact with anyone who has a different color armband. You must stay together as a group at all times; if someone in your group needs to go to the bathroom, you all must go to the bathroom together."

Laurie begins calling off names and handing out armbands. Soon, the circle around the flag has been replaced by a collection of separate groups.

Connie says it is now time for breakfast, and begins calling off the order in which the groups can head into the cafeteria. Over the course of several minutes, she calls out the following list: White, Asians, Native Americans, Malcolm (the isolate), American-born Hispanics, multiracial, Mexican-born Hispanics, and African Americans. The two Hispanic groups are the largest—they easily comprise half the participants at this program.

Inside the cafeteria, participants stand quietly in line to get their breakfast. Usually, there are two servers handing out food in the morning; today, however, there is only one. Connie confirms that this decision was made as part of the morning exercise. The presence of only one server means that it takes a remarkably long time to get food. By 9 AM, the Mexican-born Hispanics and African Americans are still standing in line while the first groups to enter the cafeteria are finishing their meals.

The cafeteria is very quiet; people aren't speaking much, and when they do speak it is in a quiet whisper. Laurie sees a lone Mexican-born Hispanic female heading to the drink machine to get a drink. "You guys have to stay together!" she says to the group. The whole group grudgingly but quietly heads over to the drink machine.

At 9:13, the African American group finally sits down at a table with their meals in hand.

At 9:14, Laurie makes an announcement. "Those who want to go outside for free time can go. Mexican-borns—remember you must stay to clean up!"

The White and Asian groups quickly get up to leave. At this point, they have had more than 30 minutes to eat breakfast.

By 9:24, only the Mexican-born Hispanics and the African Americans are left in the cafeteria. Malcolm, the lone isolate, sits alone at a table quietly eating his breakfast.

Outside, it is a beautiful, clear morning. The various groups are scattered around a fairly small area in front of the cafeteria building. Each group is studiously following the rules, and most of the groups seem to be having a good time. The Asians are playing with a volleyball. Nearby, the multiracial group is singing songs and laughing loudly. The White group, not so far away, is singing a round-robin version of "Row, Row, Row Your Boat." They keep laughing as people make mistakes. The three members of the Native American group sit together on a rock in the middle of the small field, talking quietly among themselves. Eventually, Malcolm emerges from the cafeteria and sits down on a porch, looking sad and alone.

Malcolm is sitting close to a soda machine. I notice for the first time that the machine has a handwritten sign taped on its front. The sign says, "Whites Only."

At 9:34, the African American group emerges from the cafeteria. They stand in a small circle together and begin talking about the weather. Inside the cafeteria building, the Mexican-born Hispanics are busy sweeping the floors and wiping off the tables.

Occasionally, a group heads off together toward a cabin to use the bathroom. I follow the multicultural group inside and realize that the bathrooms are also marked with handmade signs. Sinks, water fountains, and bathroom stalls are all marked as "Whites Only" or "Coloreds Only."

Because they are all standing in such a small area, the separation of the groups is striking. A few of the groups have moved to different areas of the field, but all continue to play games and talk among themselves. Because everyone seems to be following the rules, Connie and Laurie are simply wandering around the field quietly. They don't have much to say.

Eventually, at 9:50, Laurie tells the American-born Hispanic group to clean up the field area. They are given a trash bag and begin wandering among the groups picking up litter.

At 9:52, the Mexican-born Hispanic group finally emerges from the cafeteria. They find an area to stand in and begin chatting quietly among themselves.

In the small area, it is hard to miss the fact that the American-born Hispanics are cleaning up while all the other groups are busy laughing, singing, or simply standing around chatting. I hear one member of this group say to the others, "We should start marching!" But the other members of the group continue to pick up trash.

By 10:10, the Separation Exercise has been going on for nearly 2 hours. Although the groups have changed positions a few times, there have been no efforts to break the exercise. Most of the participants still seem to be having fun playing and singing within their groups.

At this time, Connie and Laurie meet near the flagpole and raise their hands to make an announcement. "It's time for our morning sing! Remember, have no contact with the other groups! Please head over to the pavilion!"

The pavilion stands right next to the flagpole field. It is a concrete patio, with a collection of picnic tables arranged in the shape of a "U" underneath a large wooden roof. The groups all head over to this area and find places to sit. The area isn't very large, so the groups have to sit right next to each other to fit. Still, the participants all stay huddled together in their assigned groups. A few staff members have handed out a bunch of songbooks containing song lyrics; they then return to sit with their assigned groups.

By 10:15, they are all settled in. Connie tells them to start with the Anytown theme song. They groups start singing with a conspicuous lack of enthusiasm:

> Anytown; Anytown; yellow, Black, White, red, or brown;
> Makes no difference when you come down to Anytown.

The contrast between the ideal of unity expressed in the lyrics and the reality of the rigidly separated groups singing the song is unmistakable. When the song ends, there is muted applause and few giggles.

Connie stands in the middle of the tables with a stern look on her face. "African Americans, I want you to lead us all in 'I Believe I Can Fly.' Please come stand here in the middle."

The African Americans make their way to the center of the pavilion, and they begin a very halfhearted rendition of the R. Kelly song. Connie is clearly unhappy.

"Come on! Lift it up!" she shouts. The singing gets noticeably stronger.

When they get to the end of the song, there is once again muted applause. Laurie walks over to where the multicultural group sits. "You guys need to pick it up!" she declares. "Why aren't you singing louder?"

The song session continues in this fashion. The Mexican-born Hispanic group is asked to lead everyone in "De Colores," a classic folk song with Spanish lyrics celebrating diversity that has become an unofficial anthem in the Latino community.

After that, Connie tells the White group to sing "Hero," by Mariah Carey. The chorus is all about strength and empowerment and the presence of heroic potential within each of us. With each song, the disconnect between lyrics celebrating unity, diversity, and empowerment and the reality of the Separation Exercise grows more and more jarring.

It is 10:25; the Separation Exercise has been going on for 2 hours. When the White group finishes singing, a young woman in the multiracial group raises her hand. "Can you clarify what you mean by 'contact'?" she asks the directors. It is the first student comment that goes anywhere near publicly challenging the rules of the exercise.

"You can sing, but don't make contact with the other groups," Connie replies. "It's really very simple."

Laurie asks the Asian group to sing a song called "I Wish." They are terrible—absolutely no energy or enthusiasm. Laurie actually stops them mid-verse and tells them to sit down.

"Asians, you are not doing it. Multiracials, why don't you take over!" she demands.

When they are done, Laurie turns to the African Americans. "A majority of you weren't singing. Why not?"

One of the participants says, "We don't know the words."

Laurie seems unsatisfied. "Is that all?"

At this point, Connie turns to Malcolm. She says, "Malcolm, lead us in 'Stand by Me.'"

Malcolm, the lone isolate in the exercise, stands alone in the center of the pavilion. He begins singing weakly, and the rest of the participants soon join him in struggling through a rendition of the classic song about solidarity and connection that is utterly devoid of enthusiasm or conviction.

The sense of frustration and sadness in the group is almost palpable. Connie turns to Cathy, one of the counselors, and asks her to stand up alone to sing a song called "Don't Give Up." Cathy is clearly on the edge of tears as she stands up in front of everyone. As she begins to sing, her voice trembles with a mix of sadness and fear.

Eventually, she stops trying to sing and just reads the lyrics, which offer a message about perseverance and hope. The sound of her lone voice in the crowded pavilion is heartbreaking. When she finishes, the silence echoes through the pavilion.

The time is now 10:35. Connie asks a male in the White group to sing "You Gotta Be." This particular participant is in a wheelchair and speaks English with a foreign accent. He wheels himself out to the center of the pavilion and struggles through all the lyrics. It takes almost 6 minutes. The song about wisdom, empowerment, and strength sounds like a funeral dirge.

At 10:43, Connie notices that a counselor in the Asian group is crying. "Kristie—you're not singing!" She tells her to come up front to lead a song.

Audibly sobbing, Kristie makes her unsteady way up to the middle of pavilion. Far too upset to sing, all she can do is stand there shaking and crying.

Finally, things seem to have gone too far. A young woman in the American-born Hispanic group speaks out. "You guys are being mean to us! That's why we're all crying! You're telling us we gotta sing louder!"

Someone in the Mexican-born Hispanic group speaks up next. "You go keep telling us to stick together and now we gotta stay separate!"

The first participant to speak up is clearly very upset. "I don't know if this is a trick, but Kristie is upset and it's not fair to put her on the spot and make us watch her cry!" There is no mistaking the anger in her voice.

One of males in the Asian group stands up and walks over to Kristie. He, too, is on the edge of tears now.

Connie keeps the pressure on. "John, sit down! This is Kristie's turn to lead the singing!"

John shakes his head. "I'm not going anywhere! This isn't fair!"

At this point, everyone has begun to chatter loudly. Laurie sees that an American-born Hispanic has ripped off his armband; others in the group decide to follow along.

"Who told you could take off your armbands?" she asks sternly.

"I'm not going to let color come between us!" he responds angrily. When he stands up and walks over to Kristie to give her a hug, several other members of the group follow.

One girl in the Mexican-born Hispanic group seems angry at the fact that everyone is breaking the rules. "I understand why they did the separation—they wanted to make us feel different! But Kristie could say no if she wanted!" She has not moved from her seat and seems to be in no rush to break the exercise.

At this point, Laurie casually removes her scarf. She and Connie step back and no longer attempt to enforce the rules.

It has only been a few minutes since Kristie was asked to stand up front, but the change is dramatic. A group of 10 or 12 participants has gathered around her; they are giving each other hugs and talking about how awful it felt to be separated all morning. Participants have also gathered in two other groups, with lots of hugging and crying occurring all around. A few individuals are still sitting in their seats, watching all the action.

An Asian boy has walked over to the Mexican-born Hispanic girl who defended the exercise, and they are in a heated debate. "How can you stand by while we can't hang with our friends? How can you let her stay up there alone? It's not right! It's not right!" In response, the girl continues to shake her head and remain in her seat.

At this point, the large group gathered around Kristie begins to sing "Stand by Me." This time, the singing is loud and enthusiastic, and before long most of the participants gathered in the pavilion are singing along.

When the song is over, Connie raises her hand to make an announcement. "OK! We want to take some time to talk about this! Let's head back to the meeting room to debrief!" The time is 10:55.

The participants are still busy hugging each other. Several are still crying. Slowly, they make their way out of the pavilion and head off to debrief the experience.

Separation Exercise 3: John and Susan's System

The exercise begins, in actuality, the night before the segregation occurs. The students are allowed to stay up late, and the staff members retreat to the staff room for a meeting, where the noise of kids laughing and singing sets the backdrop for the meeting.

John, a White male, is a codirector of the program, along with Susan, a White female. John had originally envisioned organizing an incident to kick off the exercise: There would be a (seemingly) spontaneous staff water fight that gets out of hand, providing a reason for a dramatic change in tone and policies the following morning; however, the staff members quickly agree that this ruse is not necessary. The students have not really been coming together, and their general tendency to stay up too late and arrive late to the morning circle already provide enough reason to make the segregation exercise feel justified.

John explains that the rules for the delegates are simple and clear:

1. Stay in your group.
2. Don't talk to anyone outside your group.
3. Don't make eye contact with anyone outside your group.
4. Always stay together.

He then explains that some members of the staff will be placed in groups with delegates. These staff members have their own rules:

1. No matter what, don't say anything beyond repeating one of these four rules (slight variations in wording are acceptable).

2. Staff members are absolutely not allowed to break the exercise until the last delegate in their group has broken the exercise.

He then makes it clear that the senior staff members will play the role of "enforcers." They will not be a part of any group and are responsible for enforcing the rules of the exercise. They will also hand out projects to groups designed to highlight stereotypes and distract them from taking action.

The next 30 minutes of the staff meeting involve staff members sharing their concerns about the exercise. They are afraid to act mean toward the delegates and are concerned about causing emotional pain. One of them fears she might actually enjoy the abuse of authority she is expected to display. John and Susan make it clear that they should keep in mind the big picture: This difficult exercise is done for a good cause, and there will be ample time to debrief with the participants and make the participants feel supported and understood when the exercise concludes. At 1 AM, the meeting ends, and staff members head out to get some sleep.

We arise early the next morning to a clear and beautiful day. As usual, the bell in the central courtyard is rung precisely at 7 AM, telling the delegates that they have 15 minutes to get dressed and arrive at the morning circle. This morning, a surprisingly large number of delegates seem to have overslept. The group stands in an incomplete circle in the central courtyard, as straggler after straggler walks out to the courtyard and joins the circle. There is an awkward silence to the morning.

At about 7:20, John speaks up angrily. "Everyone stay quiet until all delegates and staff members are outside!"

By 7:30, it appears as though the circle is complete. John emerges out onto the courtyard, and he doesn't look happy.

"Things are going to be different today," he says ominously. "All sorts of people have been breaking all sorts of rules. We are your state-mandated guardians for the week, and we have decided we need to make a change because of how you all have been acting. So there are some new rules we are going to follow today!"

Susan begins calling out names and gathering the students in the following groups: White males, blonde White females, non-blonde White females, Latinos, Jewish, multiracial, isolates, LGBTQ, Asians, South Asian/Middle Easterners, privileged Blacks, Black males, and Black females. Each group is given a particular color armband (yellow for the Asians, brown for the Black males, pink for the blonde women, etc.). They are told the four rules and then told to stand silently as the process continues. Within 10 minutes, the circle in the central courtyard has transformed into a field of isolated and silent groups. The silence is deafening.

Slowly, the groups are invited in to breakfast: White males first, then blonde White women, then non-blonde White women, Asians, Jews, Latinos, and so on. It is 8 AM before the last of the groups is told to leave the courtyard and head to the cafeteria.

In the cafeteria, the scene is striking. The normally boisterous and irrepressible delegates are sitting silently in segregated groups. By the time we get there, the only group that has yet to eat—the Black males—is just arriving. Kristin, one of the enforcers, speaks to them forcefully. "You guys will eat at this table."

One of them quickly points out that there aren't enough chairs for everyone in the group at the small round table.

"Then some of you will have to eat standing up. That's the way it is."

One of the members of the Jewish group speaks up. "We have some extra chairs—they can take ours if they want . . ."

Kristin's response is instant and icy. "Stay with your own group! This is none of your business!"

Another enforcer says loudly to the White men that they are welcome to go take a shower at this point if they want. The Latinos are asked to clear the White male's tables.

Seeing that one of the Black males has gone to the toaster on his own, she immediately chastises the group. "I told you to stay together! What is he doing off on his own? Can't you people follow directions? You know, you people don't even deserve this cereal. No cereal for you this morning!"

She proceeds to collect the small packages of cereal on the table, in some cases spilling milk into the laps of delegates who had only partially completed their meal.

At this point, enforcers begin sending various groups to different locations around the facility. An awkward silence fills the cafeteria.

I proceed to walk through the rooms of the conference center. Everyone seems to be looking down in silence. The multicultural group sits silent in a small conference room. The blonde females are seated on a landing at the top of the stairs. The Black females stand alone in the courtyard.

Eventually, I bump into John, who explains some of the tasks that are being handed out: The Asians have been asked to write a report about why they are the "model minority." The South Asians have been asked to write a report explaining terrorism. The blonde females have been told to apply makeup and do each other's hair. The non-blonde White females have been told to create greeting cards for various American holidays. The multicultural students have been instructed to draw a map of the world and trace their ancestor's roots. The Black females have been told to put together a "step show" dance routine.

All around the conference center, the scene is striking: silent, joyless delegates halfheartedly going through the motions of their assigned tasks.

Through a back window, I see a solitary Black delegate sitting utterly alone. I later find out that he is the only Muslim in the group and has been sent off by himself. In the front hallway, a Black female delegate sits alone on a chair, with her knees pulled up under her sweatshirt and her head covered by her sweatshirt hood.

I turn a corner and find one of the delegates talking to the LGBTQ group. He is explaining that their job is to organize a gay pride parade and that they will have to do this while standing in a broom closet. He ushers five individuals into the cramped closet and closes the door. Minutes go by, and nobody tries to leave. It is 9:17 AM.

I walk outside, and see the Black women halfheartedly teaching each other dance moves. The Black men are seated at a picnic table, and many of them seem to be staring in the same direction. I follow their gaze to where the White males are playing a casual game of Frisbee in a large field.

As the moments tick away, rumbles of discontent can be heard. One of the Black males sings "We Shall Overcome" quietly. Another one says, "Damn! The White boys get to play Frisbee and we gotta sit here doing nothing? That's *messed* up!" But the groups remain isolated, and everyone continues to follow the rules.

In the cafeteria, the mood is funereal. In one corner, the South Asians work quietly on a piece of poster board exploring the causes of terror. The Asians whisper to each other as they explore what it means to be a model minority. The non-blonde White women have created a pile of greeting cards covered with images of flowers, snow, turkeys, and other holiday images. The Jews, seated just outside at a picnic table, work on an article about reconstructionist Judaism. On occasion, an enforcer speaks up, reminding a delegate to "keep your eyes on your own group" or saying, "What are you, confused? The rules say stay together!"

The time is now close to 10:00 AM. I walk past the broom closet in the front hallway. The door is open about half an inch. I am shocked to see that the LGBTQ group is still inside, standing in complete silence.

The sense of quiet, oppressive, stasis is palpable everywhere. Nearly 2 and a half hours have gone by, and the exercise remains unbroken. Apart from some quiet grumbling and halfhearted songs of protest by an individual or two, there have been no meaningful challenges to the status quo.

Then, at 10:18, something happens. As I walk down the hall, I am passed by Eduardo, a member of the Latino group. His fellow group members are nowhere to be seen. As he walks up to the coffee station and begins preparing a cup of coffee for himself, he is spotted by an enforcer.

"Eduardo! What are you doing! You are supposed to STAY WITH YOUR GROUP! Put down that coffee!"

Eduardo is clearly nervous but also resolved to resist the rules of the exercise.

"Or what? Put down the coffee or what? I'm done following these bullshit rules!"

John suddenly appears with a look of urgency on his face. "You know the rules, Eduardo! Get with your group! NOW!"

Eduardo puts down the coffee and starts making his way outside to where the rest of the Latinos are standing. John looks furious, and Eduardo is clearly frightened. But he is determined to speak his mind. He is about to rejoin his group when he suddenly turns and heads toward the Black females, still rehearsing dance moves in the courtyard.

John gets in his face. "GET. BACK. TO. YOUR. GROUP!!"

"Or what?" Eduardo replies, growing increasingly emboldened. "What are you gonna do to me?"

At this point, Kristin joins John in trying to quash this act of rebellion.

"Eduardo, what's the problem?" she says scornfully. "You're not proud of your people? You wanna be a sellout, and just leave them all behind? You're not proud of being Latino?"

Eduardo's nervousness is gone, replaced by a clearly simmering anger. "Yo, I'm proud to be Latino. But you been telling us all week to resist oppressive systems, and that's what I'm doin' here! Yo! Everyone! Free Your Mind!!"

Both John and Kristin try to usher him back into the Latino group, but he quickly dashes around them and runs to the Black female group.

"Hey! Ladies! Join me in fighting this! Come on! Let's bring unity to Anytown!"

The group of six delegates averts their eyes. He stands with them for a few more seconds, but it is clear that none of them is going to break the rules. He runs across the courtyard to the isolated Black woman and again invites her to join him. She looks away and shakes her head. Soon Eduardo is back with his Latino group, loudly denouncing the enforcers.

More minutes more go by. The act of rebellion seems to have been ineffective. Although there is a new energy simmering across the courtyard, the groups remain isolated and obedient.

At this point, the enforcers have begun moving groups around a bit to change the dynamic. At 10:30, I see the LGBTQ group led out into the courtyard. They had remained stuffed into the broom closet for close to 45 minutes. The South Asians are led out and asked to continue working on their report at a picnic table a few yards outside of the courtyard. The Black males have begun to grow clearly restless. They emerge from one of the dorms to the courtyard bustling with nervous energy. "F—the White man!" one of them yells. Another starts singing "Wade in the Water." Still another says, "Unite like a fist!"

Across the courtyard, Eduardo sees the new possibility. He looks to his group, saying, "Come on, everyone! Stand up for what's right! Bring Anytown together!" He begins to run toward the Black males, and this time his peers follow him. Soon, the Black males and Latinos are huddled together, bursting with renewed energy.

"Come on! Let's go! We gotta get everyone together!" Whooping and hollering, the group sets out in search of other groups. As they pass the large bell in the center of the courtyard, one of the Black males yells, "Ring the unity bell!" Another Black male grabs the bell's handle and rings it loudly three times. At this point, it must be apparent to everyone at the conference center that something unplanned is going on.

Many of the groups refuse to break the rules when they are approached. The Asians, now seated at another picnic table near the courtyard, shake their heads. "There must be a reason why they are doing this," says one delegate to the Blacks and Latinos gathered next to the table. "Just follow the rules! Don't mess it up!" The South Asians also remain apart, choosing to continue working on their report. The privileged Blacks, however, do choose to break the rules and join the rebellion. When the group approaches the blonde White females upstairs, the delegates initially seem to redouble their efforts to apply makeup and style hair. After a few minutes of debate, however, this group chooses to break the rules and join the growing movement.

Moments later, the growing mass of delegates approaches the LGBTQ group, inviting them to break the exercise and join the "movement." The LGBTQ group is doing everything it can to turn their backs to the boisterous crowd. They seem to be looking to one of the staff members who was included in the group. As instructed, he is looking down silently and simply refusing to break the rules.

Somehow, word has gotten out that this group spent 45 minutes standing in a closet, and the rebels are furious at the news.

A Latino girl says to a female member of the LGBTQ group, "They locked you in a closet for 45 minutes! That's f—ed up! You gotta join us in fighting this messed up system! Come on! Join us!"

The delegate being addressed keeps her eyes on the ground and just shakes her head. "We believe in following authority," she says. Another member of the group is visibly crying but refuses to make eye contact with anyone standing around her. Finally, the delegate who spoke before looks at the large group of people standing around. "Please," she says quietly. "Just go. Please leave us alone."

At a loss for how to proceed, the individuals in the movement look around at each other in confusion. Finally, Eduardo says they should just move on, and the group departs, leaving the LGBTQ group huddled together alone.

By 11:00 AM (nearly 3 and a half hours since the start of the exercise), it appears as though the movement started by the Latinos and Blacks has attracted all the members it can. They retreat to a large conference room to discuss how to proceed. Although voices are heated and passionate, they seem to be raising their hands and having a more-or-less orderly debate.

"We need to figure out what the movement stands for!" says one Black female. "We need to bring everyone together," says a Black male.

As the group begins work on a statement of principles, I head out to explore the conference center.

The multiracial group remains in a small conference room. The room has glass doors, so they have seen and have been addressed by the large group of students who have broken the exercise. Apparently, they chose to continue following the rules.

The Jews remain outside at a picnic table. They are furious because an enforcer recently came by and tore up their report on reconstructionist Judaism. Although they are clearly furious about the exercise, they have chosen not to join the movement.

I realize that I have not seen the White males in some time, and I ask an enforcer where they have gone. He leads to me a basement room right off the courtyard, where the four members of that group are sitting in a carpeted, air-conditioned room watching a movie. Compared to the near-chaos and upheaval occurring upstairs, the calm, cool, leisurely atmosphere of this room comes as a bit of a shock. From this room, it is possible that this group may have no idea of what is happening upstairs. They may have heard the bell and seen some individuals walk past the small windows looking out at knee-level on the courtyard, and simply chose to keep watching the movie without exploring what was happening outside. The group members look at us briefly then turn back to the television.

Back in the courtyard and in the conference rooms, the enforcers continue to attempt to reinforce the rules but in a less strident manner. They are constantly milling about, reminding people to "stay in your group." It is clear, however, that it is possible to break the rules of the exercise without suffering any real consequences. However, several groups have clearly taken their stand, and they have no interest in joining the movement.

Minutes later, I return to the conference room where the movement has been developing its core principles. It seems they have agreed on their mission and have written up a sign declaring their values and purpose. The sign says:

What is the movement about?

- *Unity of all identities*
- *Respect (self and each other)*
- *Assertion of Rights*
- *Rejection of Oppression (monoculturalism)*
- *Breaking the Cycle and Categories*
- *Don't tell Anybody What to Do*
- *Tell people what they CAN do*
- *Be Peaceful and Non-violent*
- *Try hard to cause each other the least pain possible*

The movement has also agreed on a plan: They are going to hold hands and walk out among the other groups. The individuals at the front of the line will hold the sign, and individuals in the line will invite the other delegates to make the personal choice to join the movement. Within moments, a long chain of delegates has snaked its way out of the conference room and toward the remaining segregated groups.

For the next 10 minutes or so, the long chain of delegates weaves its way toward the various groups seated at picnic tables or in chairs near the courtyard. Most of the groups make it clear they have no interest in budging. When the human chain heads back toward the conference center, a handful of groups remain seated outside. The Asians, South Asians, isolated Black female, and other Black females have opted not to join the movement.

I find John and Susan gathered in the center of the courtyard. It is nearly noon, and they are deciding whether to allow the exercise to continue. Looking out around the courtyard, they agree that the groups that remain segregated look likely to stay that way for hours. Together, they make the decision to bring the exercise to a close, and they send one of the enforcers off to ring the bell for lunch.

Concluding Thoughts on the Separation Exercises

We've now followed three different Separation Exercises and watched as they unfolded in three completely different ways. Now, we'll turn our attention to exploring the lessons that emerged from researching these exercise through observation, questionnaires, and careful analysis.

6

Findings at the Interpersonal and Intergroup Levels

Now that we have had a chance to observe three distinct Separation Exercises through the eyes of the researchers, we've been able to take a high-level, 30,000-foot perspective on what happened during each of these activities. We are equally interested in zooming in, however, to explore how individuals immersed in these experiences understood what was happening. To that end, we asked participants to fill out questionnaires that would illuminate how everyone individually understood the experience, why they chose to act as they did, and what elements of the system they chose to focus on. The goal was to achieve a better understanding of this process of system-wide social change in which we could explore the unfolding events and the way individuals immersed in these systems made sense of what was happening.

In this chapter, we'll present key findings that emerged from data focused on the first two levels of analysis of this research: *interpersonal* and *intergroup*. Because there is so much richness and complexity to consider at the highest whole-system level, those findings get their own chapter (Chapter 7).

In this review of high-level findings, I'll refer to the data while trying to keep charts and tables to a minimum. For those who are interested, I've included a more detailed explanation of our research methodology in Appendix A. I've also gathered much of the raw data from all three exercises in the appendixes as well; you'll be told where to find that additional content at appropriate points in the pages ahead. Readers interested in going beyond the high-level overview offered here are invited to take a deeper dive into the raw data included in the back of the book.

The Interpersonal Level of Analysis

We'll begin our analysis of findings from this research at the interpersonal level of analysis—the level of the individual. This is, after all, the perspective that is most familiar to us each day while we make meaning of the world around us through our own individual experiences. What insights might we gain through this type of exploration?

The questionnaire that we gave to participants asked participants to share their version of what happened during the exercise and asked the following four questions intended to elicit data regarding the interpersonal level of experience (for the complete questionnaire, see Appendix B):

1. *Tell your story of what happened during this exercise and how events progressed. Be sure to include the important events that occurred over the course of the exercise.*

2. *What did it feel like being a member of your group? Why?*

3. *In your opinion, what was the most important group? Why?*

4. *Why did you not break the exercises earlier than when you did?*

5. *How did it feel to break the exercise?*

Each question was intended to elicit an answer that illuminates a different aspect of the experience, so we'll work our way through the findings in order. The one additional thought I'll offer before diving into this data is that we are going to stay focused on presenting the findings, with minimal additional analysis. Essentially, we are going to listen very carefully to the voices of the participants in an effort to understand how individuals immersed in the exercises made sense of their experiences. How the findings that emerge from this research can or should inform our understanding of real-world matters of race and social change is vitally important, and we'll dive into that discussion in earnest in Chapters 8 and 9.

The first question we asked related to the interpersonal level of analysis was this:

> *Tell your story of what happened during this exercise and how events progressed. Be sure to include the important events that occurred over the course of the exercise.*

The intention was to surface the ways that individuals immersed in these activities understood their experience. Remember: In every case, participants had woken up to what they thought would be another typical day at camp, and they unexpectedly found themselves thrust into an unequal, segregated social system. How did they explain to themselves what happened during the exercise?

It should be noted that this was not an in-depth interview; it was a question on a questionnaire that was completed prior to engaging in a lengthy and substantive multi-hour debrief session. These responses surely represent participants' early, initial approach to framing the experience before having an opportunity to reflect deeply on the matter. As such, it's a window into participants' first instincts and default tendencies when it comes to thinking about the exercise they just encountered. In all participant quotes throughout this chapter we made the choice to retain the authentic voice of participants by not correcting any spelling or grammar in their responses.

What we learned was the participants made meaning of this experience in myriad ways.

Some responses highlight a sense of confusion:

> *"Well when Thomasina and Drake read the groups off I didn't know what was going on . . ."*

Other responses reflect a strong awareness of the fact that different groups received very different treatment:

"In the morning we were split into groups . . . We ate our meals separately and were served in an order based on the social power of the groups. The groups also served people if they were Black women, swept if they were Hispanic men and were benefited [or] hurt in other ways depending on the gender race religion of the people."

Some responses emphasized a fear of getting punished:

"I think when the director told us not to bring up our dishes that's when I felt like we had to strictly follow the rules, and that 'reprimand' kind of stuck with me. I really didn't want to get in trouble."

Some simply told the tale of how events unfolded in a very straightforward and factual manner:

"We were put into certain groups and told to follow each other when we need to go somewhere. Then, we went to a breakfast, and after we were told to go in the field and stand up. During breakfast my group was told to put away everyone's dishes. Eventually, we got tired of standing up in the field and went to the discussion room to go sit down, then to get beverages, then to the cabin, then stayed in the discussion room and played jump rope and danced."

Others sought to highlight the more symbolic and systemic dimension of the experience:

"I think what happened was that they were trying to make White people rich and like first class. The spanish be maids and Black girls be clean up people too. And I think that they were trying to make Black males have no job."

Through a careful analysis of this qualitative data, the research team developed a list of 12 different ways that participants sought to make meaning of this experience. The complete list is presented in Appendix C.

The main outcome here is that although the participants were all immersed in the same activity, individuals made sense of their experiences in very different ways. It would have been fascinating to explore the correlation between understanding and action in some empirical way, but we were not able to do that, unfortunately. Instead, we were left with intriguing but unanswered questions: Were people who told stories focused on confusion, fear, or trust in the good intentions of the staff members less likely to break the system? Were people who told different stories that focused on frustration with the unfairness of the system and their excitement when others began to resist the system more likely to challenge the system themselves? It seems reasonable to suggest that the stories individuals chose to tell themselves about this experience led to either passivity and a sense of powerlessness or to a sense of agency and a commitment to work for change.

The third question on the questionnaire asked, *"What did it feel like being a member of your group? Why?"* This question was designed to explore the affective dimension of individual experience in this exercise. As part of our effort to analyze these data, we chose to organize these responses into grids that enabled us to see the responses received from members of each group. We listed the groups hierarchically in the order that was decided on by the staff members running each exercise and then listed responses from members of that group horizontally in the appropriate row. The intention here was to create a sort of x-ray view into the inner lives of individuals immersed in these systems. We wondered: Are there themes or patterns to the way that individuals at the top of these systems felt about being members of their group? How about individuals in the middle? At the bottom? What might we find by illuminating the emotional experiences of individuals at every level of these systems? What might we learn by inquiring into these inner experiences?

To give you a sense of what this looked like and how this approach illuminated themes and insights in useful ways, the grid from Separation Exercise 1 is presented in Table 6.1.

Table 6.1 Reports of Individual Experience by Group From Exercise 1

White Males	Awkward. I didn't really want the privileges I was given. I felt undeserving.	Depressing, because I wanted to follow rules.	
White Females	There are just no words. I really don't know.	Uncomfortable because we were served/had our tables cleared by the Black woman group. It was also hard to watch the Jewish group and the Black woman group bake in the hot sun.	I felt very offended because I am not all White. I'm only 25% Italian . . . I felt like they took one look at me and assumed I'm all White.
Jewish	It was uncomfortable . . . not being treated fairly. The badge, which was a Holocaust star, made me feel like less of a person. It made me identify with my ancestry and the segregation of my own people in the past.		
Latinos	Fun because I like this group.	I felt like I was appreciated for being my race.	Bad' cause they was making us clean but good' cause it was fun . . . we was just hanging out.	Fun because we found a fun thing to do.	I felt downsized. Lower than others. The only other group I felt equal to was the Black females.

Black Females	I felt like a slave because we had to put away everyone's dishes. I also felt like a child because everyone had to follow me wherever I went.	It felt good most of the time when they didn't put me down.	It was cool being in a group of people that I never got to know before.	They had us pick up everyone's dishes that's when I started thinking like why do they have all Black females picking up dishes?
Black Males	It felt the same as any other day because that is who I hang out with. We felt like we was the tightest or closest because we spent so much time together.	At first it felt good . . . because I was with . . . most of my friends. Later on it got boring because we were lonely. We felt privileged because we didn't have to clean like the others.	Kind of bad because we went last for everything.	It was true to put me in that group because of the stereotypes and how we act.
Isolates	I felt alone because there was no group and I was bored as hell.	It felt depressing because I was isolated from everything and everyone. It felt horrible because all I wanted to do was TALK!		

Note that not every participant completed a questionnaire, and not everyone who completed a questionnaire completed every question. (For questionnaire completion rates for each exercise, see Appendix A.) If we received an answer to this question from a participant, it is presented in this grid.

Presenting this data in this way enables us to develop a snapshot of the inner life of the system. Because we researched multiple instances of the activity, we were able to engage in cross-case analysis and look for themes that appeared in all three exercises (all three grids of raw data related to this question are presented in Appendix C). The view that emerged from this process tells a paradoxical story in which different individuals describe having very distinct experiences, even as system-wide patterns emerged across all three activities. Here are the key findings from this data:

First, individuals in the same group report very different feelings about their experience. Consider, for example, the responses from the four Latinos in Table 6.1. The first respondent is having fun, the second feels appreciated, the third feels a mix of "bad 'cause they was making us clean" along with "good 'cause it was fun . . . we was just hanging out." The fourth is also having fun, but the fifth clearly feels the sting of discrimination, stating, "I felt downsized, lower than the others."

Based on these results, it's clear that we cannot talk about some unified, universal Latino experience within this exercise. Different people—even when standing right next to each other and having what looks to observers to be a shared experience—have very different feelings about what happened. It's a finding that can be seen in other groups in all three exercises.

Another finding was the presence in every exercise of a handful of individuals who expressed frustration that the group they were forced to join did not honor the full complexity of their identity. Consider the response of one of the White females in Table 6.1, who stated, "I felt very offended because I am not all White. I'm only 25% Italian . . . I felt like they took one look at me and assumed I'm all White." Participants in each of the exercises expressed similar sentiments; although they may have looked like they belonged in their group, their identities were actually far more complex than these systems allowed them to express.

Another key finding was the fact that in every exercise, this experience evoked memories of a historical trauma experienced by groups in the past. In Table 6.1, this can be seen in the lone response by a Jewish participant, who explains that being forced to wear an armband marked with a yellow Jewish star evoked memories of the Holocaust. The participant states, "It made me identify with my ancestry and the segregation of my own people in the past." We also see a response from a Black female, who says, "I felt like a slave because we had to put away everyone's dishes." Similar examples appeared in all three exercises, suggesting that this experience of present injustices evoking feelings associated with historic events is a common phenomenon in these systems.

The other key finding to emerge from this data is that a fairly simple system-wide pattern appeared in all three exercises. Among individuals in groups at the top of the hierarchy, we heard themes of guilt and shame, with White participants saying things such as, "I didn't really want the privileges I was given. I felt undeserving." or (from Exercise 2) "I was ashamed because we received special privileges." This sense of guilt and shame is far less present (and often not present at all) among groups lower in the system.

As we move down the hierarchy, we encountered expressions of pain and anger. Examples include the comment from a Latino stating, "I felt downsized, lower than the others" and the comment from a Black female, who said, "I felt like a slave because we had to put away everyone's dishes." We also encountered the phenomenon of intersectionality, a term that speaks to the fact that the same individual can be simultaneously privileged in some ways and oppressed in others (Crenshaw, 1991). In this case, an individual from the Black male group at the bottom of the social hierarchy stated, "we felt privileged because we didn't have to clean like the others," meaning the Black females. It's a remark that illuminates the complex experiences of individuals immersed in this kind of hierarchical social system. It's too simple to suggest that the groups at the top are privileged and the groups at the bottom are oppressed; for many individuals, the reality is far more complex than that.

Within the groups toward the lower end of the hierarchy we found the anger and bitterness of discrimination mixed with positive emotions of belonging and friendship that were experienced by individuals able to share their experiences—good and bad—with peers. We encountered many comments along the lines of "It was fun to be with my group." This theme was far less present among individuals in groups at the top of the hierarchy.

These exercises also revealed the unique pain experienced by social isolates. For obvious reasons, the experience of isolates lacked any dimension of fun and camaraderie; in all three exercises, isolates reported feeling alone, bored, and depressed throughout the exercise. In all cases, the responses of isolates focused solely on their own personal pain and not on the injustices of the system. It seems to be the case that for individuals enduring an experience of social isolation the injustices and discrimination of the system are less salient than the pain of feeling alone and isolated for so long.

Finally, there is one slice of raw data from another exercise that needs to be highlighted here. As you may recall, Exercise 3 was the only activity that included an LGBTQ group; this was the group that spent nearly 45 minutes of the activity standing together in a small broom closet. The data from these participants are presented in Table 6.2.

Table 6.2 Reports of Individual Experience of LGBTQ Participants From Exercise 3

LGBTQ	It felt terrible being considered only a lesbian. It felt dehumanizing, degrading, and embarrassing.	Suffocating. Because I was shut in a tiny closet with four other people. Because all the seriousness and fear and unfairness felt was so overpowering.	It was sad because some people came over to us and tried to get us to break free and some of our members started to cry.	Awful—being constantly reprimanded by authority figures feels bad.

It is easy to see that the responses from this group were intensely negative. A compelling case can be made that this group endured the most challenging and difficult experience of any of the groups across all three exercises. Because of the unique treatment of the LGBTQ group in this exercise, we can't engage in any cross-case analyses of this data, but the experience of this group merits attention in this discussion of findings because it was so uniquely challenging and negative.

There is, of course, a great deal more that could be said about this set of data, because all three exercises included a different selection of groups arranged in different hierarchies, and each and every comment is illuminating in its own unique way. For our purposes here, however, we've covered the high-level findings. Again, readers eager to dive deeper are invited to check out the other grids in Appendix D.

Even though the answers here are brief and the number of participants is relatively small, it's remarkable how much complexity emerged from this data. We encountered the idiosyncrasies of personal experience, the guilt of the privileged, the anger and camaraderie of the oppressed, the experience of intersectionality among some participants, the frustration of being forced to identify with a group that does not align with the fullness of individual identity among others, and the pain of social isolation. Equally important, we gained some sense of the systemic interconnection of all these experiences. It's a perspective that offers at least a rudimentary opportunity to sense the whole elephant regarding matters of race and social change in America.

The third question, "In your opinion, what was the most important group? Why?" is discussed in further detail under "The Intergroup Level of Analysis."

Exploring the Connection Between the Individual and Systemic Change

The final two questions on the participant questionnaire were designed to explore the connection between individual experiences and the dynamics of systemic change. Questions 4 and 5 reflect a recognition that this exercise is designed to give participants experience with challenging systems of bias and discrimination and that individual actions possess an undeniable potential to generate system-wide change.

Specifically, Question 4 asked, *"Why did you not break this exercise earlier than when you did?"* It's a question intended to explore the factors that keep individuals immersed in unjust, segregated, hierarchical systems from confronting the injustices of those systems. Once again, we'll listen carefully to the voices of the participants in each exercise to see what insights, patterns, and themes might emerge from their responses.

For this question, the three-person research team reviewed the responses and generated a set of codes intended to categorize themes emerging from the responses. Once we had arrived at a set of codes, we revisited the raw data and measured the frequency of each code by counting the number of responses that fell into each category. The result is an overview of all the reasons individuals in each activity gave for not breaking the exercise sooner than they did, arranged by how many times each of those reasons was cited by participants.

The pattern that emerged from this data could not have been clearer across all three exercises. In every case, "fear of consequences" was by far the most frequently cited reason for not challenging the norms of the exercise earlier. In every case, the second reason was cited only half as frequently as the first, and sometimes far less: "confused about the exercise." Behind those top two reasons were a varied set of 7 to 10 additional reasons that were only cited by one or two individuals in each exercise.

Table 6.3 gives an overview of the top three responses from all three exercises.

The list of other reasons why some participants chose not to challenge the exercise was long and varied. Some were waiting for others to take the first step, others were waiting for help, others trusted that the program directors had a reason for doing this and

Table 6.3 Frequency of Top-Three Responses to Question About Not Breaking the Exercise Earlier

Code	Example	Ex. 1	Ex. 2	Ex. 3
Fear of consequences	"I had a sort of fear or dislike of punishment for breaking the rules."	48%	63%	28%
Confused about exercise	"I honestly didn't know what we were doing."	9%	9%	17%
Third most frequent reason	(Differed for all three exercises)	9%	4%	9%

didn't want to undermine that purpose, still others made a deliberate choice to play the role of passive observers who would simply watch events unfold without taking any stand. Each of these responses was given only by small number of respondents representing a just a few percentage points of the overall responses. In other words, the data show clearly that the most important factor by far in keeping people from taking a stand was a fear of punishment by the authorities, even they knew in their hearts the exercise was unjust and unfair.

In light of these results, it is impossible to avoid noting the relevance of the classic experiments by Milgram. As you'll recall, Milgram investigated whether individuals would harm another individual if told to do so by an authority figure; his studies revealed that 60% of subjects obeyed the commands of authority, even though they experienced intense moral anguish about their actions. Here, we see large numbers of individuals again choosing to obey the commands of authority even when those demands contradict the beliefs of their own conscience. This time, however, we gain some perspective on how the consequences of that choice played out on an interpersonal level and also on a system-wide scale.

The data also illuminate the role confusion plays in hindering action. Given the nature of this exercise, the experience of confusion is surely understandable. These participants woke up to what they thought was just another day of the program and suddenly found themselves thrust into this exercise with no warning, explanation, or context. In those circumstances, it's easy to understand why many participants felt so confused about what was happening that they weren't sure if they could or should take a stand. However, it seems reasonable to question whether some participants chose to let this state of confusion become their excuse for not seeking to address—or perhaps even just name and discuss—the unfairness of the system. To move from "I don't know what's going on" to "The way groups and people are being treated here isn't right" is a cognitive shift that could demand some kind of behavior change. It's reasonable to question the degree to which some participants chose to stay in a state of confusion as a way to avoid feeling responsible for confronting the norms of this system.

Finally, in these results, we also see the power of conformity; although it is evidently less influential than the drive to obey, it is still potent. In each exercise, we encounter participants who are clearly uncomfortable with what is happening, but they chose to wait passively until someone else made a stand. The fear of being the first to step out of line; leave one's comfortable, homogenous group; and express the truth of what they were feeling and experiencing was intense. The similarity with those subjects in Asch's experiments who chose to disregard the evidence of their own eyes in order to conform with peers is undeniable. And again, here we see how those choices had implications that play out not only in interpersonal relationships but also on a system-wide scale.

As we know from the narratives in Chapter 5, however, eventually some small subset of individuals summoned the courage to risk disobeying authority, stopped conforming to passive peers, and moved out of a state of paralyzing confusion. And once that choice was made, it had the potential to catalyze a remarkable process of change that could transform the entire system. How did participants experience that part of the social change process? We now turn our attention to exploring that important question.

Breaking the Exercise

Question 5 on the questionnaire asked, *"How did it feel to break the exercise?"* In the spirit of honesty and transparency, I need to note that we quickly learned that in an important sense, this was a poorly worded question. The intention here was to explore each participant's feelings in the moment when they personally made a choice to break the exercise. It turns out, however, that many individuals appeared to read it as "How did you feel when the exercise ended?" In other words, the question was written in a manner that made it sufficiently ambiguous that it resulted in multiple interpretations. Nevertheless, the responses generated by this question still prove illuminating.

For this question, the research team once again generated a set of codes that reflected themes that emerged from the data, and then went back and counted how often each theme appeared in the data. Table 6.4 presents the themes and how frequently they appeared in each exercise.

Although all responses don't appear at the same rates in all three exercises, the most frequent response is the same in all three cases: It felt great and empowering once the decision was made to take a stand against these unjust norms. Many participants, it seems, experienced a strongly positive—if not cathartic—release once they began to challenge the rules of the system in an effort to promote greater equality and justice among the groups. It's important to note, however, that there was also a sizable percentage of participants who experienced ambivalence about the break. As once respondent stated, "[I]t felt liberating to join hands with the peace chain. At the same time, I felt like I was betraying the groups that had chosen to stay separate." In a system with this level of complexity, some participants who made the choice to break the exercise found themselves struggling simultaneously with feelings of joy and betrayal.

Other responses to this question appeared less frequently, but—as always—merit some attention because they compel us to confront

Table 6.4 Frequency of Responses to Question About Breaking the Exercise

Code	Example	Ex. 1	Ex. 2	Ex. 3
Great! Empowering!	"Excellent! Once we realized we were right it felt empowering!"	41%	53%	29%
No answer	—	23%	7%	13%
Ambivalent	"[I]t felt liberating to join hands with the peace chain. At the same time, I felt like I was betraying the groups that had chosen to stay separate."	18%	9%	8%
We didn't break it	"We didn't break it."	14%	2%	19%
Other	—	5%	4%	2%
Disappointed	"I was disappointed in myself and my group that we didn't break it on our own."	0%	2%	19%
Relieved	"I felt relieved."	0%	20%	8%
Angry at non-breakers	"I felt bad since some groups did not join the movement, and the fact that they were persecuting themselves when they could be themselves just upset me."	0%	2%	2%

myriad ways individuals might react to this element of the experience. Some participants were relieved instead of joyous; others expressed anger at individuals who refused to challenge the rules, even though those rules discriminated against them ("I felt bad since some groups did not join the movement, and the fact that they were persecuting themselves when they could be themselves just upset me."). Still others expressed disappointment in themselves because they never attempted to challenge the norms.

It's worth taking a closer look at the differences between the responses from individuals who did break the exercise and those who didn't. Among individuals who did not break the exercise, the sense of regret, disappointment, and frustration is unmistakable. Consider the following few responses from individuals who declared themselves to be in this category:

> "We didn't, and I am ashamed of that."

> "It was nice to finally end this exercise, but I was disappointed in myself and in the group that we didn't break it on our own and depended on our counselors to do it for us."

> "Well we didn't and it felt really bad."

> "Discouraging—like I am not capable of accomplishments. I feel like I let everybody down but this is an experience I will grow/learn from and I am glad we did it."

> "I felt bad we didn't break it and I was disgusted that I let myself get demeaned and degraded for four hours."

These comments illuminate the negative emotions experienced by those who endured the injustices of this exercise without ultimately making an effort to challenge the system. It is important to remember, however, that not everyone in the system had this type of difficult experience. As indicated in Table 6.4, by far the most frequent response to Question 5 in all three exercises was that it felt "Great! Empowering!" to have made an effort to challenge the unjust norms in an effort to bring more justice, equality, and unity to the system. Here's a sampling of just a few of the many responses expressing these sentiments:

> "Excellent! Once we realized we were right it was empowering!"
>
> "If felt very liberating and exciting to break the exercise."
>
> "It felt good, productive, and empowering."
>
> "When I joined the 'revolution,' it was like a weight was lifted off me and I started speaking up about them mistreating us and I tried to convince others to do the same."

For these individuals, the Separation Exercise provided a powerful lesson in the possibility of overcoming fear in order to take a stand for greater equality, freedom, and unity. The fact that these sentiments were so widespread is also a notable finding. Each of these exercises began as oppressive, segregated hierarchies that were eventually challenged by a few individuals from the lower end of the social system. Inevitably, however, these movements for justice and unity involved more and more individuals and generated significant changes in the structure and organization of the social system. In each case, large numbers of individuals from every level of the system as it was originally designed expressed joy and excitement at having taken a stand for a more just, equal, and unified community.

As a final thought here, it's worth reiterating that this exercise took place in the context of a week-long program run by experienced staff members. Immediately following each exercise, all participants engaged in an extended (close to 2-hour) processing session. Although it was surely challenging to experience some of the dark emotions evoked by this exercise, participants had a chance to reflect on their experiences, engage deeply with the perspectives of others who were in different groups in the system or who made different choices, and consider the relevance of this simulated experience to real-life events. Through these processing discussions, participants deepened their understanding of the nature of these systems, recognized the possibilities that did exist to create change, and gained deeper insight into consequences that ensue from choosing passivity or agency, fear or courage, conformity or responsibility.

One Additional Inquiry: Exploring Agency

At this point, we have reviewed the results from the answers to the five questions on the participant questionnaire intended to illuminate the interpersonal level of analysis of the system. The results have simultaneously revealed some common themes and patterns occurring across all three exercises, compelling us to confront the remarkable diversity and complexity in the ways that different individuals experienced and reacted to these exercises. Before we turn our attention to the next level of analysis, however, there is one more inquiry to conduct here.

As discussed in Chapter 4, the purpose of Camp Anytown in general is to empower participants to challenge problematic dynamics of bias, bigotry, and discrimination. The Separation Exercise is designed to give participants a chance to demonstrate their ability to act in the face of these social dynamics. Equally important, my own interest in this work as a focus of research is to attain a deeper understanding of how we might empower a larger number of citizens to understand and confront this kind of systematic injustice out in the real world. For this reason, it seems reasonable to inquire into the degree to which each exercise succeeded in empowering participants to feel capable of creating change.

In an effort to clarify the concept of empowerment, we chose to review this data one last time to explore how many participants demonstrated what we chose to call *agency*. Table 6.5 shows how we defined our terms for this additional analysis.

Our intention with this analysis was to explore the effectiveness of the senior staff members' efforts to generate agency within the

Table 6.5 Example Responses Indicating Degrees of Agency

Code	Definition	Example
Agency	A narrative describing a clear, proactive action that was taken to change the system	"At one point, we heard people singing 'We shall overcome' and *I joined the revolution.*" [italics added]
No Agency	A narrative describing passively watching others take action or actively refusing to get involved with changing the system	"Some individuals from the Hispanic group took off the armband . . . soon after everyone followed." "A group of people came to my group trying to get us to rebel but I did not participate."
Unclear/ No Answer	It is unclear whether the individual was active or passive during the exercise or there was no answer given to Question 1	—

system. Given the purpose of the exercise, the argument can be made that exercises with higher levels of agency are more effective in that they empowered more participants to take action.

The results comparing all three exercises are shown in Table 6.6.

According to this analysis, the differences in levels of agency produced in each exercise were dramatic. Exercise 2 generated the lowest level of agency (7%), and Exercise 3 generated the highest (43%). As you'll recall, Exercise 3 resulted in the formation of a movement, development of a nine-point mission statement, and a nonviolent protest involving nearly half the participants. The other two exercises did not generate such complex behaviors involving so

Table 6.6 Frequency of Responses to Question About Agency Across all Three Exercises

Code	Exercise 1 (n=22)	Exercise 2 (n=44)	Exercise 3 (n=47)
Agency	32%	7%	43%
No agency	59%	89%	47%
Unclear/no answer	9%	5%	10%

many participants, so this outcome makes sense in the light of observable events that occurred in each exercise.

The findings regarding Exercises 1 and 2 are somewhat surprising. As you'll recall, Exercise 1 was run by Thomasina, and not much happened beyond the Black males and the Black females coming together to socialize. Given the minimal amount of activity that occurred at this event, this level of agency is fairly high. This might be related to the fact that this exercise had the lowest level of questionnaire responses; only 55% of participants in this exercise (23 of 42 individuals) completed the questionnaire compared to a 96% response rate in Exercise 2 and a 98% response rate in Exercise 3. It may be the case that the individuals who did choose to fill out the questionnaires were the individuals who felt a sense of agency during the exercise, which might account for the high percentage.

For Exercise 2, the number is surprisingly low (7%). This may be a function of the setup of the program; this was the exercise in which all the participants were gathered together to participate in an all-group song session fairly early in the exercise. When the Asian participant broke down and cried and another participant came to her defense, the whole group experienced the episode at once. Within a matter of minutes, the groups came together and the exercise was called to a close. Although the experience surely had educational value, this analysis suggests that almost nobody felt personally empowered to create change after participating in an exercise executed in this manner. It's a phenomenon we'll explore in more detail in Chapter 7, when we focus on the whole-system level of analysis.

The Intergroup Level of Analysis

In this next section, we leave behind our focus on individual experiences and zoom out a level to seek some insights into dynamics that emerge between groups. As you'll recall, this level of analysis has been explored by classic social psychology experiments of the past, including the Stanford Prison Experiment, the Robbers Cave Experiment, and the Blue Eyes/Brown Eyes Exercise. It's a level that includes the interpersonal dynamics we've already explored, yet also transcends those dynamics by bringing into focus the higher, intergroup-level dynamics.

The question that we chose to ask participants in our effort to explore this level of analysis was, *"What other groups were most important during this exercise? Why?"* The intention here was to gain some insight into any patterns and themes that might be found regarding which groups individuals chose to focus on in these exercises. Were participants more inclined to focus on the groups at the very top of the system? At the very bottom? Were they more inclined to focus on the groups immediately above or below them? Were certain groups more likely to be largely ignored during the exercise? Did individuals try to divide their attention among all the groups in the system? In this situation—so analogous to real life—when there is more than just one group that could be considered as the "other" in a system, which groups do we choose to focus on?

And—an equally important question—*Why?*

Before diving into the data, it is important to note that the findings from the previous section of this chapter illuminated this intergroup level of analysis in important ways. As we have seen, the individuals in each group clearly responded differently to each exercise, despite the shared elements of their experience. So all Latinos, for example, experienced discrimination in a way that all White males did not, but that did not mean that there was one universal, shared Latino perspective on the experience (or, for that matter, a monolithic White male perspective). It's a finding from the previous section that should inform our thinking about this intergroup level of analysis right from the start; we must remain awake to the shared elements within each group and the diversity of individual perspectives evoked by those experiences.

In the attempt to explore this research question, we analyzed the responses to Question 3 on the participant questionnaire that asked *"What other groups were most important during this exercise? Why?"* Our first approach to analyzing this data involved organizing the quantitative data into attention distribution charts for each exercise, which provided a quick visual overview of how often each group was mentioned as "most important" by someone in the system. In reading these charts, keep in mind that individuals could—and often did— highlight more than one group in their responses. Also, some individuals did not answer this question at all, so the number of responses does not necessary equal the number of participants in the group.

For a complete overview of this data, see Appendix E. We'll present an abridged version of the data from each exercise here. Let's take a look at the results from Exercise 1 in Figure 6.1.

As you can see, some groups received considerable attention, and other groups were essentially ignored by the other individuals in the system. In this case, the White males at the top of the system were mentioned eight times, and the Black females and Black males were both mentioned four times. The White females were not highlighted as most important by any group, and the isolates were not mentioned either. Latinos were mentioned twice, Asians and Jews were both

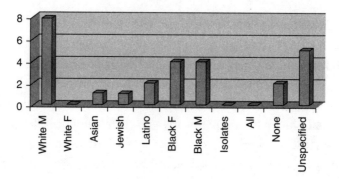

Figure 6.1 Separation Exercise 1 Quantitative Attention Distribution

mentioned once, "none" was mentioned twice, and five comments were coded as "unspecified," meaning they didn't explicitly mention any particular group.

Do similar patterns of attention appear in the other exercises? Let's take a look at the chart presenting the data from Exercise 2 in Figure 6.2.

Once again, it's clear that some groups receive considerable attention, and other groups are not mentioned at all. We can also see, however, that beyond that obvious similarity with Exercise 1, the pattern of attention distribution here is quite different. In this case, the assertion that "All groups were important" received the most comments here; in Exercise 1, not a single participant listed that answer in the comments. There was some sort of powerful consciousness of the whole system that was present in Exercise 2 and absent in Exercise 1.

To complete our review of this set of data, let's take a look at results from Exercise 3 in Figure 6.3.

Here again, we see a widely uneven distribution of attention, but once again the pattern is unique. In this case, it is the Black males who receive most of the attention, with multiple groups (multiracial, isolates, Asians, and South Asians) not being mentioned at all.

The primary story told by the quantitative data, it seems, is this: In these complex social systems, attention is always distributed

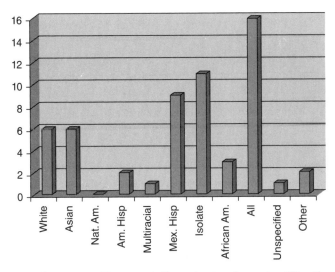

Figure 6.2 Separation Exercise 2 Quantitative Attention Distribution

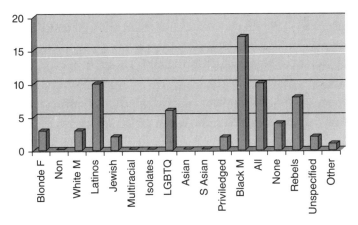

Figure 6.3 Separation Exercise 3 Quantitative Attention Distribution

unequally, with some groups getting a great deal of attention, some getting just a little attention, and some subset of groups being completely ignored or overlooked by others in the system. The patterns of attention distribution were not the same across cases;

however, one system was intensely focused on the group at the top, another was focused on the group at the bottom, and another believed strongly that all groups were equally important.

What leads to this type of variation? Why do individuals choose to focus on whatever groups they report here? We can explore these important questions by taking a look at the qualitative data we gathered here.

For our effort to analyze this data, we once again took participant responses and organized them into qualitative attention distribution grids enabling us to see the reasons participants gave for focusing on various groups. In these grids, we were not focused on who *wrote* each comment; instead, we were focused on *which group is mentioned* in each comment. The result is an overview of the reasons that various participants gave for focusing on each particular group.

Table 6.7 shows one of these grids—from Exercise 1—to provide a sense of what this data look like and how these grids illuminate system-wide dynamics. The grids for the other two exercises are available for review in Appendix F.

This effort to illuminate the inner life of the system in yet another way offers a new set of insights. Here are some key findings that emerge from analyzing this data across all three exercises.

First, it's clear that in some cases, attention gravitated toward the groups that either enjoyed the most conspicuous privilege or that suffered the most apparent oppression. We've already discussed that in Exercise 1, attention was disproportionately focused on the White males at the top of the system. It's apparent from this qualitative data that the conspicuous privilege of this group was what led to this attention; all the comments highlighting the White males as most important included sentiments along the lines of "they were the most privileged" or "they were treated like kings." Most of the other comments from this instance of the exercise highlighted visible examples of discrimination: "They had to clean" or they had to "sit in the hot sun."

Table 6.7 Separation Exercise 1 Qualitative Attention Distribution Grid

White Males	"[T]hey were all treated like kings got their food given to them and didn't do anything. Which I think is just wrong."	"[They] had the most privilege."	"They got to go to breakfast first and had their food set up already."	"The White group was favored and was most important because their food was prepared . . ."
	"Because they are so set on obeying the rules and having things given to them and my group have to fight for the stuff we do here."	"People set their table for breakfast."	"It was as if they were masters, and everyone else were slaves."	"[They] had the most freedom."
White Females				
Asians	"People sometimes forget them . . . Asians are not bad people . . . they are nice."			

(continued)

Table 6.7 (Continued)

Jewish	"It was hard to watch the Jewish group . . . sit in the hot sun . . ."		
Latinos	"[T]hey were the only people that cleaned."	"[T]hey did the most cleaning."	
Black Females	"[T]hey were the only people that cleaned."	"[T]hey were the only people that cleaned."	"[They] cleaned up after [the White males]."	"[T]hey did the most cleaning."
	"Both the African-American groups were the most important because those participating in those groups broke the segregation barriers . . ."		
Black Males	"We had the most people."		
	"They have become go-getters from years of internalization and they were able to help somewhat break up the group"		

Isolates	
All	
None	"No group was important. Not even mine because we should be together."	"[T]here are no other important groups . . . I was only thinking about our group and getting out of the sun . . ."
Other	"Others, because they are people I know."

A similar pattern appeared in Exercise 2. We again heard comments highlighting the White males as most important because "they got all the privileges" and "they were treated better than all the other groups." Nearly all the other comments focused on visible experiences of discrimination endured by other groups. A comment about the Mexican Hispanics noted that "they did all the dirty work"; the isolate was "treated badly alone"; and the African Americans "were the last to eat."

In Exercise 2, however, some additional reasons for attention appeared. As you'll recall, this was the exercise in which all participants were gathered together for a song session, and the break occurred when an Asian woman was told to sing alone in front of the group and visibly broke down in tears. In this system, the Asian group received attention for this reason: "Without them, no one would have had the courage to stand up and break the rules." Here, then, is another reason why a group may get attention: It plays a role in catalyzing change in the system.

That theme comes through even more clearly in Exercise 3. That was the exercise that generated a self-organized movement advocating for nonviolent social change. In that system, the Black males received a great deal of attention, but mostly it was not because of the discrimination they experienced. Rather, it was because they so obviously played an important role in creating change. Responses here noted that "[t]hey started the revolution," "they broke the rules," and "they were the ones who made us realize what we were being forced to do."

In the data for Exercise 3, we also found a group—"the rebels"— that did not appear in the other two exercises. It's clear from the comments that this referred to the coalition of groups that collectively challenged the rules of the segregated system. Comments focused on this group noted that the rebels "were the ones that changed the course of the exercise"; they were "the first ones to walk out. They started the domino reaction" and "They abolished my ignorance."

It's interesting to note the variations in why groups got attention in the exercises. These differences seem to be a function of the overall level of dynamism and change that unfolded in each exercise—a topic we'll explore in much more detail in Chapter 7, when we dive into our discussion of the whole-system level of analysis.

Another finding that emerged from analysis of this data was a pattern of evidence suggesting that individuals miss or distort the facts of what happens in these exercises. One goal of this research was to be able to explore the relationship between the high-level observation of events presented in the narratives and the way individuals in those systems understood what happened. We learned that individuals often have a distorted or false understanding of events. For example, there is a comment in the data from Exercise 1 asserting that in that system, the Latinos were the only group forced to clean, and another comment making the same claim about the Black males. The truth is that both groups were forced to clean during the exercise. Here's another example: In Exercise 3, it was a Latino participant (Eduardo) who was clearly responsible for cata- lyzing the social change movement, but the Black males received more comments highlighting the pivotal role they played in rebelling against the system. Given the complexity of these systems—which are, of course, dramatically simplified versions of real-world social systems—it is perhaps not surprising that individuals immersed in events can't and don't see everything. It's a finding that suggests that when discussing complex social systems, curiosity rather than cer- tainty is almost certainly a more appropriate stance to take.

This analysis also compels us to grapple with the disconnect that exists between intentions and impact in segregated, hierarchical systems. In Exercise 2, someone asserted that the White male group was most important because "they made us feel like s—." We know from the narrative that although the enforcers may have been aggressive toward the lower groups in the system, the White males were not actively focused on shaming or mistreating any other groups; they—similar to essentially everyone else in the system— were simply obeying the rules and not challenging the enforcers. Surely, those White males could honestly and sincerely claim that they were in no way engaged in malicious, intentional efforts to make anyone feel bad. Yet we must also grapple with the fact that people of color who are forced to do menial work while White males enjoy free time and abundant resources have cause to feel that they have been treated unfairly. The race-based, segregated system is unjust, and as long as it endures, people of color will feel justifiably mistreated, even if those with privilege are not actively, intentionally acting with malice. Individuals at the top may be genuinely well-intentioned, with deeply held values about equality and inclusivity, but if they are not confronting the unjust structure of the system, they are perpetuating and passively supporting a structure that is unequal and not inclusive.

Yet again, there is much more that could be said about these data from the intergroup level of analysis, and interested readers are welcome to review the raw data from all exercises in the appendixes. Now we will turn our attention to insights that emerged from the third and highest level of analysis: the whole system.

7

The Whole System
Level of Analysis

In this chapter, we zoom out once again and focus on a third and final level of analysis. This higher-level perspective is largely unexplored in social psychology literature and research. As you'll recall from our discussion of classic experiments in Chapter 2, this level of analysis includes and transcends the interpersonal dynamics of obedience and conformity, as well as intergroup dynamics of conflict, cooperation, privilege, and oppression. The Separation Exercises enable us to empirically observe and investigate dynamics unfolding at this highest level of analysis, providing a remarkable opportunity to observe the "whole elephant" of race and social change.

We live immersed in the interpersonal dynamics that govern the individual level of analysis as well as the intergroup dynamics that govern the interpersonal level. We understand obedience and conformity, because we spend our lives navigating those social forces. We also grasp intergroup conflict and competition, as well as privilege and oppression, because we are immersed in those dynamics every day. Studying those issues may lead to powerful insights and deeper understandings that change the way we understand human relations. A powerful encounter with these social dynamics—such as that experienced by participants in the Blue Eyes/Brown Eyes Exercise— can lead to epiphanies and new depths of empathy and understanding regarding the feelings and experiences of "the other" and the impact of dynamics that we may not have fully understood before. These experiences help us achieve higher levels of consciousness regarding our long-standing relationships. This learning experience can feel like seeing a light go on or having a blindfold removed. We were blind, but now we see.

When it comes to the highest, whole-system level of analysis, it has been my experience that epiphanies are harder to achieve. The whole-system level of analysis is governed by dynamics that are counterintuitive and often surprising. Although we are immersed in these dynamics every day, just as we are with individual and intergroup dynamics, events at this level transcend the level of consciousness that we usually bring to our lives and push us to think differently about our world and our place within it.

At this level of analysis, we encounter the need to explore two compelling research questions. First, *What themes and patterns emerged across all three instances of the Separation Exercises?* In searching for these patterns, we hope to illuminate some empirical truths about the ways in which large-scale social change can happen. And second, *Why did all three of these Separation Exercises unfold so differently?* Given the obvious differences in the events that transpired across all three exercises, it is clear that there can be dramatic variation in the process by which this sort of change occurs. How do we even begin thinking about the factors that generated these different outcomes?

It turns out that the first question—the search for common patterns—is far easier to answer than the second, so we'll begin our analysis with a review of patterns and themes encountered across the exercises.

Patterns That Appear Across All Three Exercises

Although all three of the Separation Exercises that we observed progressed in different ways and resulted in different outcomes, there were clearly some patterns that appeared. Each exercise began as a segregated, hierarchical social system by design. Then, the system entered a long period of stasis. Although the enforcers were kept busy policing minor infractions of the rules during the early hours of the exercise, the system in general felt static. There was near-perfect obedience to the rules and almost complete conformity within each of the separated groups.

Eventually—after nearly 2 hours in all three cases—an individual from one of the lower groups in the social hierarchy began to challenge the rules of the system. This may have involved a public effort to criticize the system and reach out to other groups, or it may have been a more subtle effort to connect with another group. Multiple small violations of the norms occurred without causing any real change in the structure of the system. Then a particular act of rebellion triggered a more significant reaction from others, and this act represented a sort of tipping point in the development of the system. After this initial act of rebellion, the underlying social structure of the complex system began a process of rapid and dramatic change. Coalitions began forming: In Exercise 1, the Black females, Black males, and Latinos gathered together in a meeting room. In Exercise 2, an American-born Hispanic participant made a strident challenge to the system in defense of an Asian peer who was too upset to sing during the group song session. In Exercise 3, the Latinos, Black males, and blonde women gathered together to organize a movement, create a mission statement, and initiate a nonviolent protest against the rules of the system.

The formation of these coalitions was just the first step. Soon, most groups were affected by the changes occurring in the system. As the minutes passed, the separated, hierarchical system evolved toward a complex, interconnected, and interdependent network. Each group—actually, each individual in each group—was faced with a decision: Should I connect with the network, or should I maintain my separation? In all three of the exercises, the majority of groups elected to join the integrated network, and a few groups and individuals remained disconnected. At this point in the development of each system, the staff members ended the exercise and invited everyone back to a meeting room to process the experience.

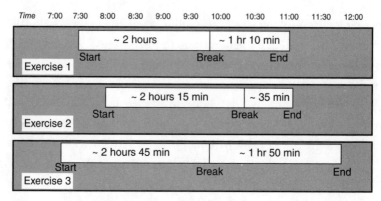

Figure 7.1 Cross-Case Analysis: Development of Whole Systems Over Time

A very simplified analysis of this process of development over time is presented in Figure 7.1. The figure presents the start time of each exercise, the amount of time before the first significant "break" in the exercise, and then the time until the conclusion of the exercise.

This basic developmental narrative appeared across all three exercises, suggesting that it may be generalizable to real-world complex systems; in Chapter 8, I'll offer some thoughts on how to think about the relevance of these experimental findings to dynamics of social change in the real world.

At this point, we have identified what patterns appeared across all three exercises. Now we must turn our attention to why each exercise unfolded so differently. This is a far more complex question to answer.

Exploring the Different Outcomes of the Exercises

Our first step here is to look to the literature on complex systems that we explored in Chapter 3 for guidance. Although the staff at Camp Anytown surely did not understand their work in these terms, they were engaged in a real-life educational analogue to the challenge faced by the computer scientists working on the Game of Life, which was an attempt to develop a computer simulation of a system that exhibited qualities of a living system. The goal was to design a system that would neither settle quickly into a frozen, unchanging stasis nor explode into formless chaos; instead, the system would exhibit the sorts of qualities that we see all the time in real-world living systems: self-organization, adaptation, creativity, and ongoing evolution. In the Game of Life, computer scientists established a set of rules governing relationships between agents in the system as well as rules governing the process by which agents changed states over time. They would then establish the system in its initial state, press go, and then watch what happened. They were on a quest to discover a set of rules and conditions that would give rise to the qualities of life itself.

The program staff members at Camp Anytown were not thinking about their work in these terms. They were out to achieve the organizational mission of confronting discrimination and bias by creating an educational activity that would be provocative and uncomfortable but ultimately productive and illuminating for participants. As a researcher in search of some way to explain the dramatic differences in how these three exercises unfolded, however, I found the Game of Life analogy to be invaluable in analyzing these systems. It suggested what I found to be the most powerful way to frame a useful research question to explore dynamics at the whole-system level of analysis: *How do you design and implement a simulated social system that exhibits the qualities of a real-life living system?*

The goal of these activities, after all, was to give participants a chance to practice challenging unjust, hierarchical, segregated social systems in ways that mirrored the actions taken by citizens involved in America's civil rights movement. The hope was that participants who found themselves unexpectedly immersed in a static, unjust status quo would eventually challenge the norms of obedience and conformity on which the system depended and begin to self-organize a movement for change. After reviewing all three exercises, it is clear that the different exercises demonstrated very different levels of success in achieving this goal.

The systems revealed by the Game of Life simulation and discussed in Chapter 3 provide us with a way to think about how events unfolded in these activities. Four categories of systems emerged from the simulations. Category I systems are doomsday systems, in which all the agents in the system quickly die. It's a bit of a stretch to suggest that any of the Separation Exercises exhibited this behavior. Category II systems, however, are systems that go through some flux before settling into stable, unchanging patterns. They don't die, but neither do they exhibit all that much life. It seems reasonable to suggest that Separation Exercise 1—Thomasina and Drake's system—falls into this category. There was a bit of movement and action, but compared to Exercise 3 the overall energy was much lower and there was far less self-organization, individual agency, and overall system-wide transformation.

Separation Exercise 2 is interesting to examine through this lens. It is unlike the other two exercises because codirectors Connie and Laurie managed the program in a manner that differed significantly from the other directors. In the other two programs, the staff members introduced the rules and then enforced the rules and made minor changes, such as asking certain individual groups to move to different locations. Throughout, groups engaged in different activities, then reinforced the hierarchical nature of privilege and oppression (for example, White males played Frisbee while Latinos cleaned dishes) and did so while remaining physically in separate locations.

Connie and Laurie handled things differently. After a relatively brief period of time in which the staff members enforced the rules, the codirectors pulled the whole group together in a pavilion for a morning song session. This was a programmatic choice that may have advanced the desired educational goals of highlighting the pain and injustice of segregation in productive ways. It had the effect, however, of constraining the degrees of freedom available to participants, who were all gathered together in a shared activity. Separation Exercise 2 evoked an intense emotional response from participants, but again, in comparison with Exercise 3, it just didn't exhibit the same level of self-organization, creativity, personal agency, and evolution.

Category III systems are systems that are chaotic and devoid of any sort of order or pattern; as with Category I, none of the Separation Exercises exhibited these conditions. Category IV systems, however, live in that magic sweet spot in between static order and formless chaos; these are the systems that produce "coherent structures that propagated, grew, split apart, and recombined in a wonderfully complex way. They essentially never settled down" (Waldrop, 1992, p. 226). These are the systems that exhibit the qualities observed everywhere in real-life living systems: an ability to self-organize in complex ways, a remarkable balance between order and creativity, and an ability to continue changing and evolving without end.

Separation Exercise 3 falls into this category of system. Unlike the other two systems, it produced an emergent, nonviolent social change movement that self-organized, developed its own purpose and goals, and then deployed creative tactics—marching around to engage with groups and individuals who remained segregated—in an effort to unite the system. Exercise 3 didn't settle into a stable, low-energy state like Exercise 1, and it unfolded with an entirely different level of self-organization and creativity than Exercise 2, in which the outcome of the system—the group united following a song session—was clearly a direct result of top-down choices made by the codirectors.

When I began this research, I did not anticipate the need to pursue this whole line of analysis. I thought I would be exploring systems of privilege and oppression, acts of resistance, intergroup conflict and cooperation, and the like. With the whole-systems level of analysis, however, it becomes clear that we can't discuss those dynamics without recognizing the reality of a larger context. All those individual and group interactions happen within a whole system whose dynamics influence events occurring within it. *How do you design and implement a simulated social system that exhibits the qualities of a real-life living system?* was not a question I expected to ask, but it's apparent that we can't really understand the interpersonal and intergroup dynamics already discussed in previous chapters without finding a way to think about events unfolding at this higher level that includes and transcends them.

The Paradox of Structure and Freedom

The lowest hanging fruit available to investigate this research question is the rules used to design and implement each exercise. Program staff members developed different sets of rules for each exercise, and it's reasonable to believe that those variances played a key role in the diverse ways that each exercise unfolded. In a sense, these rule sets are analogous to lines of code used by computer scientists in the Game of Life to design different simulated universes. If different rules inevitably produce dissimilar system outcomes, what might we learn from an analysis of the rules governing these various Separation Exercises?

An overview of the different rule sets appears in Table 7.1, which presents the number of rules created by the designers of each system along with the details of what those individual rules stated.

This presentation of the rule sets governing the different exercises reveals a paradoxical finding: The exercise with the greatest number of rules and most developed structure was also the exercise that generated the highest levels of self-organization and individual agency. Exercise 3—the sole activity that had generated an emergent, self-organized, nonviolent protest movement—had 22 rules, compared to just 13 for Exercise 2 and 10 for 1.

I recall that the first time I encountered this finding that I reacted with a sense of "Hey . . . that's a surprise!" It seemed counterintuitive to me to that the system that generated the most self-

Table 7.1 Cross-Case Analysis of Rules Used in Design of Separation Exercises

	Exercise 1	Exercise 2	Exercise 3
Initial Status (*same for all exercises*)	1. Individuals separated into hierarchically organized groups 2. Individuals given armbands or patches		
Initial Instructions to Participants (*same for all exercises*)	3. "Don't talk to anyone outside your group." 4. "Don't make eye contact outside of your group." 5. "Stay with your group at all times."		
Specific Guidelines for Counselors	6. "Be filler. Be sheep."	6. "Just follow the rules." 7. "If a student is very upset, pull him or her aside." 8. "Watch for when I remove my scarf."	6. "Reinforce the rules by repeating instructions when appropriate." 7. "Only break when the last member of your group breaks."
Privilege and Resource Allocation	7. White group eats first, gets double servings for breakfast. 8. Black women clean up plates. 9. Latinos sweep cafeteria floor.	9. White group eats first. 10. Asians get ball to play with. 11. Mexican-born Hispanics pick up trash. 12. "White's only" bathrooms, soda machine	8. White groups eat first, get double servings. 9. Black males do not get enough chairs to sit in. 10. Black males do not get to finish meal. 11. White males get to play Frisbee, drink water, watch movie.

(continued)

Table 7.1 (Continued)

	Exercise 1	Exercise 2	Exercise 3
Formal Activities Assigned or Organized During Exercise	10. Black males get ball to play with.	13. Morning song session (all groups brought together for sing-along)	12. Blonde females put on makeup, write report about women in media. 13. Non-blonde females design greeting cards. 14. Latinos translate English songs into Spanish. 15. Jews write report about reconstructionist Judaism. 16. Multiracials draw maps of where their ancestors came from. 17. LGBTQ persons organize gay pride parade.
Formal Activities Assigned or Organized During Exercise (continued)	(none)		18. Asians write report about being model minority. 19. South Asian/Middle Easterners write report about terrorism. 20. Privileged Blacks write report about affirmative action. 21. Black Females do step routine. 22. Black males do step routine.
Total Number of Rules	10	13	22

organization and individual agency was also the system with by far the most structure. Prior to this research, I had not spent a lot of time thinking deeply about the relationship between structure and freedom, but this research pushed me to realize that I held an assumption that these forces were incompatible. If you wanted more freedom, you had to reduce structure; if you wanted less freedom, you would naturally increase structure. Yet the data from this research suggested this assumption of an either-or relationship between these two dimensions was deeply mistaken. It would not be the last time I discovered that my hidden, unexamined assumptions about how the world works were challenged by findings from this research.

Quantitative Metrics as a Manifestation of the Quality of Presence of Directors

In interpreting this finding, it is almost surely the case that there is something deeper and more important here than the simple matter of the number of rules. The list of rules reflects a quantitative measure of something important yet less tangible. If we could travel back in time and encourage Thomasina from Exercise 1 to add 12 more rules to the design of her exercise while changing nothing else about her approach, would we see higher levels of agency and creativity emerge among the participants in her exercise? We can never know the answer, of course, but the question is helpful in that it pushes us to look past the simple numbers to consider why those numbers were so different.

After much dialogue and reflection, I have come to the belief that the staff members of each program generated a different number of rules *because they personally were present in notably different ways*. The quantity and the quality of the rules they chose were, in a very real sense, a manifestation of their different ways of being. Furthermore, in some clear and significant ways, the behavior of the whole system somehow mirrored the quality of presence of the staff members who designed and then implemented the exercise.

Consider Exercise 1. At the morning staff meeting in which the exercise was introduced, Thomasina said, "Participate as if you have no idea of what it is about. You are not to shift the dynamics. You are neutral. Filler. Sheep. It will be as if all the camp stops leading except for me and Drake."

Just a while later, when she greeted the participants and introduced them to the exercise, she said, "We are going to have an exercise this morning. Drake doesn't know a lot about it; I will explain it to you all at the bottom of the stairs." In light of the choices made by staff members in other exercises, Thomasina's decision to neither delegate nor collaborate with other staff members—including her second-in-command, Drake—is striking. From her words and actions, it is clearly Thomasina's intention to be the sole source of power and authority over the course of this exercise. Everyone else is—in her own words—"filler" and "sheep."

Furthermore, as we now know, Thomasina created the fewest rules. Although she put some effort into crafting a hierarchy of privilege and resources, she made little effort to engage the different groups during the activity. While the activity was unfolding, she made the surprising choice to spend much of the morning hanging out in a cabin with Drake. After making it clear that she alone was in charge of this provocative activity, she was absent for much of the morning.

Essentially, Thomasina had a quality of presence that was simultaneously dictatorial and disengaged. When we compare her presence with that of the directors of other programs, she stands out in the degree to which she insisted on total control and also in the degree to which she made a minimal effort in the planning and implementation of this experience. It seems reasonable to suggest that the small number of rules is a manifestation of her way of being; she appeared to have less engagement, focus, and presence than the other directors.

If we had only examined one Separation Exercise, I would question the empirical validity of this analysis. In an activity this complex, one can question whether it was just a coincidence that there seemed to be such a connection between the number of rules created to govern the system and the quality of presence—the overall way of being—of the senior staff member(s). It seems to be the case, however, that this dynamic emerged across all three of the exercises. In each case, metrics such as the number of rules generated and the number of participants demonstrating agency seem to be quantifiable manifestations of the quality of presence of the program directors.

Consider the ways that Connie and Laurie, the codirectors responsible for Separation Exercise 2, showed up in their roles. Here's a passage from the narrative in Chapter 5 that explains how they introduced the activity to their staff members:

> Connie and Laurie make it clear that they will be in charge during this activity; however, they have a list of guidelines for the staff members to follow. Connie tells the staff members, "No lying. If someone asks you when it will end, say that you don't know." Also, no military-style tactics. Apparently, both directors have seen the exercise run in a very aggressive, militant style, and they do not want to emulate that here. They insist that there be no berating of participants or other sorts of staff activism. Essentially, the staff members are just to follow the rules obediently, making no effort to break the exercise or go beyond Connie and Laurie's efforts to enforce the rules. . . .
>
> Finally, Connie tells the staff members that some participants may be upset by the exercise. She says that if one of the members of their group is really angry or disturbed, the staff member should try to have a one-on-one conversation with the participant to try to calm him or her down.

Once again, senior leadership took clear responsibility for running this activity. However, instead of emphasizing their authority (by calling on fellow staff members to view themselves as "filler" or "sheep"), Connie and Laurie emphasized the need to minimize confrontational or aggressive behavior: There were to be no "military-style tactics," and staff members were explicitly told to offer support and compassion to any participants who seemed particularly distressed by the activity.

Although Connie and Laurie took a stern tone with some participants early in the exercise, they made a choice to gather all the groups in a pavilion for a song session. It was a pedagogical decision that minimized the hierarchical differences in privilege and oppression among groups while highlighting the experience of frustrated empathy and denied communal connectedness. Groups and individuals were told to stand before their peers singing songs about community and togetherness while experiencing isolation and segregation. When a counselor was compelled to stand in front of the group unable to do anything but cry, the participants finally broke the rules.

To be sure, there were acts of resistance, and a process of breaking the exercise took place to reestablish a sense of community and connectedness. Compared to the complexity that emerged in Exercise 3, however, this activity generated far less dynamism and creativity among participants. Connie and Laurie showed up in ways that emphasized empathy and connection while minimizing hierarchy and power, and the system they created manifested those forces in clear and powerful ways. From an educational perspective, this was a powerful learning experience for participants. From the whole-system perspective that we are exploring here, however, this exercise produced only a limited degree of life in the sense of self-organization, creativity, and evolution. As you'll recall from our analysis in Chapter 4, only 7% of the participant responses from this exercise were coded as having "agency" compared to 32% in Exercise 1 and 42% in Exercise 3.

How, then, did the senior leaders in that third exercise show up? As you will recall, the codirectors of Exercise 3 were John and Susan. Here's the text from the narrative explaining how they introduced the activity to their staff members:

> John explains that the rules for the delegates are simple and clear:
>
> 1. Stay in your group.
>
> 2. Don't talk to anyone outside your group.
>
> 3. Don't make eye contact with anyone outside your group.
>
> 4. Always stay together.
>
> He then explains that some members of the staff will be placed in groups with delegates. These staff members have their own rules:
>
> 1. No matter what, don't say anything beyond repeating one of these four rules (slight variations in wording are acceptable).
>
> 2. Staff members are absolutely not allowed to break the exercise until the last delegate in their group has broken the exercise.
>
> He then makes it clear that the senior staff members will play the role of "enforcers." They will not be a part of any group and are responsible for enforcing the rules of the exercise. They will also hand out projects to groups designed to highlight stereotypes and distract them from taking action.
>
> The next 30 minutes of the staff meeting involve staff members sharing their concerns about the exercise. They are afraid to act mean toward the delegates and are concerned about causing emotional pain. One of them fears she might actually enjoy the abuse of authority she is

expected to display. John and Susan make it clear that they should keep in mind the big picture: This difficult exercise is done for a good cause, and there will be ample time to debrief with the participants and make the participants feel supported and understood when the exercise concludes. At 1 AM, the meeting ends, and staff members head out to get some sleep.

In this exercise, we see some of the same messaging that appeared in the other two exercises. The basic rules for participants about staying in their group were the same, as was the message to staff members that the codirectors are clearly in charge; staff members are not to take any initiative other than repeating the rules. What happened next, though, was unique. In Exercise 1, Thomasina's message to the staff members was simply to be "filler" and "sheep," and there was no dialogue about what that meant or how it might feel. In Exercise 2, Connie and Laurie explicitly rejected forceful, aggressive use of authority by the staff members, making it clear that this exercise would unfold with as much empathy and support as possible given the nature of the activity. Here, in Exercise 3, we encounter an embrace of a strong, bold use of authority and a genuine commitment to engaging empathically with each other in the process. John and Susan owned that they were in charge, and accepted that the powerful use—some might even say abuse—of authority is required of staff members given the educational goals of this activity. But this message was then followed by an opportunity for the whole staff to engage with and process the emotional challenges and moral implications of treating participants with this kind of harshness and severity. It was not a comfortable role to play for the staff members, and they were invited to be honest about their doubts, fears, and concerns about having to engage with participants in this way. After nearly 30 minutes of this kind of processing, the codirectors encouraged the staff members to "keep in mind the big picture." The goal here ultimately was not to treat participants poorly; it was to help them understand how social systems work so that they could take positive, proactive steps to transform these systems in the future. This was an approach to implementing this exercise that embraced a willingness to use power and a willingness to listen to and support each other in ways that went beyond what we saw in the other two exercises.

Equally important, John and Susan developed a much more comprehensive design for this exercise than we saw in the other examples. Each group was given a task that in some sense represents stereotypical cultural expectation of that group, and the two codirectors spent the morning enforcing the rules with a level of energy and commitment that went beyond what we saw in the other examples (consider, for example, Susan spilling milk in the lap of participants as she confiscated cereal boxes from the Black males at breakfast). Their actions were provocative, intense, and upsetting to be sure, but the comprehensiveness of the programming and their in-the-moment actions reflected a level of engagement that went beyond what we observed in the other two exercises. Quite simply, John and Susan showed up more fully and powerfully than the directors of the other two exercises.

There appears to be meaningful connection between the quality of presence of the directors and the dynamics that ultimately emerged in this exercise. The way of being of the director(s) created an energetic field in which all the events of the Separation Exercises would unfold. The overall energy of Exercise 1 was low; participants were standing around a soccer field feeling mostly bored, and not much happened. Even when a few participants broke the rules and connected with other groups, the effect was minimal; they ended up hanging out together instead of hanging out apart. Compared to the other two exercises, the field generated by Thomasina, with her mix of being dictatorial and disengaged, was comparatively low energy, and the dynamism and creativity of that system were comparatively minimal.

The experience in Exercise 3 was completely different. John and Susan were notably present and deeply engaged, and they were able to integrate a willingness to exercise authority and a willingness to treat each other with empathy and compassion. Perhaps the most notable aspect of that exercise was the animated quality of the program; the entire camp felt as if it were crackling with energy that shifted and changed in palpable ways as events unfolded. When Eduardo took the first action to break the rules—by going to get coffee alone and boldly inviting the Black females to join him in challenging the system—you could feel the shift in the energy across the system. This particular act of resistance by Eduardo could be viewed as a failure of the exercise; after all, none of the Black females chose in that moment to join him in breaking the rules. But this seemingly ineffective effort was actually quite impactful in that it created a shift in energy that made future change more likely. Other groups had seen what happened, and after more than 90 minutes of stasis across the system, the possibility of choosing something other than complete obedience to the rules and conformity with peers had been glimpsed. It wasn't at all clear what was going to happen, but the sense that something—possibly something big—*could* happen was palpable.

Ultimately, something big did happen. Eduardo reunited with his fellow Latinos, and they joined him in connecting with the Black males. The movement for change had begun, and it developed with a speed and a depth of creativity and individual agency that was lacking in both the other activities. The coalition of the Latinos and Black males began inviting everyone to break the rules, and before long there was a diverse and intensely engaged self-organized, nonviolent protest movement that soon dedicated itself to articulating its own mission and value statements.

There can be no doubt that these activities unfolded without the direction and control of the staff members; this was a case in which the participants stepped up to take on a new level of agency. After an extended period of obedience and conformity, they became self-authorizing and self-directed over the course of a process that did not emerge in either of the other two activities.

This sort of shift in levels of responsibility and agency is exactly the point of every Camp Anytown program. The goal of all of these programs is to develop young people to not only achieve a higher level of consciousness about the nature of these unjust systems but also to realize a higher level of self-authorization and personal empowerment in being able to resist, challenge, and transform unjust systems. The reason why this third exercise was so much more effective and successful in producing this shift is an important one. There was something about the way the senior leaders showed up—their quality of presence—that was deeply connected to the dynamics that emerged in the system.

The Paradox of Holding Power and Love

Thus far, I have talked about this phenomenon of way of being of the directors in terms such as *level of engagement* and *quality of presence*. This concept of way of being goes beyond merely being engaged and present, however; there is a deeper dimension to this phenomenon that we must explore to fully understand how these different directors called forth different degrees of "aliveness" across these three exercises. We have already discussed the counterintuitive finding that Exercise 3 generated the greatest amount of creativity while having the greatest amount of structure. Exercise 3 demonstrated another paradoxical quality that played an integral role in the energetic quality—the aliveness—of the system. When viewed alongside the other two activities, Separation Exercise 3 was unique in the way it was able to paradoxically hold both *power* AND *love*.

Thomasina told her staff members to behave like "filler" and "sheep," and that was basically the end of the conversation about their involvement. She showed up with a focus on single-handedly controlling the whole exercise and made minimal effort to support or even just connect with her staff members on an emotional level. For her, this activity was all about power, with a notable absence of love. Connie and Laurie, however, expressly told their staff members to avoid "military-style" aggressiveness and encouraged them to offer empathy to any participants who seemed visibly upset by the experience. They also made a pedagogical decision to gather the community for a song session in a way that minimized the hierarchical nature of the system (everyone was at that point engaged in the same collective activity) while emphasizing the segregated, disconnected aspect of the experience. For them, this activity was all about *love*, with a notable absence of *power*. John and Susan, however, modeled a way of exercising authority that was strong, purposeful, and forceful, while simultaneously being empathic, supportive, and emotionally connected. For them this activity was about *power* AND *love*. It's a unique element of Exercise 3 that is worth exploring in more depth.

In America's real-life civil rights movement, this question of how to think about the connection between power and love was important. In a speech he gave in 1967, Martin Luther King Jr. discussed this topic in depth:

> Now the problem of transforming the ghetto, therefore, is a problem of power, a confrontation between the forces of power demanding change and the forces of power dedicated to preserving the status quo. Now, power properly understood is nothing but the ability to achieve purpose. It is the strength required to bring about social, political, and economic change. . . . What is needed is a realization that power without love is reckless and abusive, and that love without power is sentimental and anemic. Power at its best is love implementing the demands of justice, and justice at its best is love correcting everything that stands against love. And this is what we must see as we move on . . . Now what has happened is that we've had it wrong and mixed up in our country, and this has led

Negro Americans in the past to seek their goals through love and moral suasion devoid of power, and White Americans to seek their goals through power devoid of love and conscience . . . It is precisely this collision of immoral power with powerless morality which constitutes the major crisis of our times. (King, 1967)

In this speech, King offers a framing of the central challenge of social change that is relevant to the findings of our research. In his analysis, he does not frame the "major crisis of our time" as the struggle of Black people against White people or the privileged against the oppressed; it is the "collision of immoral power with powerless morality." When people with power—whoever they may be—seek to dominate and control without compassion, and those who are dominated appeal to compassion without seeking to exercise power to demand change, all parties involved collude to perpetuate an unjust and unchanging status quo. The work of creating social change involves simultaneously challenging those with power to embrace love and those who are oppressed to embrace power, so that everyone throughout the system is engaged in the challenging work of holding *power* AND *love*.

Author and social activist Adam Kahane wrote a book-length exploration of this challenge in *Power and Love* (2010). His insights are so relevant to this research that I quote him at some length. In the introduction to his book, Kahane explains his thinking on these matters as follows:

Power and love are difficult to work with because each of them has two sides. Power has a generative side and a degenerative side, and—less obviously—love also has a generative side and degenerative side. Feminist scholar Paola Melchiori pointed out to me that we can see these two sets of two sides if we look at historically constructed gender roles. The father, embodying masculine power, goes out to work, to do his job. The generative side of his power is that he can create something valuable in the world. The degenerative side of his power is that he can become so focused on his work that he denies his connection to his colleagues and family, and so becomes a robot or a tyrant. The mother, by contrast, embodying feminine love, stays at home to raise the children. The generative side of her love is that she gives life, literally to her child and figuratively to her whole family. The degenerative side of her love is that she can become so identified with and embracing of her child and family that she denies their and especially her own need for self-realization, and so stunts their and her own growth. . . . Love is what makes power generative instead of degenerative. Power is what makes love generative instead of degenerative. Power and love are therefore exactly complementary. In order for each to achieve its full potential, it needs the other. . . . If we are to succeed in co-creating new social realities, we cannot choose between power and love. We must choose both. (pp. 7–9)

Given the intangible quality of these two forces, talk about power and love often feels like a philosophical or theological discussion; the challenge of operating with these two forces in balance requires engaging with what seems a mystical dimension of the work of social change. This cross-case analysis of three Separation Exercises offers empirical evidence supporting the notion that it takes power and love to catalyze significant social change. Each force on its own generated notably static systems devoid of real creativity, self-organization, and change. The one activity that effectively held love and power in an integrated way generated a system that crackled with creativity, dynamism, and change.

Illuminating the Connection Between the Inner and Outer Worlds

With this insight, we arrive at perhaps the most important finding of this research: the profound interdependence between our inner and outer worlds. It is easy to believe that these dual dimensions of our experience are essentially disconnected. When we look inward, we encounter our thoughts, feelings, beliefs, stories, perceptions, and overall way of being in the world. We experience this inner world as intensely personal, and we constantly experience the truth that although we may have an intense desire for the world around us to be different from the way it is, our simple desire for a change to occur does not by itself transform the world. Given this daily experience, a belief that the world within us and the world outside of us are separate and distinct is understandable.

Yet this research suggests that this experience of separation is an illusion. In all three Separation Exercises, the systems and structures experienced by participants were outer-world manifestations of the inner ways of being of the program directors. A key reason why each exercise unfolded so differently was the fact that each program director was in the world in such a different way.

It would be a mistake, however, to get overly fixated on the power and influence of the program directors. Another reason why the exercises were different was that each participant in the system showed up with a particular way of being, and those inner qualities had a very real potential to transform the structure of the whole system. In Exercise 3, Eduardo showed up with a level of courage and commitment that was exceptional and stepped into his own power, and over time his efforts to act from that place of purpose catalyzed a dramatic shift in the entire structure of the system. One can't help but wonder: What if Eduardo wasn't there or had acted differently? What if there were two or three others who challenged the norms early on alongside him? What if any one of the individuals in that exercise had spoken up or acted out in a different manner? Although we can never know for sure how the system would have responded to any individual act of courage or resistance, we know for certain that at least in the case of this simulated social system, there is no doubt that anyone and everyone could have *tried something different,* and the system would have responded *somehow.* The reality of individual agency is an inescapable fact, as is the possibility that individual actions could affect the whole system.

It's a finding that aligns with an idea that has been explored recently by leadership scholar and MIT professor Otto Scharmer, who speaks eloquently about the "blind spot" of leadership: http:// www.ottoscharmer.com/sites/default/files/2003_TheBlindSpot.pdf

> There is a blind spot in leadership theory, in the social sciences as well as in our everyday social experience. This blind spot concerns the inner place from which an action—what we do—originates. In the process of conducting our daily business and social lives, we are usually well aware of what we do and what others do; we also have some understanding of the process: how we do things, the processes we and others use when we act. And yet there is a blind spot. If we were to ask the question, "Where does our action come from?" most of us would be unable to provide an answer. The blind spot concerns the (inner) source from which we operate when we do what we do— the quality of attention that we use to relate to and bring forth the world.
>
> I first began thinking about this blind spot when talking with the former CEO of Hanover Insurance, Bill O'Brien. He told me that his greatest insight after years of conducting organizational learning projects and facilitating corporate change was that "the success of an intervention depends on the interior condition of the intervener." That sentence struck a chord. What counts, it dawned on me, is not only what leaders do and how

they do it, but that "interior condition," the inner place from which they operate. I also realized that organizations, institutions, and societies as a whole may have this blind spot—not only individuals. Maybe, it occurred to me, what really needs to be done in response to the current world crises—political, social, and spiritual—has to do with changing that interior condition: collectively shifting the inner place from which a person, an organization, or a system operates. (2003, p. 2)

Scharmer argues that our innermost way of being plays a vital role in leadership in ways that we too often ignore or fail to understand. It is important to highlight his statement that each of us shows up with a quality of attention that does more than influence our own personal experience; it plays a critical role in how we "*relate to and bring forth the world.*" With this research, we are invited to take seriously the notion that in each of these exercises, the program staff members had unique, distinctive ways of being that, quite literally, "brought forth a world." Program staff members were not like computer programmers who designed a system, crafted the rules, hit run, and then had no influence on the unfolding of events. In a meaningful sense, the social systems created in the Separation Exercises ended up being manifestations of the interior ways of being of those individuals.

Why, then, did each exercise unfold so differently? Because each activity was essentially a "world" brought forth by different individuals, whose ways of being generated the design choices and quality of presence that played such a central role in the unfolding of each system.

Of course, this perspective has a simple yet profound implication: If we are able to shift our innermost way of being, we are sure to start bringing forth different kinds of worlds. This perspective raises a great many questions. What if participants experienced this activity, debriefed the whole experience, and then found themselves once again being separated into segregated groups the next morning when they showed up for morning circle? Although we can't know for certain exactly what would happen, we can assume that participants operating with a much deeper level of understanding and much higher consciousness about the nature and impact of these segregated, hierarchical systems would respond in a much more immediate and forceful way to challenge the norms.

If we take seriously the notion that the inner world and the outer world are in fact too interconnected to separate, then it follows that transformations in inner-world consciousness must produce transformations in outer-world structures—and vice versa. It's an implication that we will explore in more detail in Chapter 8. It is also the deepest motivation informing the writing of this book. Perhaps, if a wide enough circle of individuals can shift their consciousness—and thus their way of being—about how these systems work, we can begin to collectively call forth transformations in the systems around us in the years ahead.

How Wholeness Challenges Us to Radically Reframe Our Understanding of Events

A final insight that emerges is that this whole-system perspective on events challenges us to radically reframe the way to think about the nature of the events that unfolded in each Separation Exercise. At the interpersonal and intergroup levels of analysis, it seemed perfectly reasonable to think of the different groups in the system as being separate and disconnected; it was clear that participants experienced a visceral sense of being part of an "us" that was separate and distinct from "them" (actually, from multiple "thems").

When we make the jump to viewing the system from the whole-system level of analysis, however, we are challenged to confront the reality that these powerful experiences of separation turn out to be, in essence, false perceptions that reflect a limited grasp of the true nature of the system. At this highest level, we are compelled to take the deep interdependence and interconnectedness of the entire system as a given. From this perspective, a system in which individuals are gathered together in homogeneous, segregated groups is not, in reality, a collection of disconnected, independent parts. Rather, *it is an interdependent whole that is blind to the reality of its wholeness*.

It's a perspective that compels us to revise the way we understand all of the dynamics that unfolded in these exercises. For example, until now it seemed reasonable to suggest that when a participant such as Eduardo (from Exercise 3) broke the rules and spoke with members of another group, he was forging connections across disconnected groups and "bringing people together." From the whole-systems perspective, this is a problematic way of understanding events. The system always was whole and interdependent, and the experience of separation was an illusion resulting from a limited and incomplete understanding of the true nature of the system. It makes more sense to say that Eduardo *awakened the system to a higher level of conscious awareness of dynamics of interdependence that were always present*. Or that Eduardo *shattered an illusory experience of isolation and disconnection and called into being a more accurate understanding of collective interdependence*. As more and more individuals break the rules and come together, the system is not so much "coming together"—it has always been together—as it is arriving at a deeper understanding and higher consciousness of its true nature.

The emergence of this higher consciousness has important implications. With greater insight into its own interdependence, a system can begin self-organizing with greater self-awareness. Eventually, the system can become self-transforming: Instead of having systems and structures that emerge from the self-organized actions of individual agents who are essentially blind to the way their individual actions cocreate the systemic whole, the agents in the system can begin working together to self-consciously call forth systems and structures that more accurately promote the health of the whole system's sustainability.

In other words, this whole-systems perspective challenges us to grapple seriously with a simple yet profound truth: Although the lived experience of individuals and groups in these systems is one of separation and disconnection, in a very meaningful sense, there is no "us" and "them" in these systems; there is only "us." We arrive at a perspective that has been advocated by many of the world's most ancient wisdom traditions. Consider, for example, the relevance of the insight offered by the Dalai Lama in his best-selling book *Ethics for the New Millennium* (1999):

> When we come to see that everything we perceive and experience arises as a result of an indefinite series of interrelated causes and conditions, our whole perspective changes. We begin to see that the universe we inhabit can be understood in terms of a living organism where each cell works in balanced cooperation with every other cell to sustain the whole. If, then, just one of these cells is harmed, as when disease strikes, that balance is harmed and there is danger to the whole. This, in turn, suggests that our individual well-being is intimately connected both with that of all others and with the environment within which we live. It also becomes apparent that our every action, our every deed, word, and thought, no matter how slight or inconsequential it may seem, has an implication not only for ourselves but for all others as well. (pp. 40–41)

With this research, then, we are compelled to confront the challenge of learning how to think about events unfolding in a system that always was, always is, and always will be inviolably whole.

Awakening to Inner Wholeness

We have already talked about the ways that this research illuminates the interconnectedness of our inner and outer worlds. It is important to recognize that along with this act of awakening to a new consciousness regarding the wholeness of the world around us, we must also awaken to a new depth of consciousness regarding the wholeness of the world within us.

This process of awakening to inner wholeness is a theme that has been explored extensively by Parker Palmer. Palmer is an author and educator who writes eloquently about the inner life; a central component of his work is the search for wholeness within the self, and he highlights a clear connection between the inner work of achieving wholeness within ourselves and the outer work of confronting systems of injustice. In his book *Healing the Heart of Democracy* (2011), he illuminates this connection when he notes that movements for social change always begin with an inner choice that he calls the "Rosa Parks decision." In a passage with clear relevance to the Separation Exercises, he explains this as follows:

> The first stage of all social movements lies in what I have called the "Rosa Parks decision." Rosa Parks did not launch the American civil rights movement by herself, to say the obvious. She became the public icon of a long line of oppressed African Americans who had an "imprisoned image" of themselves as free women and men while being externally imprisoned by cultural and institutional racism. Rosa Parks spoke for all of them when she made the decision to "live divided no more," to act outwardly in a way that reflected the truth that she knew inwardly: that she was nothing less than a human being, whole and worthy and free . . .
>
> That decision is often made at personal risk—the risk of losing your reputation, your friends, your livelihood,

and sometimes even your life. We cannot find the courage to take such risks by calculating the odds that our actions will trigger something big. There is no guarantee that anyone will stand with us or that what we do will release larger energies.

We have only one guarantee: the knowledge that by living divided no more, we are claiming our own identity and integrity in the midst of a hostile world. (pp. 184–185)

In another book, A Hidden Wholeness (2009), Palmer explores the same themes:

The divided life is a wounded life, and the soul keeps calling us to heal the wound. Ignore that call, and we find ourselves trying to numb our pain with an anesthetic of choice, be it substance abuse, overwork, consumerism, or mindless media noise. Such anesthetics are easy to come by in a society that wants to keep us divided *and* unaware of our pain—for the divided life that is pathological for individuals can serve social systems well, especially when it comes to those functions that are morally dubious. . . .

No one wants to suffer the penalties that come from living divided no more. But there can be no greater suffering than living a lifelong lie. As we move closer to the truth that lives within us—aware that in the end what will matter most is knowing that we stayed true to ourselves—institutions start losing their sway over our lives. (p. 20)

It's a perspective that illuminates the results of this Separation Exercise research in myriad ways. Palmer states that when we live a divided life in which we are disconnected from our own truth, we experience a sort of spiritual pain. In the research, we saw this reflected by participants who chose not to break the exercise, and as a consequence they experienced dark emotions of guilt, shame, disappointment, and anger. By contrast, individuals who did choose to break the exercise reported feeling happy, strong, energized, and proud. Palmer also notes that the choice to live "divided no more" is risky, and there can be no guarantee that our inner choice will unleash energy in the world outside ourselves. We saw this in the actions of Eduardo in Exercise 3, who simply refused to disconnect from his own truth and took many courageous, risky actions that seemed to generate no response . . . until the moment when he was finally able to tip the system.

Most significantly, Palmer's perspective here reinforces the deepest insight that emerged from this research: that the connection between our own innermost ways of being and the systems and structures in which we are immersed is too interconnected to separate. When we turn inward and seek to heal the divisions within ourselves, we begin calling forth and cocreating systems that are more healthy and whole than they once were.

In other words, we must grapple seriously with the deepest implications of the finding that the systems and structures of the outer world are really a manifestation of our own inner worlds. If we embrace this perspective, then it is no mystery why we find ourselves immersed in an outer world that is divided, separated from itself, blind to its own true nature, and afraid of confronting its own pain and its own sources of strength and resilience. Such a world is really just a reflection of our own innermost condition, and the work of transforming all that pain and separation begins by turning inward and undertaking a journey toward wholeness and healing within ourselves.

With that insight, we conclude our in-depth analysis of the findings from this research. We now turn our attention to the question of how these findings relate to the real world. How should we understand the relationship between these simulated exercises and real-life matters of race and social change? What are the key lessons and insights we should glean from this research? Now that we have engaged in a rigorous and in-depth analysis of all three levels of the Separation Exercises, we are now ready to turn our attention to these important questions.

8

Lessons for the Real World, Part I: Seeing the System and the Process of Awakening

In this chapter, we leave behind the analysis of the data from the Separation Exercises and consider the implications that this research has for matters of race and social change in the real world. Clearly, the Separation Exercises are a simulation of historical social dynamics; one can reasonably question the degree to which any insights that emerge from these educational activities can or should inform our understanding of race and social change. Engaging with this question will enable us to unpack the lessons this research holds regarding dynamics of race and social change in our lives, communities, and nation.

Seeing the System

In 1990 an MIT Professor named Peter Senge wrote a book called *The Fifth Discipline* that went on become a best-seller and is considered classic in the literature on organizational development. The title of the book refers to an important new discipline that organizations need to develop if they want to survive and thrive in our modern, complex world: *systems thinking*. Senge (1990) states:

> Business and other human endeavors are also systems.
> They, too, are bound by invisible fabrics of interrelated

actions, which often take years to fully play out their effects on each other. Since we are part of that lacework ourselves, it's doubly hard to see the whole pattern of change. Instead, we tend to focus on snapshots of isolated parts of the system, and wonder why our deepest problems never seem to get solved. (p. 7)

As Senge suggests, this discipline does not just apply to business and organizations; it's the mental shift we need to make if we are to begin to understand matters of race and social change. It's a perspective that leads directly to the first key lesson we must take from this research: A system of racial privilege and oppression exists.

A System of Racial Privilege and Oppression Exists

This is the first and perhaps most important lesson of the Separation Exercise research. The whole point of these activities was to illuminate the experience of living within an unjust system organized according to the logic of a racial hierarchy, with Whites and lighter-skinned people enjoying privilege and Blacks and darker-skinned people experiencing various degrees of discrimination. Within this system, individual character, experience, achievement, and motivation are essentially irrelevant; the most salient aspect of the identity of all participants is the superficial detail of skin color and physical appearance. To be sure, these simulations did not capture the full complexity of this system as it exists in the real world, but it was sophisticated enough to enable us to study this type of system in some rigorous and meaningful manner. After all, Stanley Milgram did not need to fully re-create a totalitarian dictatorship in order to conduct experiments that illuminated the dynamics of obedience to authority.

I recognize that this claim that a system of racial privilege and oppression exists can be critiqued as a statement of something so obvious that one might wonder whether it merits being mentioned, never mind highlighted. After all, in the context of this research, the presence of an unjust system is not so much a finding as a basic description of the design of all three activities. And in the context of the real world, for people of color who continue to experience discrimination on a daily basis, to assert that such a system exists is to state something along the lines of "the sky is blue" or "water is wet." It is a statement of something so obvious and apparent that it seems almost bizarre to present it as an insight that emerged from years of research and rigorous analysis.

However, there may be no greater barrier to progress toward racial equality and social change than a lack of awareness on the part of those with racial privilege that this system exists. This lack of consciousness about the existence of a system of racial discrimination is a large part of what makes dialogue about race so contentious and progress in bringing about change so slow.

One of the most important moments of this research for me was the moment, in Exercise 3, when I went looking for the White males and found them all sitting comfortably in a quiet, carpeted, air-conditioned basement room deeply engrossed in a movie. I had spent the last hour observing events unfolding with all the other groups in the system. Part of what I saw was a litany of systemic indignities: Black kids forced to clean floors, brown kids forced to clean dishes, LGBTQ kids forced to stand in a broom closet. Part of what I saw were acts of courage, resistance, creativity, and compassion: participants challenging the unjust norms of the system, participants coming together in solidarity, participants debating the principles on which they would ground their nonviolent movement for social change. It was an intense and dramatic experience, and the White males in that basement room had no idea that any of it was going on.

That moment in the research evoked a powerful memory for me: I remember being in high school—the same age as the participants in this program. I was sitting in my bedroom in my family home in a predominantly White middle class Connecticut suburb, and I was asking myself the question at the heart of this book: *What's true about race and social change?* I recall wracking my brain for evidence that race mattered at all in my life . . . and I couldn't find any. I couldn't remember a single instance in which I had been stopped, or questioned, or challenged, or in any way troubled by my race. Although I was aware of America's history of slavery and racial discrimination, I came to the conclusion that racism had to be a dynamic perpetrated by racist individuals. Because I myself wasn't a malicious racist, I wasn't implicated, involved, or responsible for racism at all. As I sat in my room in a middle-class suburb, the systemic nature of racial discrimination was utterly invisible and unfathomable to me.

Now, as I think back to that moment, I am struck by the contrast between the nobility of my intentions and the falseness of my conclusions. I may have been genuine in my desire to understand "the other," and I was unquestionably motivated by a passion to promote social justice and a yearning for racial equality. But I see now that I was similar to the White males comfortably enjoying a movie in the basement, oblivious to the workings of a vast system of racial privilege and discrimination that was invisible to me and others who look like me because we enjoy a position at the top of the system. It's not that a system of racial discrimination didn't exist; it's that systems of discrimination are invisible to those who benefit most from those systems.

Over the course of my quest to explore these matters, I have heard many people of color say that in some important ways they actually prefer the clarity of dealing with White people who are blatantly, explicitly racist to dealing with White people who claim to be progressive yet remain largely blind to the reality of systems of privilege and oppression. I can now understand why it must be maddening to encounter people who believe themselves to be compassionate and open-minded and committed to racial progress, yet dispute and deny even the most basic truths of the experiences of people of color. Although this blindness may not be a reflection of malicious or explicitly racist intentions, it has the effect of sustaining and perpetuating the injustice, privilege, and discrimination of the status quo. I see now how well-intentioned individuals (such as my younger self) who remain blind to the workings of these systems end up holding beliefs and taking stands that actually serve to support and perpetuate the very injustices they claim to find so intolerable.

The fact is that for those of us who are metaphorically similar to the White males sitting in that comfortable basement, there can be no full understanding of the experiences of "the other" until we recognize that there is far more at play than just our personal intentions and interpersonal interactions. Once we learn to see the system, we must recognize some hard truths: It doesn't matter that we don't consider ourselves to be racist. It's not enough to work hard to treat others with respect and dignity, especially if the only people we ever encounter are also metaphorically sitting with us in that comfortable basement. When it comes to promoting or hindering social change, what *does* matter is our unwillingness to step out of our comfort zones where we are surrounded by the pleasant and familiar, our desire to travel in social circles in which we are surrounded by others just like us, and our misguided belief that we can understand anything about race and social change in the absence of authentic and meaningful encounters with people of color.

If we are not working in some way to understand and transform the structural injustices of the system, we are at best passively perpetuating systems and structures that privilege White people while discriminating against darker-skinned "others." And if we are not even aware of the fact that those systems exist—or actively insist that they don't—then we are not only not transforming those systems but also we are—however unintentionally—actually impeding the efforts of others who are trying to do so.

The Process of Awakening for White People

Based on my own journey toward a deeper understanding of these matters, and after having listened carefully to experiences shared by others and having read a great deal, I have discovered a word that reappears again and again to describe the experience of transforming one's consciousness regarding matters of race and social change: *awakening*. One does not learn about race and social change the way one learns multiplication tables or the rules of proper punctuation. This is not a process of digesting new facts; it is a process of becoming able to see through an all-encompassing illusion to begin perceiving what feels like a whole new reality.

In her book *Waking Up White, and Finding Myself in the Story of Race*, author and educator Debby Irving describes her personal search for a deeper understanding of race and social change as a White woman. As the title of the book makes clear, the notion of awakening is central to her experience:

> Waking up felt like stepping out of a dream, a fantasy world I'd been living in since birth. In fact, in her book *The History of White People*, Nell Irvin Painter uses the term "cultural fantasy" to characterize the system of racism that's evolved around skin color interpretations. Leaving behind the bubble of White ideology and stepping into a new shock-wave-laced reality came with a strange mix of alarm and wonder. I couldn't shake the feeling there must be more I didn't know. What other errors and omissions might I stumble upon?
>
> [. . .] Learning about how racism works didn't challenge me just because it was new information. It was completely *contradictory information*, a 180-degree paradigm reversal, flying in the face of everything I'd been taught as a child and had believed up to this moment. America's use of racial categories seemed fraught with unfairness, cruelty, and dishonesty. Yet my parents', grandparents', and entire extended family's life philosophy, as I understood it, had revolved around fairness, compassion, and honor. This was my legacy, the one I

took the most pride in passing on to my children. Discovering I'd been complicit in perpetuating a system that
was so very terribly bad flew in the face of all I'd understood about myself. (2014, p. 95)

Irving's words resonated powerfully with me, because they so
clearly articulated my own experiences on my journey to greater
understanding of race and social change. Early on, my implicit and
unexamined assumption was that the work I had to do to promote
racial equality and reconciliation was to be vigilant about being a
good person, because I was unaware of any dynamics at work beyond
the level of my own interpersonal interactions. And given my social
location as someone with privilege, I believed that it was also
incumbent on me to find opportunities to "help" those who are
"less fortunate." As I described in Chapter 1, however, I soon found
myself immersed in a steady stream of experiences that forced me to
confront the problematic assumptions buried deep in that way of
framing reality.

It wasn't so much a process of *learning* as much as a process of
unlearning: of interrogating ideas and assumptions that I had once
held without question and discovering, again and again, that my
patterns of thought and ways of framing reality distorted or rendered
invisible vitally important truths. I was similar to the White males
sitting in the comfortable basement room watching a movie, believing that my politeness in offering to get more popcorn for others
when I went to grab some more for myself was evidence of my
inherent goodness. It's not that this belief was outright false or that
good manners and interpersonal politeness are insignificant. It's
that this way of thinking about how the world works obscures the
truth that that group of White males were able to watch a movie only
because Black and brown people were busy cleaning the plates they
had eaten off of and sweeping the floors they would walk across again
soon for lunch. The illusion—the dream—is that they are separate
and independent from "the others," and that there is no connection

between the privileges they enjoy and the discrimination that those others endure.

Discovering this difficult truth is not pleasant, and once an individual with racial privilege glimpses this truth, he or she faces an inescapable choice: Which path will I choose to walk from here on out? Will I awaken to the uncomfortable truth or remain asleep in the comfortable dream?

In his best-selling book *Between the World and Me*, journalist Ta-Nehisi Coates offers a relevant story. Coates is a Black journalist whose book is a long letter to his son, a Black boy growing up in 21st-century America. Coates offers his insight and hard-won wisdom to his son who is coming of age in a country where Black men are routinely being killed by police and then—time and time again—not brought to justice. The book opens with Coates relating a story of a recent appearance on a TV show during which the White female host asked him to explain one of his ideas about what's true about race and social change. The notion of *dreaming* is central to his response:

> Specifically, the host wished to know why I felt that White America's progress, or rather the progress of those Americans who believe that they are White, was built on looting and violence. Hearing this, I felt an old and indistinct sadness well up in me. The answer to this question is the record of the believers themselves. The answer is American history . . . (2015, p. 6)

He continues:

> I realized then why I was sad . . . It was like she was asking me to awaken her from the most gorgeous dream. I have seen that dream all my life. It is perfect houses with nice lawns. It is Memorial Day cookouts, block

associations, and driveways. The Dream is treehouses and the Cub Scouts. The Dream smells like peppermint but tastes like strawberry shortcake. And for so long I have wanted to escape into the Dream, to fold my country over my head like a blanket. But this has never been an option because the Dream rests on our backs, the bedding made from our bodies. And knowing this, knowing that the Dream persists by warring with the known world, I was sad for the host, I was sad for all those families, I was sad for my country, but above all, in that moment, I was sad for you. (pp. 10–11)

It's a clear testament to the ubiquity and persistence of dreaming in White America. And as Coates phrases it, "the Dream persists by warring with the known world"; it rests on an unwillingness to acknowledge systems, structures, and experiences that have endured in this nation for centuries.

These systems and structures are inescapable for people of color, who find their lives constrained, limited, and affected by these systems on a daily basis. As Coates states, remaining blind to the truth is not an option for people of color. No matter how much they might want to, they cannot "escape into the Dream."

It's too simple, however, to suggest that only those at the highest levels of the system must undergo a process of awakening. It turns out that people of color must undergo a similar process that is distinct and different but also related and complementary to the awakening that those with racial privilege must undergo. We turn our attention to that related process now.

The Process of Awakening for People of Color

Towards the end of *Between the World and Me*, Coates describes his experiences on a trip abroad to Paris. He tells the story of making a friend who was as eager to practice English as Coates was eager to practice French. They agreed to meet for dinner for the purpose of practicing their languages together; they met as planned, had an enjoyable conversation, and after dinner the friend took him on a brief walk to take a look at a notable building a few blocks away. Then the evening ended without further incident.

The event is significant because Coates realizes that he spent the whole time leery that he was going to be somehow taken advantage of by his new friend. He states, "Watching him walk away, I realized that I had missed part of the experience because of my eyes, because my eyes were made in Baltimore, because my eyes were blindfolded by fear" (p. 126).

Here, then, we encounter a window into the process of awakening as it unfolds for people of color. For White people, this awakening begins by attaining a new consciousness regarding the existence of systems at work in the world beyond the self. For people of color, awakening involves attaining a new consciousness regarding the ways those systems of discrimination and oppression have been internalized *within the self*.

A classic example of this phenomenon can be found in the *Autobiography of Malcolm X*. The boy who would become Malcom X was a promising student in school who dreamed of becoming a lawyer. In his teenage years, however, he was told by a teacher that he could never become a lawyer and should look into careers in plumbing or carpentry (the echoes of the roles given to participants of color in the Separation Exercises are apparent here). Eventually, as a result of that indignity, combined with some challenging life circumstances, he chose to drop out of high school in Michigan and move to Boston, where he began trying to find his way and make a name for himself on the streets of Roxbury. He bought himself a zoot suit—a colorful and ostentatious suit worn by the flashiest and highest-profile young men at that time, and before long he decided it was time for a conk.

A conk was the name used to describe the hairstyle that was popular among his peers, in which the natural curls and frizz of Black hair were chemically treated to become straight or wavy similar to the hair of White people. The process to achieve a conk was fairly expensive, because it involved buying several chemicals that had to be mixed together. It was time-consuming, because the chemicals took a while to transform the hair. Most significantly, it was *painful*: the chemicals burned not just the hair but also the scalp, and the process involved leaving them in for as long as possible before rinsing them out when the pain became unbearable. It was considered something of a test of masculinity to see how many minutes you could last before going for the rinse.

Here's how a grown-up Malcolm X looks back at his first conk, which was applied by a friend named Shorty:

> The congolene felt warm when Shorty started combing it in. But then my head caught fire.
>
> I gritted my teeth and tried to pull the sides of the kitchen table together. The comb felt as if it was raking my skin off.
>
> My eyes watered, my nose was running. I couldn't stand it any longer; I bolted to the washbasin. I was cursing Shorty with every name I could think of when he got the spray going and started soap-lathering my head.
>
> He lathered and spray-rinsed, lathered and spray-rinsed, lathered and spray rinsed maybe ten or twelve times . . .
>
> "The first time is always the worst. You get used to it before long. You took it real good, homeboy. You got a good conk."
>
> . . . The mirror reflected Shorty behind me. We both were grinning and sweating. And on top of my head was this thick, smooth sheen of red hair—real red—as straight as any White man's. (pp. 55–56)

Then, with the next line, Malcolm X shifts from this vivid description of the process to the understanding he attained regarding that experience years later, as a far more race-conscious adult:

> How ridiculous I was! Stupid enough to stand there simply lost in admiration of my hair looking "White," reflected in the mirror in Shorty's room. I vowed that I'd never again be without a conk, and I never was for many years.
>
> This was my first really big step towards self-degradation: when I endured all that pain, literally burning my flesh to have it look like a White man's hair. I had joined that multitude of Negro men and women in America who are brainwashed into believing that the Black people are "inferior"—and White people "superior"—that they will even violate and mutilate their God-created bodies to try to look "pretty" by White standards. (X & Haley, 1992, pp. 56–57)

I'm aware that the question of hairstyle is a very sensitive matter in the Black community, and I should state that my intention here is not to suggest that any person of color choosing a straight hairstyle today should be viewed as suffering from internalized oppression and a low level of race consciousness. My point here is simply to highlight a moment of awakening to higher levels of awareness regarding internalized oppression in the life of an iconic Black activist in our recent history.

Here's one more: Nelson Mandela was one of the most courageous, conscious, and effective activists and statesmen of the 20th century. He is an exemplar of the truth that people of color can resist the pressure to internalize the oppressive and discriminatory messages of a blatantly racist society and—in doing so—transform the outer-world structures in which they are immersed. Yet even he discusses moments of awakening to new levels of consciousness regarding just how pervasive and insidiously internalized racism can be. In his autobiography *Long Walk to Freedom*, Mandela relates this brief but telling anecdote about getting on a plane to travel from Sudan to Ethiopia on one his international tours to generate support for the anti-apartheid movement:

> We put down briefly in Khartoum, where we changed to an Ethiopian Airways flight to Addis. Here I experienced a rather strange sensation. As I was boarding the plane I saw that the pilot was Black. I had never seen a Black pilot before, and the instant I did I had to quell my panic. How could a Black man fly an airplane? But a moment later I caught myself: I had fallen into the apartheid mindset, thinking Africans were inferior and that flying was a White man's job. I sat back in my seat, and chided myself for such thoughts. Once we were in the air, I lost my nervousness and studied the geography of Ethiopia, thinking how guerilla forces hid in these very forests to fight the Italian imperialists. (p. 292)

Awakening as an Ongoing Journey

Once again, it would be a mistake to depict the process of awakening as unfolding in these overly simplistic terms, with White people awakening to oppressive structures in the outer world and people of color awakening to internalized oppression in the inner world. The truth is more complex, because the process of awakening is always ongoing, and in time it unfolds in the inner and outer dimensions for White people and people of color. Consider, for example, the experience of Michelle Alexander, author of the highly influential best-seller *The New Jim Crow*. In the book, she explains that the journey to that book began when she was an experienced lawyer already deeply involved in racial justice work for many years:

> When I began my work at the ACLU, I assumed that the criminal justice system had problems of racial bias, much in the same way that all major institutions in our society are plagued with problems associated with conscious and unconscious bias . . . By the time I left the ACLU, I had come to suspect that I was wrong about the criminal justice system. It was not just another institution infected with racial bias but rather a different beast entirely . . . Quite belatedly, I came to see that mass incarceration in the United States had, in fact, emerged as a stunningly comprehensive and well-disguised system of racialized social control that functions in a manner strikingly similar to Jim Crow. (2012, pp. 3–4)

Over the course of the book, Alexander presents a thoroughly researched case illuminating the existence of an oppressive social system that had long been invisible to her, despite her high level of race consciousness and years of work promoting racial justice. Although a complete review of her thesis is beyond the scope of this book, the basic idea is highly relevant to this discussion. She argues that today's criminal justice system represents a new way to maintain and enforce exactly the sort of segregated, hierarchical, unjust system of racial privilege and oppression we encountered in the Separation Exercises, using language and methods that have morphed and evolved to preserve this system in terms that are acceptable in our supposedly color-blind modern era. As a result, she points out that today there are more Black adults under the control of the criminal justice systems (in jail, on probation, or on parole) than were enslaved in 1850, just a few years before the start of the Civil War.

In one of the many journal articles she has written exploring the subject of mass incarceration, she reaches for some familiar language to describe how it came to be that even highly engaged, informed, and professional racial activists somehow missed the fact that the elements of this vast system were slowly being put into place:

> Many of us—myself included—slept through a revolution. Actually, it was a counterrevolution that has blown back much of the progress that so many racial activists risked their lives for. This counterrevolution occurred with barely a whimper of protest, even as a war was declared, one that purported to be aimed at "drugs" . . .
>
> I am listening carefully at my window now. I hear that rumbling sound, signs of an awakening in the streets. My heart leaps for joy. People of all colors are beginning to raise their voices a little louder; people who have spent time behind bars are organizing for the restoration of their civil and human rights; young people are becoming bolder and more defiant in challenging the prison-industrial complex; and people of faith are finally waking up to the uncomfortable reality that we have been complicit in the birth and maintenance of a system predicated on denying to God's children the very forms of compassion, forgiveness, and possibilities for redemption that we claim to cherish. (Alexander, 2014, p. 1)

Here, then, is an example of people of color awakening to a higher consciousness regarding the workings of a system outside of the self.

On the matter of the process of inner awakening that White people must undertake, I can offer two examples drawn from my own experience. I present them in the hopes that sharing my own stories might serve to help some of the White readers of this work undertake a similar journey of inner awakening in their own lives.

Awakening to Internalized Privilege

The first of these two moments of inner awakening occurred during a class on moral development at Harvard. The professor, feminist psychologist Carol Gilligan, was facilitating a discussion of the notion of "double consciousness" presented by W.E.B. Du Bois in his seminal work *The Souls of Black Folks*, originally published in 1903. He explains it this way:

> It is a peculiar sensation, this double-consciousness, this sense of always looking at one's self through the eyes of others, of measuring one's soul by the tape of a world that looks on in amused contempt and pity. One ever feels his two-ness,—an American, a Negro; two souls, two thoughts, two unreconciled strivings; two warring ideals in one dark body, whose dogged strength alone keeps it from being torn asunder. (1999, p. 11)

There were many students of color in the class discussing their own experience of this phenomenon, in which they operated constantly with an understanding that there were at least two sets of rules at work in the world. There were the rules that governed what was acceptable to think, say, and do while among family and peers and a different set of rules governing what was acceptable to think, say, and do when interacting with White people. And these two ways of being were clearly valued in very different ways. To be among White people and use the speech used among communities of color was to risk being judged for speaking poorly or incorrectly; to be among White people and use the mannerisms or social norms used among communities of color was to risk being judged for behaving abnormally or inappropriately. Although White people never really had to learn these different ways of being because they were never compelled to live and work in communities of color, people of color were forced to grapple with these different rules whenever they had to interact with institutions or people with power.

Listening to the personal testimonies of my peers, it became clear to me that this concept of double consciousness was not some abstract notion; it was a daily reality for many of my fellow students. It did not resonate for me, personally, however. I did not live with such a vivid and intense awareness of "doubleness"; for me, there was one set of rules—one way of being—that applied everywhere at all times.

At some point in that class discussion, I was struck by an insight that challenged me to reframe the whole way I experienced my own inner life. If these peers of color lived with "double consciousness," didn't that mean that I had been operating up to that point in a state of "single consciousness"? As a straight White male, I moved through the world with a perpetual sense that there was one "correct" way of behaving—my way—and any individuals who deviated from that norm could be described (and dismissed) as "abnormal," "inappropriate," "wrong," or "problematic." In this moment of awakening, I was suddenly open to considering the possibility that this dimension of my inner experience was not objectively true; there was not, in fact, one single proper way of being in the world. There were other, alternative ways of being, and for the first time I found myself considering the possibility that my foundational inner experience of "single consciousness" could be more accurately described as a facet of "internalized privilege." In other words, the belief that there is really only one "correct" way of being in the world was not an objective truth; it was simply a facet of my place in the system that had become internalized.

Awakening to Internalized Hierarchy

This experience of awakening to an internalized dimension of my own privilege laid an important foundation for another insight that occurred in a different course that I was taking that same semester. At the same time that I was grappling with the implications of double consciousness in my moral development class at the school of education, I was also deeply engaged with learning about civic leadership in a class called "Exercising Leadership, Mobilizing Group Resources" I was taking at the school of government. This was my first encounter with the adaptive leadership model referenced in the introduction to this book, and it was nothing less than life changing. Here's why:

The leadership course included large-group sessions in a lecture hall and the small-group "consultation sessions" involving a diverse group of 8 to 12 fellow students. At each of these small-group sessions, one member of the group would present a real-life leadership failure, and the rest of the group would try to help the presenter think about how he or she might have addressed that situation differently using the concepts and insights of the adaptive leadership model. After each of these sessions, every member of the small group would write a paper responding to a set of questions asking us to reflect on the group dynamics that occurred during the session. In other words, there were two dimensions of learning occurring simultaneously in these sessions: We were learning from real-life failures, and we were also learning from the dynamics that unfolded as we strived to learn from those failures.

Similar to each of these small groups, my own group was highly diverse. Our group included individuals who were male and female, gay and straight, Black, Brown, White, and Asian, and a mix of Americans and foreign students from places such as Japan, Europe, and South America. Over the course of the semester, we shared our failures with each other while diving ever deeper into an understanding of our own group dynamics.

Early on, I loved these sessions. I felt like each failure presented by a fellow student represented a sort of intellectual puzzle—a game that I could "win" by discerning the key mistakes they made that led to the failures. It was my habit to arrive early, grab the spot at the head of the small conference table, and do my best to use logic and intellect to drive the group rapidly and confidently toward uncovering the flawed belief or action that produced the failure. If I felt that colleagues were pursuing lines of questioning that I thought were not fruitful, I redirected the discussion. If I thought that presenters were resisting my interpretation of events, I challenged them aggressively. When I arrived at an insight that I believed represented the key flaw in the presenters thinking or actions, I declared it boldly, proud that I had "won" the game of solving the puzzle.

A few sessions into the semester, however, it became clear that my fellow students were growing more and more resistant to my style of participation. Some of the women found my aggressive style to be deeply upsetting; they accused me of being callous, heartless, and needlessly cruel and accused me of "holding myself above the group." Other peers—male and female—expressed increasing frustration with my tendency to dominate the discussion and control the flow and direction of the group dialogue. The foreign students were noticeably silent as the tension—and vocal disagreement—among the Americans in the group grew stronger and more polarized. And everyone—even the foreign students—accused me of "holding myself above the group."

I found myself growing angrier and more frustrated as the semester continued. Metaphorically speaking, my inner dialogue began to occur in all caps. I was SOLVING THE PROBLEMS! I was WINNING THE GAME! I was LEADING THE GROUP! What was the PROBLEM with these PEOPLE?!? The more my peers challenged my approach, the more entrenched in my understanding of the situation I became, and the more righteous and justified I felt in being angry about it.

Then—within a few weeks of the moment when that insight about "single consciousness" happened in the moral development class—something very strange occurred at a moment when I happened to be standing in my kitchen cooking up some mac and cheese (a very common occurrence in my grad school days). I was standing there raging against the foolishness of my peers in my mind when suddenly and abruptly something shifted in my consciousness. The best metaphor I can find for the experience was that it was like I was one of the *Apollo* rockets traveling through space, and suddenly one of the stages of the rocket detached itself and began to float away from the main body, slowly twisting and turning as it drifted away, enabling me to view it from all angles as it slowly rotated in space. The remarkable thing was that I had not known that this thing now floating in space was detachable; I was utterly surprised to discover that it had been a part of me, and I was only able to awaken to that reality in the moment that it separated itself and enabled me to see it from a distance.

The "thing" in this metaphor was an assumption, buried so deep and held so tightly in my consciousness that I had no idea how powerfully it was informing and influencing my actions. And that assumption was this: *The purpose of life is to climb as high as you can in the hierarchy*. This was not as much a belief or an attitude as it was a *way of being in the world*. If I was in a social situation, I was busy climbing the hierarchy—with no awareness of the fact that that was what I was doing.

Suddenly, I was able to hear the criticisms of my peers in a whole new way. I realized that they were right: I *was* holding myself above the group, because I assumed that that was the only way to relate to a group of people. I *was* dominating the discussion, because I was focused on seizing my classmates' attention and constraining the way issues were framed. I *was* being aggressive and ruthless, because I assumed that all social interactions represented games to win, not relationships to deepen and cultivate. These were strategies I had to use to maintain dominance and control. All of this became clear in an instant as I stood there preparing my mac and cheese.

At the next small-group consultation session, I showed up in a completely different way. I sat at the side of the table instead of at the head, and I focused on listening as opposed to arguing. It quickly became clear that my choice to step back (way, way back!) created a space that enabled others to step up. Other members of the group had far more opportunities to speak up, including the foreign students whose perspectives pushed our thinking in unexpected and useful ways. Other students raised issues that I thought were pertinent, but they did so with far more empathy and compassion than I would have summoned had I chose to make similar points. There were also multiple perspectives that I would not have personally considered that illuminated the case in valuable ways. As a result of my choice to step back, presenters were able to hear and work with a wider array of insights than I would otherwise have allowed to surface and to do so in far more productive ways.

Today, I consider this moment of awakening to be perhaps the single most important insight I gained over the course of my six years of doctoral work. Since that moment, I have been able to intentionally choose how to relate to a social system, as opposed to instantly and unquestioningly seeking to climb the hierarchy inherent in that system. I have been able to partner with others—as opposed to holding myself above them—and seek connection and understanding instead of dominance and control. I have come to see my own comfort with holding positions of authority as a valuable resource, and I've learned that many people struggle with power and authority in the same ways that I have struggled with partnership and connection. With this awakening, however, I found myself able exercise an entirely new degree of freedom regarding whether or not I should deploy this resource in any given situation. I now had a choice regarding how to behave, whereas before I had none.

Equally important, it was immediately clear that my own transformation in consciousness directly resulted in a transformation in the social system in which I was immersed. As long as I was busy struggling to maintain dominance and control, others members of my group had to fight for the right to be heard. In hindsight, I realize that I was playing a major role in keeping my group stuck at the level of a simple hierarchy. Once I achieved a change in consciousness, the group was able to make a leap forward toward becoming a more interconnected and interdependent network, in which individuals experienced far more equality, partnership, collaboration, and understanding. I see now that the group's collective process of developing toward higher levels of complexity was hindered and delayed as a result of my own blindness to the workings of the system as a privileged White male.

I've also come to appreciate the interrelatedness of individual transformation and the fractal nature of social change. For me, this moment of awakening occurred while I was immersed in a small-group discussion at grad school; in terms of fractals, this experience unfolded at the scale of interpersonal relationships. Soon after grad school, I landed a job at City Year, and over the course of several years was able to move up the organizational hierarchy, eventually rising to the level of vice president of leadership development. In that capacity, I was able to create developmental experiences for corps and staff members that were grounded in an awareness of interconnection and interdependence. In other words, I arrived at a place where I was able to influence dynamics at a higher level of fractal organization, the organizational scale. In my current position at the New Politics Leadership Academy, I am working on creating similar experiences all across the country for thousands of alumni of service programs who are interested in running for political office. Although we are still in the early stages of the effort, our aspirations are to influence events at the national scale.

The point here is that over the course of time, I have found myself with opportunities to influence and be influenced by different fractal scales of organization. With hindsight, I can see clearly how my own personal journey of awakening has, with the unfolding of time, enabled me to consciously seek to call forth and cocreate more interconnected and interdependent networks at higher scales of fractal organization. My point is not to claim any unique power or special abilities here; there is nothing particularly unusual about this story of gradually achieving an enlarged sphere of influence over the course of one's career. What I'm highlighting here is the relationship between our own individual processes of awakening and the way that our personal journeys influence the networks in which we are immersed. The fact is that we are all influencing our own corners of the world every day in our families, places of work, and communities, and there is a connection between where we stand on our own journeys of awakening and the worlds we call forth in the world around us.

Final Thoughts on Awakening to the System

Here, then, is what I have come to understand as a result of my own journey of awakening and through the empirical research into the Separation Exercise at the center of this book:

> *A system of racial privilege and oppression exists, and we not only live within that system but that system also lives within each of us.*

When we remain unaware of that system—when we dream—we sustain and reinforce a segregated and unjust system in ways that are significant and unintentional. When we awaken to that system within and around us, we participate in a process of transforming that system toward greater equality and justice. Whatever path we choose, we can be sure that in the vast web of interdependence, our actions, our choices, and our consciousness of the world in which we are immersed ripple out to influence others in ways we may scarcely understand.

9

Lessons for the Real World, Part II: On Power, Control, and the Interconnectedness of Our Inner and Outer Worlds

I n Chapter 8, we discussed the need to recognize the existence of a system of racial privilege and oppression, and we explored the process of awakening that we must undergo to achieve a higher level of consciousness regarding the impact this system has on our outer and inner worlds. In this chapter, we continue this effort to illuminate the implications that this Separation Exercise research has for matters of race and social change in the real world by investigating some related questions. Who designed this unjust system? Who controls it? And how should we understand the interrelatedness of the inner and outer dimensions of this system? In the pages ahead, we turn our attention to these important matters.

Who Designed It? Understanding the Origins of the System

Once we embrace the truth that this system exists and understand more clearly how it works, we must confront a two related questions. Who designed it? And who is in charge of it? Within the context of the Separation Exercises, the first question is an easy one to answer: The program directors designed the system, and we know that each of them made somewhat different design decisions even as they preserved the underlying framework of creating an unjust segregated system. With the help of fellow staff members, they then spent their time enforcing the rules they had created for the activity.

In the real world, the answer to this question is not so clear. Who designed the racially segregated, hierarchical, unjust systems at work in real life? Was there a designer? After contemplating this issue, I believe that what we need to do here is zoom out—way out—to view today's state of race and social change in this country as the current moment in a vast process of human development that has been unfolding not just for centuries but for millennia.

In thinking about these matters, we must revisit the discussion from Chapter 3 regarding the evolution over time of simple hierarchies into much more complex networked systems. As you'll recall, we discussed how this is a helpful framework for understanding the evolution of human civilization as a complex system. At the dawn of human history, we organized ourselves in much the same way that our nearest evolutionary ancestors organized themselves: in small groups structured as simple hierarchies governed by mature, strong males who were expected to provide direction, protection, and control. Although human communities grew in size, they remained organized as simple hierarchies for tens of thousands of years, with the age of pharaohs and god kings evolving into monarchies believed to be divinely inspired. Eventually, humanity reached a tipping point, and we saw the emergence of a wave of democratic revolutions that in some important ways continues to this day. Just a couple hundred years later, we are witness to the emergence of fully networked systems, which represent a natural continuation of this evolution toward higher levels of complexity.

At every stage of this developmental process, we see a transformation of power relationships in which those with authority experience a relative decrease in their power and influence, whereas "the people"—whoever they may be—experience a relative increase in their power and influence. Because human systems—similar to so many other living systems—are organized according to the logic of fractals, we see this evolution unfolding with symmetry across scales. So we can zoom in to observe this transformation unfolding at the interpersonal level, zoom out to see the dynamic at the organization or communal level, keep on zooming out to the national level, or zoom all the way out to the geopolitical level. Once we learn to see it, it's hard to miss.

This is a long-term process; in many ways, this basic evolutionary process is the hidden, underlying story behind all of human history since its beginnings shrouded in the mists of time right up to this morning's headlines. Each of us appears in the world at some moment in this unfolding, and our lives are but a momentary blip in the overall process.

In other words, we are all in a condition very much like the participants in these Separation Exercises, who wake up one day to find ourselves embedded in an unjust, unfair, hierarchical system that we played no role in creating and—because we are so deeply immersed in it—find it hard to fully understand.

In my own efforts to understand the implications of this perspective, I have found it helpful to conduct playful thought experiments. Imagine, for example, being able to travel back through time to, say, Europe in the 1400s. Seeing that society through our modern eyes, we would no doubt be shocked by the rigid hierarchies and rampant injustices of that age. This was before the notion of a social contract, before the notion of inalienable individual rights, during a long era in which the worldview of enlightened humanism was not active. We would encounter masses of people living as voiceless, powerless subjects of absolute monarchs who could exploit, oppress, and kill at will.

The important thing to realize here is that at that moment in the development of human civilization, the great masses of peasants and ordinary people were *not* enlightened citizens whose dreams of freedom had to be crushed under the boot of oppressive monarchs. Such a belief would surely be an anachronism—a mistaken

234 RACE AND SOCIAL CHANGE

projection of our own worldview as modern citizens onto people living in an era in which nobody had yet achieved the levels of consciousness that are widespread in our world today. In that era, it was the view of essentially everyone that their condition—the status quo of that era—was the natural order of things. Hereditary rulers exercised absolute power and dominance over powerless, voiceless masses. Everyone knew their role; everyone played their part. This was how it had always been; this was how it would always be.

I should note here that I would respectfully push back on any criticism that this underlying social architecture was unique to Europe, the West, or White people at that moment in history. We can add some adventure and perspective to this thought experiment by teleporting ourselves to the Far East, the Middle East, South America, Africa, India—anywhere, really—in that same era. Underneath the dazzling diversity of cultures and histories we would encounter on such a trip, we would find societies operating at roughly the same level of social complexity. Although the notion of the simple hierarchy represents a broad stroke that obscures a great deal of the nuance in all these societies, a compelling case can be made that this essential point holds true for the vast majority of the world of that era. The belief that individuals could and should live as empowered citizens with inalienable rights protected by systems and structures that constrained the power of rulers to act on even their smallest whims did not yet exist. And the systems and structures of societies around the world of that era reflected that fact.

Looking out at the world of the 1400s, we would see relationships of absolute power and dominance at every scale of analysis: husbands ruling over powerless wives, feudal lords ruling over powerless vassals, hereditary monarchs able to dominate everyone in their kingdom, kings engaged in endless battles and wars in an endless effort to dominate and control other kingdoms. As moderns taking in this state of affairs, it would be very clear to us that the systems and structures of society of that era were a reflection of the level of consciousness of the people living in that era. It would be apparent to us that the conditions of that day were not in truth some "natural" state of affairs; they were not some inevitable and inalterable condition of humankind. On the contrary, we would understand the status quo of that moment to be just a snapshot in a developmental process unfolding across time. And it is the evolving consciousness of humanity—the growing numbers of individuals awakening to their own innate dignity, potential, and value— that precedes and eventually manifests transformations in the systems and structures of the social hierarchy.

Continuing this thought experiment, we could imagine ourselves choosing to fast-forward through the years, watching these relationships shift at every scale of analysis from absolute dominance and dependence to something closer to equality and interdependence. We could pause in the era of slavery in America, and listen as slave owners justify the owning of sentient human beings as the natural order of the world. We could move on to the era of Jim Crow and listen as White Americans justify institutions such as segregated schools and bus stations as the natural order of the world. The falseness of these claims would be readily apparent to us.

Of course, we could continue right up through the present day, when the implications of this thought experiment become clear. After returning from this journey through time we must hear the debates in today's headlines with a new level of consciousness of the truth behind all the noise and rancor. The high rates of incarceration of people of color, police brutality, the academic achievement gap and the low levels of high school graduation among minority students, disproportionately high unemployment rates . . . all of the present day manifestations of a system of privilege and oppression would surely appear to us in a new light.

None of this is natural, inevitable, or unchangeable. It is just the moment in this millennia-long developmental process into which we happened to have been born. Although none of us living today created this reality, every one of us has a very real power to either preserve and support the status quo or step into our responsibility to work for change. After all it is a mistake to think that this development toward higher complexity simply happens; each generation must struggle to advance the cause of more freedom, justice, and opportunity in its day. And the efforts of each generation bring forth the world that will be left to their children and grandchildren.

The question of how each of us can exercise power and influence in these systems is important, but we're not quite ready to move on to that matter yet. First, we have to confront the historical legacy of this long march toward freedom. One of the findings of this Separation Exercise research is that William Faulkner (2012, p. 73) was most definitely right: "The past is not dead; it's not even past." Understanding how this works is another vital undertaking in the quest to discover what is true about race and social change.

Understanding Historical Traumas and Glories

One of the clear findings of the Separation Exercise research is the fact that present-day experiences of oppression and discrimination frequently evoke memories of historic traumas that occurred at some prior moment in this long process. This was a dynamic that appeared across all three exercises: When Black participants were forced to clean floors or stand in the hot sun against their will, the experience evoked shared memories of the horrors of slavery for at least a few of them. When Jews were forced to wear armbands marked with a yellow Star of David, the experience evoked the horrors of the Holocaust. When Latinos were forced to clean dishes or engage in manual labor, the experience evoked memories of discrimination against their ancestors. All of these participants were teenagers who had not personally experienced these traumatic events; in the case of the Blacks and Jews, they were referring to events that were decades or centuries in the past. And yet those historical events played a significant—sometimes central—role in the way individuals responded to experiences of oppression and discrimination in the present day.

Why does this happen? How does this work?

As I explained in Chapter 1, in the early years of my quest to understand what is true about race and social change, I felt that the more I learned, the more confused I became. My reading and studying spanned across a great many subjects and disciplines, and although all of it seemed relevant and important, I couldn't figure out how any of fit together. I encountered scholars and researchers from vastly different fields who had discovered eerily similar dynamics, and I struggled to understand how and why this could be happening. Eventually, however, I encountered the literature on complex systems and fractals, and suddenly an elegant simplicity underlying all that complexity popped into view. A significant example of the power of this new clarity relates to this question of historical traumas and glories.

At some point in my studies, I encountered the work of John Gottman, a professor at the University of Washington in Seattle who is among the best-known and most influential marriage researchers working today. Gottman is a psychologist who uses scientific research methodologies to illuminate the dynamics of marriage. At the University of Washington, he has created what he calls a "love lab"; it looks like a normal apartment, but it is wired with cameras, microphones, and sensing equipment that can measure heart rate, skin temperature, and other related factors. Over the years, Gottman has had large numbers of real-life married couples enter the lab and go about their lives as normally as possible, while being carefully observed and measured.

Gottman (1999) pulls together this research and his related advice in *The Seven Principles for Making Marriage Work*. For anyone interested in learning more about lessons gathered through this kind of rigorous scientific inquiry into marriage, I highly recommend the entire book and all seven principles it presents. For our purposes here, though, it will suffice to review only the first of these principles, which Gottman describes as "enhance your love maps."

Gottman begins the chapter explaining this principle by telling the story of a couple in which the workaholic husband simply did not know the names of any of his children's friends, the name of the family dog, and where the back door to the house was. This lack of knowledge—and the lack of emotional connection that it implied—was deeply unsetting to the wife. Gottman (1999) states:

> I have found that many married couples fall in to a similar (if less dramatic) habit of inattention to the details of their spouse's life. One or both partners may have only the sketchiest sense of the other's joys, likes, dislikes, fears, stresses. The husband may love modern art, but the wife couldn't tell you why or who his favorite artist is. He doesn't remember the names of her friends or the coworker she fears is constantly trying to undermine her. (p. 48)

Based on findings from his research, Gottman has found that this kind of blindness to what matters most to one's spouse is among the biggest predictors of divorce. Naturally, the practical response to this finding is to encourage couples to "enhance their love maps" by taking the time to deliberately discuss and explore these matters.

Gottman offers several detailed exercises in this section of the book with long lists of questions that couples can discuss as part of an intentional effort to strengthen their relationship. For our purposes here, one of those exercises in particular is worth highlighting. It is a reflection exercise called "Who am I." and Gottman (1999) explains it this way:

> The more you know about each other's inner world, the more profound and rewarding your relationship will be.

This questionnaire is designed to guide you through some self-exploration and to help you share this exploration with your partner. Work on this exercise even if you and your spouse consider yourselves open books. There's always more to know about each other. Life changes us, so neither of you may be the same person who spoke those wedding vows five, ten, or fifty years ago. (p. 56)

He then introduces a series of five reflection questions. For reasons that will become apparent soon, I present the full details of the first two here.

My Triumph and Strivings

1. What has happened in your life that you are particularly proud of? Write about your psychological triumphs, times when things went even better than you expected, periods when you came through trials and tribulations even better off. Include periods of stress and duress that you survived and mastered, small events that may still be of great importance to you, events from your childhood or the recent past, self-created challenges you met, periods when you felt powerful, glories and victories, wonderful friendships you maintained, and so on.

2. How have these successes shaped your life? How have they affected the way you think of yourself and your capabilities? How have they affected your goals and the things you strive for?

3. What role has pride (that is, feeling proud, being praised, expressing praise for others) played in your life? Did your parents show you that they were proud

of you when you were a child? How? How have
other people responded to your accomplishments?

My Injuries and Healings

1. What difficult events or periods have you gone
   through? Write about any significant psychological insults and injuries you have sustained, your
   losses, disappointments, trials, and tribulations.
   Include periods of stress and duress, as well as
   any quieter periods of despair, hopelessness, and
   loneliness. Also include any deep traumas you
   have undergone as a child or adult. For example,
   harmful relationships, humiliating events, even
   molestation, abuse, rape, or torture.

2. How have you survived these traumas? What are
   their lasting effects on you?

3. How did you strengthen and heal yourself? How did
   you redress your grievances? How did you revive
   and restore yourself?

4. How did you gird and protect yourself against this
   ever happening again? (Gottman, 1999, pp. 57–58)

Gottman offers these questions as a way of strengthening the
relationship between partners in a marriage. Because his research
makes it clear that the absence of this sort of in-depth understanding
of a spouse's experiences is a cause of marital discord, partners seeking
to forge a stronger relationship are encouraged to take time to explore
these matters.

Gottman's research also highlights the very clear consequences of
troubled, poor relationships between partners. He presents six signs
that he uses to predict divorce, and one of them has measurable
physiological symptoms. He calls it *flooding,* and it's the physical
sensation that partners feel in a troubled marriage when faced with

expressions of criticism or contempt by one's partner. Gottman explains the phenomenon this way:

> Recurring episodes of flooding lead to divorce for two reasons. First, they signal that at least one partner feels severe emotional distress when dealing with the other. Second, the physical sensations of feeling flooded—the increased heart rate, sweating and so on—make it virtually impossible to have a productive, problem-solving discussion. When your body goes into overdrive during an argument, it is responding to a very primitive alarm system we inherited from our prehistoric ancestors. All those distressful reactions . . . occur because on a fundamental level your body perceives your current situation as dangerous. (p. 36)

All this is fascinating for anyone interested understanding what rigorous empirical research can teach us about what makes for a healthy or troubled marriage. But what does any of this really have to do with what's true about race and social change?

Not long after encountering Gottman's work, I served as a teaching assistant for a course at the Kennedy School of Government called "Managing Intractable Conflict," taught by my mentor and friend Hugh O'Doherty. The topic was O'Doherty's area of expertise, because he had grown up Irish Catholic in Northern Ireland during the time of "the Troubles," and his professional experience and academic research was focused on peace building and conflict resolution between Catholics and Protestants in his homeland.

It was during that course that I first encountered the work of Vamik Volkan, a professor of psychiatry at the University of Virginia and founder of UVA's Center for the Study of Mind and Human Interaction. His research involved exploring the psychological dimensions of intractable conflict between ethnic groups such as the Serbs and Croats in Yugoslavia, Hutus and Tutsis in Rwanda, and

Jews and Palestinians in the Middle East. He presents his findings in a book called *Bloodlines* (1998).

I think it's probably safe to say that Gottman and Volkan don't cross paths very often, because the professional networks of marriage researchers and ethnic conflict researchers most likely don't overlap much. But once we take a look at what Volkan found in his research into the causes and dynamics of ethnic conflict, I suspect you might agree that these two might have something to talk about if they ever scheduled time to grab a cup of coffee together.

Over the course of his exploration of ethnic conflict, Volkan relates the story of when former US president Jimmy Carter traveled to Bosnia-Herzegovina in 1994 to attempt to stop the civil war raging at the time between Bosnian Muslims and Bosnian Serbs. Volkan notes that a considerable amount of time and energy at these meetings was devoted to an event that had occurred in 1389—more than six hundred years in the past! He explains that the event was the Battle of Kosovo, when Prince Lazar, a Serbian, clashed with the Ottoman Turkish Sultan, Murat I. It was a brutal battle in which both Lazar and Murat were killed and both armies decimated. The Ottomans had a many more troops in reserve, however, and in the decades after this battle conquered much of Serbia. The Battle of Kosovo, then, was a critical battle that marked the beginning of centuries in which the Ottomans ruled over the Serbs.

It turns that when one studies the dynamics of these kinds of ethnic conflicts, events from the past—sometimes even the very distant past—remain intensely alive in the minds of members of the conflicting groups. Volkan calls them "chosen traumas," and he explains that they influence group identity and intergroup relationships in much the same way that individual trauma influences individual identity and interpersonal relationships. He highlights examples such as the assassinations of John F. Kennedy and Martin Luther King Jr. and the explosion of the space shuttle *Challenger* as examples of such traumas in American life (the book was published in 1998, several years before the events of September 11, 2001, which surely merit being mentioned on such a list). Events such as these have the potential to remain a potent, emotionally charged dimension of group identity for generations or even centuries.

The same goes for positive events, which Volkan (1998) explains as follows:

> The mental representation of a historical event that induces feelings of success and triumph, what I call a "chosen glory," can bring members of a large group together . . . Chosen glories are reactivated as a way to bolster a group's self-esteem. Like chosen traumas, they become heavily mythologized over time. The Jews remember the legendary story of the Maccabees, who restored the defiled Temple of Jerusalem and lifted the spirits of an oppressed group, and the British remember the Battle of Britain, in which the Royal Air Force successfully held Hitler's forces at bay. (p. 81)

Volkan's research suggests that these traumas and glories play a vital role in the identity of various ethnic and national groups. When these traumas and glories are honored and understood by other groups, peaceful coexistence is possible. However, when these historic experiences of pain or joy are not recognized, members of a group experience themselves as fundamentally unsafe in the present moment. When this happens, a phenomenon that Volkan (1998) calls a "time collapse" may appear. He explains this as follows:

> The interpretations, fantasies, and feelings about a past shared trauma commingle with those pertaining to a current situation. Under the influence of a time collapse, people may intellectually separate the past events from the present one, but emotionally the two events are merged. (p. 35)

We saw exactly this phenomenon unfold during all three Separation Exercises, when the experience of oppression in the current moment evoked memories of historic events such as slavery, the Holocaust, and other examples of ancestral oppression. Although nobody claimed that the exercise *was* slavery or the Holocaust, their responses suggest that there was a merging of the emotional experience in the present moment with the experience of trauma experienced by the group decades—even centuries—ago.

There are a few important implications to this analysis. First, I have endeavored to make the case that human social systems are organized according to the logic of fractals, meaning that similar relational dynamics reappear across multiple scales. Here, we find compelling evidence to support this theory. Both Gottman and Volkan are researchers whose work presents findings grounded solidly in data gathered over the course of years of investigation. It is difficult to dispute that although they have turned their attention to vastly different scales of human interaction, they have discovered similar dynamics. Whether you are seeking to find out what's true about marriage or what's true about ethnic group relations, you discover that these kinds of historic traumas and glories play a key role in how those relationships unfold.

It's important to highlight that the mere presence of traumas or glories does not, in itself, cause conflict. Rather, it is how those traumas or glories are treated in the context of relationship that has the potential to lead to conflict. At both the interpersonal and intergroup levels, when chosen traumas and glories are understood, respected, and honored, strong and positive relationships are possible. When chosen traumas and glories are ignored, dismissed, or disparaged, an intense emotional response is triggered; Gottman talks about it as "flooding" within the context or marriage, and Volkan talks about it as "time collapse" in the context of ethnic conflict. In both scales of analysis, it's clear that when an individual or group encounters an "other" who dismisses or ignores a trauma or glory, that individual or group is likely to respond viscerally, as though they are physically unsafe in the manner related to whatever caused the original trauma. After all, if some "other" does not recognize and validate one's own trauma, there is reason to suspect that person might be liable to perpetrate something similar soon or in the future.

Here was an insight from my scientific inquiry that brought a whole new level of consciousness to my own personal journey of awakening about what's true about race and social change. I have already discussed how, as a young adult, I was unable to perceive the systemic nature of racial privilege and oppression because I could find no evidence of the impact of such a system on my own life. With this understanding of how historic traumas and glories work at the interpersonal and intergroup scales of organization, I see now that stating this out loud in the presence of a person of color would not be experienced as merely an intellectual oversight or academic debate; it represents a fundamental dismissal and denial of trauma in that person's life as an individual (possibly) and in the historic experience of that person's group (certainly).

I see now, in a way I did not before, how the lack of the fifth discipline—that is, system thinking—in those with White privilege can evoke a sense of anger, fear, vulnerability, and experience of not being truly seen or understood in people of color. It provides a whole new way to think about the sort of emotional volatility we saw in the response to the killings of Black and Brown men in places such as Ferguson, St. Paul, and Baton Rouge. Here, then, is an insight into what's true about race and social change in America. Year after year, decade after decade, privileged Americans who are blind to the workings of the system create experiences of fear, anger, and alienation in people of color. And in the absence of the achievement of a higher consciousness around how all this works, the cycle is likely to repeat endlessly, with generation after generation stuck in the same painful cycle.

Of course, this need not be the case. With a higher level of consciousness about these matters, we have the ability—and I would strongly argue the responsibility—to begin making more informed, intentional, and wiser choices that begin to produce different dynamics. After all, Gottman's book is testament to the fact that with greater awareness and intentionality, married couples can have the kinds of conversations that strengthen their connection and reduce the likelihood of one of the partners feeling unseen or misunderstood by the other. Similarly, history is full of examples of nations taking related steps to produce the same relational benefits at the intergroup level.

Surely one of the most notable examples is South Africa, which emerged from decades of brutal apartheid and embarked on a process of truth and reconciliation, in which the trauma of the apartheid era was directly addressed and confronted in a cathartic public process that took years to unfold. Although no such process is perfect, none can dispute that it shows a clear intention to directly confront—and therefore heal—historical traumas. Rwanda is another example of a nation that chose a path of truth and reconciliation after the bloody, murderous slaughter of ethnic Tutsis by ethnic Hutus. Nations need not be trapped eternally in a cycle of blindness and pain when it comes to these matters; there is a way forward that embraces healing and strengthening of relationships between groups that have histori-cally done great violence to each other.

It is interesting to note that the United States and Canada have a nearly identical history of grave mistreatment of indigenous peoples. Both nations waged wars against these communities, forcibly relo-cated entire indigenous nations to impoverished reservations, and forcibly removed indigenous children from their families in order to place them in boarding schools whose official purpose was to "kill the Indian in order to save the man." The practice continued well into the 20th century. Both countries embraced policies at the national level that were deliberate, systematic efforts to achieve cultural genocide. However, the choices in how to deal with this history could not be more different.

In 2008, Canada launched a Truth and Reconciliation campaign dedicated to fully confronting this dark history. A website devoted to the initiative prominently displays the following statement: "Reconciliation is about forging and maintaining respectful relationships. There are no shortcuts." The process lasted seven years, and its final report was recently released in 2016. No similar effort has been made in the United States. If you were a Native American or member of an indigenous tribe, which country would you rather live in?

The fact is that although we can do nothing to change the past, we do have a choice about how courageous and compassionate we are in seeking to confront, transform, and heal the pain of historical traumas. Once we achieve a higher consciousness about how all this works, it becomes clear that the choice is to either confront and heal the past or endure an endless cycle of ignorance and suffering in which the pain of the past is evoked constantly for some groups, generation after generation.

This insight leads to our second question about systems of privilege and oppression. Who's in charge? Who is directing the action and pulling the strings? To whom do we look to bring about change?

Who's in Charge? Understanding Individual Power, Responsibility, and Influence in the System

These questions are important and strategic. Once we know who's in charge, we can figure out the leverage points for creating change. We know whom to protest, whom to pressure, whom to rant against, whom to demonize, whom to co-opt, whom to flatter. After all, these systems don't just organize themselves. Right?

Once again, within the context of the Separation Exercises, answering this question is fairly straightforward. The program directors designed the initial conditions of the systems and set the rules. Then, with the assistance of the staff members, they enforced the rules. Essentially, they embody the beliefs and forces that serve to preserve a segregated, hierarchical, and unjust status quo. As far as the participants are concerned, they just showed up for breakfast and suddenly found themselves thrust into an experience they did not choose or understand.

Within the context of these exercises, we can definitively state that the White males at the top of the system were not in charge of these systems. They were no more responsible than any other group for creating, enforcing, and maintaining the system that everyone found themselves immersed in that morning. Similar to everyone else, they were basically just following the rules, although the new status quo meant that they spent their time enjoying privileges such as playing Frisbee or watching a movie while other participants cleaned floors or washed dishes.

Within the context of these educational simulations, it is clear that having privilege and actively enforcing segregation and discrimination were two separate things. Although it's true that the White males went a long time without challenging the system, that same critique can be made of all the groups in the system. In other words, in these simulations, the unjust, hierarchical, segregated status quo endured not because of the active efforts of the group at the top but because of the fact that everyone at every level of the system obeyed the rules—enforced by the staff members—that served to preserve the status quo. Indeed, within the context of the Separation Exercises, it was clear that anyone at any level had the power to potentially transform the system.

How should we understand the relationship between the truth of these matters in the Separation Exercises and the truth of these matters in the real world? After all, in the real world, there are billionaires, super PACs, lobbyists, CEOs, and politicians pulling the strings. In the real world, it's naive to suggest those with the most privilege are not in charge of the system, right?

When it comes to matters of race and social change, maybe not. I'm aware that this is a sensitive point. We live in a moment of extreme economic inequality, in which a small handful of the ultra-wealthy control as much wealth as 75% or more of the rest of the population, and rigorous studies have proven that wealthy interests have an outsized influence on American policy. If racial discrimination and systemic injustices exist today, it's their fault, right?

Based on this research, I would argue that this analysis of the situation is problematically simplistic. I'm not suggesting that extreme economic inequality doesn't exist or doesn't matter, and I'm not making a naive assertion that money doesn't influence politics or that everyone in the system has the same ability to create change. I am saying that there is a difference between having power within the system and being able to control the system, and we need to be aware of the difference.

I am conscious of the fact that I am a middle class White male making an argument that privileged White people are not really in charge of creating these unjust systems. Has my own privilege made me blind to the truth? Or am I just subconsciously reaching for an analysis that serves to reduce my own sense of guilt? Maybe there is some of that going on. But maybe not. Over the course of my years of studying the field of complex systems, the central insight that kept surfacing again and again and again was how these systems challenge our understanding of who is in charge and who brings about order and change. If we want to understand what is true about race and social change, then we must avoid the conceptual trap of equating power and privilege with control over the system.

It's a perspective shared powerfully by Peter Senge early on in his book *The Fifth Discipline* (1990). In the introduction, Senge makes a case for understanding how the structure of whole systems influences the behaviors of individuals immersed in those systems. Once again, we encounter a perspective that is so relevant to our discussion here that it merits being cited at some length. Senge offers his own thoughts interspersed with insights from other authors, including an extended quotation from Leo Tolstoy's *War and Peace*. Here's how Senge makes the case:

> The systems perspective tells us that we must look beyond individual mistakes or bad luck to understand important problems. We must look beyond personalities and events. We must look into the underlying structures which shape individual actions and create the conditions where types of events become likely. As Donella Meadows expresses it:
>
>> A truly profound and different insight is the way you begin to see that the system causes its own behavior.
>
> The same sentiment was expressed over a hundred years ago by a systems thinker of an earlier vintage. Two thirds of the way through *War and Peace*, Leo Tolstoy breaks off from his narrative about the history of Napoleon and czarist Russia to contemplate why historians, in general, are unable to explain very much:
>
>> The first fifteen years of the nineteenth century present the spectacle of an extraordinary movement of millions of men. Men leave their habitual pursuits; rush from one side of Europe to the other; plunder, slaughter one another, triumph and despair; and the whole current of life is transformed and presents a quickened activity, first moving at a growing speed, and then slowly slackening again. What was the cause of that activity, or from what laws did it arise? asked the human intellect.
>>
>> The historians, in reply to that inquiry, lay before us the sayings and doings of some dozens of men in one of the buildings in the city of Paris, summing up

those doings and sayings by one word—revolution. Then they give us a detailed biography of Napoleon, and of certain persons favorably or hostilely disposed to him; talk of the influence of some of these persons upon others, and then say that this it is to which the activity is due; and these are its laws.

But, the human intellect not only refused to believe in that explanation, but flatly declares that the method of explanation is not a correct one . . . The sum of men's individual wills produced both the revolution and Napoleon; and only the sum of those wills endured them and then destroyed them.

"But whenever there have been wars, there have been great military leaders; whenever there have been revolutions in states, there have been great men," says history. "Whenever there have been great military leaders there have, indeed been wars," replies human reason; "but that does not prove that the generals were the cause of the wars, and that the factors leading to warfare can be found in the personal activity of one man . . ."

Tolstoy argues that only in trying to understand underlying "laws of history," his own synonym for what we now call systemic structures, lies any hope for deeper understanding:

For the investigation of the laws of history, we must completely change the subject of observations, must let kings and ministers and generals alone, and study the homogeneous, infinitesimal elements by which the masses are led. No one can say how far

it has been given to man to advance in that direction in understanding the laws of history. But it is
obvious that only in that direction lies any possibility of discovering historical laws; and that the
human intellect has hitherto not devoted to that
method of research one millionth part of the energy
that historians have put into the description of
the doings of various kings, ministers, and generals.
(pp. 42–44)

It's a powerful quotation that compels us to question our belief—
so often unchallenged—that some small cabal of individuals with
power and privilege are fundamentally in control of the systems in
which we are immersed. With this Tolstoy quote, Senge invites us to
consider the possibility that perhaps those few men in Paris are
merely responding to systemic forces that emerge from the actions of
millions of individuals. Senge continues:

The nature of structure in human systems is subtle
because *we* are part of the structure. This means that
we often have the power to alter structures within which
we are operating.
However, more often than not, we do not perceive
that power. In fact, we usually don't see the structures at
play much at all. Rather, *we just find ourselves feeling
compelled to act in certain ways*. [Italics his] (p. 44)

A similar point is made in a context that is more current and more
topical in Ta-Nehisi Coates's *Between the World and Me* (2015). In
the book, he relates the true story of how a friend from his days at
Howard University, Prince Jones, was killed by a Black police officer
in the predominantly Black Maryland suburb of Prince George's
County. Prince had been a deeply religious Christian, extremely

ethical, and high achieving. He was unarmed and was walking into the house of his pregnant fiancé when he was shot and killed by a police officer with a history of unethical and violent conduct. After an investigation, the officer was not indicted and was soon back on the job. In his response, Coates (2015) invites us to think about the true dynamics of power and responsibility that lay behind these events:

> The need to forgive the officer would not have moved me, because even then, in some inchoate form, I knew that Prince was not killed by a single officer so much as he was murdered by his country and all the fears that have marked it from birth.
>
> At this moment, the phrase "police reform" has come into vogue, and the actions of our publicly appointed guardians have attracted attention presidential and pedestrian. You may have heard the talk of diversity, sensitivity training, and body cameras. These are all fine and applicable, but they understate the task and allow the citizens of this country to pretend that there is a real distance between their own attitudes and those of the ones appointed to protect them. The truth is that the police reflect America in all of its will and fear, and whatever we might make of this country's criminal justice policy, it cannot be said that it was imposed by a repressive minority. The abuses that have followed from these policies—the sprawling carceral state, the random detention of Black people, the torture of suspects—are the product of democratic will. And so to challenge the police is to challenge the American people who send them into the ghettos armed with the same self-generated fears that compelled the people who think they are White to flee the cities and into the Dream. (pp. 78–79)

In any given situation there are clear power structures and lines of responsibility. In this case, this specific police officer was an employee of the state, charged with protecting and defending the citizens. He had a supervisor, and his supervisor had a supervisor, and so on, and all of them were ostensibly constrained by the laws of the state and the laws of the nation. But Coates is making the same argument that Tolstoy made and that Senge highlighted. Is it really accurate to say that the police chief in Prince George's Country was in charge of the state of race relations that—at the deepest level— resulted in the death of Prince Jones? The governor? The judges and lawyers involved in the case? The US president? Or does this "understate the task," as Coates phrases it?

As we discussed previously, this question of who's in charge is important and strategic. If we can understand who wields the power, then we can determine the greatest leverage points for change. If people with power create the system, than we need to focus on confronting those with power. If, however, the system creates those with power, then we need to focus on awakening to the true nature of that system and our own involvement in it if we want to get to the root of the challenge.

For those who might suggest that this focus on the system is academic and philosophical and naively disconnected from the work of creating real-world change, consider this perspective from Nelson Mandela (2013) soon after his release from prison. After 27 years in jail, he had plenty of time to think deeply about the root causes of injustice, and he emerged with this insight:

> I was asked as well about the fears of Whites. I knew that people expected me to harbor anger towards Whites. But I had none. In prison, my anger towards Whites decreased, but my hatred for the system grew. I wanted South Africa to see that I loved even my enemies while I hated the system that turned us against one another. (p. 568)

The research presented in this book—and the complex systems perspective in which it is grounded—aligns with Mandela's understanding of circumstances. We are challenged to honor the truth that, in a complex living system, it does not make sense to ask, "Who's in charge?" *No one is charge*. Individuals at all scales of fractal organization are working mightily to exercise influence, but living systems are not machines, and they do not always simply do as they are told. Instead, the world in which we find ourselves every day reflects the emergent properties that manifest from millions of autonomous agents—each of us—with a way of being that calls forth an entire world.

When we understand this truth, we must recognize that the question of "Who's in charge?" is perhaps not the most useful question to ask. Instead, we might take seriously Gandhi's assertion that "We must be the change we wish to see in the world." What insights might we gain by asking *"What world am I calling forth right now at the scales I most directly influence with my own way of being?"* Whether we are influencing the dynamics of our family, our organization, our community, our nation, or our world, this research challenges us to recognize that we are calling forth and cocreating systems and structures that are direct manifestations of our own innermost ways of being. We must recognize that if we spend all of our time, energy, and attention looking outside of ourselves, either trying to influence those with power or support those at the margins, then we are ignoring the vital work of looking inward and trying to deliberately, intentionally cultivate a way of being that calls forth the type of world that we hope to see manifest at larger scales (i.e., at higher levels of the fractal).

It's helpful here to revisit the cellular automata concept we encountered in our exploration of complex systems in Chapter 3. As you'll recall, the cellular automata work involved creating computer simulations composed of vast grids in which each individual square on the grid is an individual agent that is influenced by the states of surrounding agents. The example we reviewed involved a model in which each agent could be in either a state of calm or a state of panic; researchers could then set parameters along the lines of "If four or more surrounding agents are in a state of panic, then an agent in a state of calm will switch to a state of panic." Researchers would cue the system up in some initial state, press go" and then watch as, over time, system-wide patterns emerged as a result of changes in state unfolding at the individual level.

It goes without saying that the real world is vastly more complex than this simple panic-calm cellular automata simulation, but it suggests a whole way of thinking about how the world works that should inform our thinking about what is true about race and social change. Imagine if, instead of the binary states of calm or panicked, we could run the simulation with states that reflected a bit more of the insights emerging from this research. For example, what if individual agents could alternate between the states of dreaming and awake. Agents in the dreaming state are blind to larger system dynamics and unaware of the way that their own inner state contributes to those larger patterns. Agents who are in the awake state recognize the existence of system-wide dynamics and understand the connection between their inner state and those larger patterns.

Just as in the calm-panic version, we could assume that each agent would be influenced by the state of surrounding agents and that over the course of multiple iterations, we would start to see the appearance of stable, system-wide patterns that emerge as a result of the aggregated ways of being cultivated by vast numbers of individuals. Whatever those global patterns might look like, they would not be the result of direction and control wielded by some central authority.

Of course, the key difference between human beings and computer simulations is that human beings have conscious awareness and choice. Although we may often simply react mindlessly to the states of those around us, we have the potential within us to do otherwise; we can consciously cultivate intentional ways of being within ourselves that enable us to transcend a condition of unthinking reactivity. Indeed, in this vast, interdependent, evolving sea of a multitude of agents, the only thing that any of us have the ability to truly, fully control is our own inner state.

With this insight, I believe, we take an important step closer to understanding what's true about race and social change. At the deepest level, our current state of race relations is not being directed and controlled by some all-powerful cabal, nor is it the "fault" of some elected official or local authority. It is the emergent property of a vast interconnected system in which we are immersed and that we cocreate every day through our own innermost ways of being. Our work, then, is not to figure who to blame and who's at fault; it is to awaken to a higher level of consciousness regarding the existence of the whole system and our place within it. And although none of us can unilaterally control or transform the whole system, we can join the growing number of awakened souls seeking to consciously cocreate conditions in the whole system that are more fully aligned with our espoused values.

This, then, is the key insight from this Separation Exercise research: Our innermost ways of being and the outer world systems and structures in which we are immersed are deeply interconnected and interdependent. It's a dynamic that is difficult to discern at the interpersonal and intergroup levels of analysis, but it pops into view at the highest whole-system level of analysis. Whatever the condition of our inner lives may be, it calls forth and cocreates a world of systems and structures at whatever fractal scale we are influencing at any moment in time. This insight has important implications to which we turn our attention now.

Understanding Inner Ways of Being and Outer Change

When thinking about the inner and outer worlds, we must recognize that they are interdependent but also distinct. The landscape of the outer world comprises systems and structures, laws and policies, data and metrics, statistics and findings. The landscape of the inner world features emotions and meaning, thoughts and feelings, will and purpose—ways of being that may not be objectively measurable but that nevertheless represent powerful forces in the world. The two worlds influence each other in profound ways, but it is not unusual for individuals to focus on one of these worlds and largely ignore the other. This inability to hold both dimensions of experience in our view at the same time can be highly problematic.

Consider, for example, the experience of a privileged White person awakening to a higher level of consciousness regarding the systemic nature of racial privilege and oppression. This is the path I have walked, and I have learned a great deal about the dangers and challenges of this journey of awakening over the course of my own quest. At the start of my journey, I believed that the world was essentially fair and just, that my own good intentions meant I was not contributing in any way to experiences of discrimination or oppression, and that America offered a level playing field in which anyone could achieve his or her goals if he or she just worked hard.

Through a long process of inquiry into the world outside myself, I began to awaken to the truth. Powerful systems of privilege and oppression existed but were largely invisible to me because of my place at the top of those systems. The limits of my own good intentions became clear to me; I discovered that to simply focus on being a good person while not confronting those systems was in fact a choice to perpetuate and reinforce those systems. And America was definitely not a level playing field; I was immersed in systems that privileged me while discriminating against others, and the belief that I was somehow neutral, uninvolved, or outside or beyond these systems was an illusion. A dream.

This encounter with the truth of the outer world had a significant impact on my inner world. Specifically, my awakening was accompanied by what felt like a tidal wave of guilt and shame. The more I learned, the more I realized how blind I had been to the reality of privilege and oppression, and how powerfully my whole way of thinking about the world and my place within it had served to obscure uncomfortable truths. This journey of awakening was not pleasant, and I found myself battling mightily with some very dark emotions as a result of what I was learning. On several occasions, I lost that battle for a while, and in those times I shifted from *grappling with feelings* of guilt and shame to *becoming* guilty and ashamed. The dark emotions became the ground of my being. I was in the world as a guilty person.

But here is the rub. *If our inner lives do not merely reflect the world around us but actively call forth and cocreate the world around us, then we must be conscious of the implications of allowing dark emotions to become the ground of our being.* What world was I creating through being in the world as a guilty person?

Looking back at those times in my life when I allowed the magnitude of the pain and injustices of these systems to overwhelm me, I realize now that this way of being was counterproductive. Just as the panicked agents in the cellular automata simulations would spread their state of panic to nearby agents, I spread my state of guilt to those around me. I was very good at making privileged people in my orbit feel as bad about themselves as I felt about my own self, and I was very focused on letting people of color I encountered know how terrible I felt about my unearned privilege. None of this served to bring about any sort of positive productive change; on the contrary, it was a way of being that actively perpetuated the systems I aspired to transform.

Consider the following example: A dear friend of mine is the founder of a 10-month service learning program that is intensely focused on working with a particular urban community with a deep sense of partnership and equality. The participants on this program live and work in the neighborhood where they serve, and great effort is put into listening carefully to the host community and collaborating on projects identified by the locals as being a genuine priority.

She tells the story of the day when a bus pulled into the neighborhood and a group of unknown White young adults stepped off the bus with paint brushes and paint cans in hand. They proceeded to paint an exterior wall of a building in the community for several hours, and when they were done, they packed up, climbed back on the bus, and drove away. Nobody in the community knew who they were; nobody had asked them to come, and nobody saw any real burning need or genuine value in having that wall painted. It was clear that some group from a more privileged area had decided to "help" the "needy," and they had decided completely on their own that painting that wall was a worthy project. No doubt they felt virtuous about themselves on the ride home, and they believed that they were "doing good" and "making a difference."

But let's take a closer look at what happened here. The privileged painters managed to preserve their ignorance about the authentic experiences and true needs of the local community and drove away having learned nothing about "the other." Their actions were clearly more focused on assuaging their own feelings of guilt than on actually serving the local community in any meaningful way. And the locals were left feeling invisible and used—invisible because their own hopes, fears, needs, strengths, and aspirations were in no way seen by the visitors and used because some busload of strangers had essentially treated their neighborhood as a place to engage in some bizarre practice of poverty tourism and exercise in guilt reduction.

If our innermost way of being calls forth outer world systems and structures, then this is the world we call forth when we are in the world as individuals who are feeling guilty and ashamed: We engage with the world in ways that reinforce our own ignorance and blindness regarding actions that make "the other" feel unseen, uncared for, used, and somehow "less than" as a result of our choices. This is the world called forth by guilt, and it is a world in which dynamics of ignorance, separation, hierarchy, and discrimination are reinforced, not diminished.

People of color face a challenge that is distinct yet related. As the Separation Exercise revealed, although those with privilege struggle with guilt, those who encounter discrimination and oppression struggle with anger. Because of the complexities of intersectionality, many individuals may grapple with some mix of both of these dark emotions. Although anger is an understandable response to systemic injustice, we must again confront the question of what it means to allow the dark emotion of anger to become the ground of one's being. What world do we call forth when are in the world as an angry person?

On December 20, 2014, a 28-year-old man named Ismaaiyl Brinsley shot and killed two on-duty New York City policemen in Brooklyn. The shooting occurred in the weeks after two separate grand juries had decided not to indict the police officers who had killed Eric Garner and Michael Brown. It was an act of revenge motivated by outrage at the fact that across America, police officers could kill unarmed Black men and not be brought to justice. After shooting the two policemen, Brinsley ran into a subway station and shot himself, making this an act of murder-suicide.

This act was the rancid fruit of anger, and it's important to discern clearly the world it called forth. The shooting left police feeling even more justified in viewing young Black men as violent criminals, making acts of police brutality against men of color even more likely in the future. Neither the police nor communities of color emerged with greater clarity regarding the conditions that produced systematic police brutality that focused on people of color, and it is certain that none of those conditions was meaningfully transformed through this act. And three individuals were now dead, adding to the circle of individuals, families, and communities traumatized by racial hatred and violence. This is the world called forth by anger, and it is a world in which the dark forces of separation, hatred, violence, and trauma are repeated, reinforced, and strengthened, not diminished or transformed.

These two examples illuminate the implications of the finding that our innermost ways of being call forth the systems and structures in the world around us. It turns out that, in an important sense, it doesn't matter whether we find ourselves at the top of these systems of privilege and oppression or at the bottom. In either case, if we aspire to transform these systems in positive ways—to leave the world more equal, more just, more compassionate, and more fair than we found it—then there is simply no way to avoid waging a spiritual struggle within the self. We must confront clearly and directly the truth that we are immersed in a vast, terrible, cruel, and unjust system . . . without allowing the dark emotions evoked by that encounter with truth to become the ground of our beings.

Perhaps the best-known example of an individual who successfully waged this inner battle is Nelson Mandela. He spent 27 years—a lifetime, really—imprisoned in a small cell at Robbin's Island for his resistance to the injustices of apartheid in South Africa. He was a man with a wife and family, a man who loved children, a man with an education and a career as a lawyer, and a man whose only "crime" was a belief that he and the other dark-skinned people of South Africa should be treated with dignity and equality as full human beings. I honestly can't imagine the depths of anger, bitterness, hatred, and despair one must feel over the course of nearly three decades in prison. Yet somehow, Mandela did not allow the darkness to become the ground of his being. He did not allow himself to become an angry, hateful person. He famously explained his thinking this way: "As I walked out the door toward the gate that would lead to my freedom, I knew if I didn't leave my bitterness and hatred behind, I'd still be in prison."

Mandela was soon elected the first Black president of South Africa, and in those early months after the end of apartheid, it was clear that the country was poised on a razor's edge. After enduring generations of violence, cruelty, and oppression, would the newly empowered Black citizens of South Africa choose the path of anger, hatred, and revenge or compassion, cooperation, and reconciliation? It could have gone either way.

It is fascinating to apply the findings of this Separation Exercise research to this historical example. If Mandela had emerged from his cell as an angry, bitter, vengeful person, would South African have been able to take the path of cooperation and reconciliation? Based on the findings we've explored here, the answer would be no. Mandela was a remarkable man who somehow managed to endure 27 years of prison while sustaining a way of being grounded in compassion, understanding, and forgiveness. We are invited to consider the truth that it was Mandela's innermost way of being that called forth the possibility of reconciliation, forgiveness, and cooperation among South Africans during his tenure as president. Had he not found this capacity within himself, he would not have been able to call it forth from the people of South Africa.

Mandela is such a towering figure of history that it is easy to believe that we could never be like him. That would be a mistake. It's true that most of us will never be tested as he was, and it's true that most of us will never attain a position of authority at the national level, as he did. But this research suggests that in our own humble ways, we can indeed be like Mandela. We can confront the unjust systems of our age with clarity and courage. We can wage a struggle within ourselves to be in the world as compassionate, courageous, and forgiving souls, even as we experience the dark emotions that are the inevitable and understandable responses to seeing systems of oppression for what they really are. And each of us can—indeed, every day we do—call forth worlds at whatever fractal scale we have a chance to influence. Whether it is at the scale of our group of friends or family, our organization or community, or something even larger, we are creators of worlds. Inspired by Mandela's example, let's support and challenge each other to create worlds of cooperation, reconciliation, compassion, and love at whatever scale is available to us.

Understanding the Self in the System

Given the reality of the interconnectedness of our inner lives with the outer world in which we live, a key personal challenge for each of us is the struggle to understand and manage our inner lives while immersed in a vast, interconnected, unjust system. It's a challenge that I and my fellow researchers directly confronted in the process of completing this research. It was hard—often extremely hard— to observe the events of these Separation Exercises unfold. (I suspect many readers find it hard to even read about them.) Because this research was done as part of a small, diverse research team, it quickly became clear that each member of the team resonated to different events and dynamics. For example, I was powerfully affected by that moment in Exercise 3 when I walked down into that air-conditioned, carpeted room and encountered the White males quietly engrossed in a movie, oblivious to the social upheaval occurring among their peers outside. The recognition that this was a metaphor for my own life experience of race hit me like the proverbial ton of bricks. Also, in multiple exercises, I found it extremely disturbing to watch the Jewish group don armbands marked with a yellow Star of David. Although none of the ancestors of my immediate family perished in the Holocaust, my whole life I have grown up with a strong consciousness of this historical trauma experienced by my own people. It was impossible to watch that moment and not connect with the horror of Jews in concentration camps and gas chambers. Even knowing that the whole thing was just a simulated educational exercise, I felt like I had been hit in the gut seeing adolescent Jews in armbands with yellow stars.

Over the course of the many conversations with my fellow researchers, however, it quickly became clear that they responded with different moments. Derria, a Black female, responded powerfully to the experiences of women and Blacks in these exercises. For Dumisani, a Black male, it was the experiences of Black and Brown men that hit the hardest. It wasn't that each didn't see or respond at all to other injustices; it was clear, though, that certain events—the events that struck closest to our own individual identities—evoked uniquely powerful emotional responses.

Leadership scholar Ronald Heifetz (1994) offers a useful metaphor for understanding how this works. He suggests that it is helpful to think of each of us as being like a stringed instrument; each of us has a unique tuning, and our "strings" inevitably resonate based on what we encounter in our environment. He explains it this way:

> As you go through life, your strings resonate with the environment based on your own particular tuning. Your tuning derives from many different things: your childhood experiences, genetic predispositions, cultural background, gender, and loyal identifications with various current and historical groups. Your tuning in your professional life may also be affected temporarily or long term by what is happening in your personal life.
>
> Those strings vibrate continuously, communicating to those around you who you are, what is important to you, where your sensitivities lie, and how you might be vulnerable. When something happens in your environment, your strings may respond more or less strongly, depending on whether the events stimulate a powerful memory or aspiration. Being caught up in the action of everyday events, you may find it difficult to understand just how your strings are being stimulated at any particular moment. But knowing how the environment is pulling your stings and playing you is critical to making responsive rather than reactive moves.

He continues:

> For many people, the idea that you are always powerfully influenced by your surroundings and history challenges dearly held notions of free will. Yet if you can get on the balcony and observe the forces acting on you, you actually are exercising free will. You have

acknowledged the reality that you are embedded in a web of relationships and are influenced by those relationships, so you create more freedom for yourself to act with understanding of those influences rather than merely react unthinkingly to them. (pp. 195–197)

Heifetz provides a powerful way of understanding the experience of the self in the system. The encounter with the reality of dynamics such as privilege, segregation, and discrimination are almost guaranteed to trigger intense emotional reactions. The challenge, however, is to develop a level of self-awareness and self-control that enables us to honor our inner experiences without getting lost in them. Without this self-awareness and control, we run the risk of being blind and reactive—blind in the sense that we are unable to see or empathize with the experiences of others in the system and reactive in the sense that we just act on our sense of anger, pain, or injustice with no intentionality or mindfulness.

This ability to honor one's own experience while remaining open enough to see and honor the experiences of members of other groups can be challenging. In my own journey, I have experienced many times when dialogues exploring these various intergroup experiences veered into something that can best called "victim Olympics," a sort of twisted game in which members of different groups get very focused on trying to "prove" that their own history of injustice and oppression is somehow more real, more valid, and more painful than that of other groups. This is, somewhat ironically, an attempt to create a kind of segregated, hierarchical social system organized according to righteous validity of suffering.

There is another, wiser path. Instead of allowing these intense emotional reactions to keep us separate, alone, disconnected, and in pain, we can learn how to work with our own suffering in ways that cultivate compassion for others. Thich Nhat Hanh, the Vietnamese

Buddhist monk who was nominated by Martin Luther King Jr. to win a Nobel peace prize, explains that challenge this way:

> I think that we need a "policy" for dealing with our suffering. We do not want to condone it, but we need to find a way to make use of our suffering, for our own good and for the good of others. There has been so much suffering in the twentieth century: two world wars, concentration camps in Europe, the killing fields of Cambodia, refugees from Vietnam, Central America, and elsewhere fleeing their countries with no place to land . . . We need to use the suffering of the twentieth century as compost, so that together we can create flowers for the twenty-first century. (1992, pp. 133–134).

How, then, do we "create flowers for the twenty-first century"? With this question, we turn now to a call to action—actually, a *dual* call to action—for all who aspire to bring about "a more perfect union" that narrows the gap between the daily lives of our citizens and our nation's espoused noble ideals. In this final chapter, we explore what we as individuals and we as a nation can do to bring about positive change, given this understanding of matters of race and social change.

10

The (Dual) Call to Action

For we move—each—in two worlds; the inward of our own
awareness, and an outer of participation in the history of our
time and place.
—JOSEPH CAMPBELL

N ow that we have gained insights into matters of race and social
change, how can we put them to use? What can we do?

Based on the insights that emerged from this research into the interconnected nature of our innermost way of being and the systems and structures in the world around us, I conclude this book with a *dual call to action*. Given the fact that each of us encounters these systems first and foremost at the individual level, the first call to action is *personal*. I offer an invitation to each reader to undertake an inner journey of personal transformation and awakening informed by the insights presented in this book.

Although this kind of inner journey is essential, however, we must recognize that individual transformation alone is not sufficient to address the fullness of the challenges that we confront today. We must honor that the oppressive and discriminatory systems and structures in their current state are the legacy of centuries of injustice, and they operate not only at the interpersonal and organizational levels of fractal organization but also at the national scale, and therefore they require an appropriately large-scale response. Thus, the second element of this dual call to action is *national*. I call on the nation to dramatically expand voluntary national service so that it becomes a universal rite of passage for every young American. As I will explain, this is a public policy approach that responds to many of the deepest insights about race and social change that emerged from this research. It has the potential to meaningfully transform some of the most problematic and intractable systemic injustices at work in our nation today in a manner that is demonstrably impactful, cost-effective, and aligned with our highest ideals. At its best, national service has the potential to integrate personal and national trans-formation, producing a generation of conscious and awake citizens while measurably affecting structural inequalities on a national scale. This book will conclude by making the call—and making the case—for national service in detail.

This dual call to action is deeply influenced by the thinking of Joseph Campbell, whose quote opens this chapter. Campbell was a comparative mythologist who studied the myths told by cultures all around the world since the dawn of human history right up through modern times. One spark of wisdom that emerged from this lifelong quest to understand the deeper truths revealed by myth was the notion captured in this quote:

> For we move—each—in two worlds; the inward of our
> own awareness, and an outer of participation in the
> history of our time and place. (1995, p. 92)

The implication here is that right now, at this very moment—as in every moment—each of us engaged simultaneously in two distinct but related worlds: the *inner world* of our own individual thoughts, emotions, values, beliefs, and overall way of being . . . and the outer world that we encounter when we walk out our door in the morning and that we read about in the daily headlines. It's a profound insight that resonates powerfully with the findings of this research, and it informs this dual call to action in fundamental ways.

The Individual Call to Action: Undertake a Journey of Personal Awakening

Whether we came into the world rich or poor, White, Black, or Brown, lavishly privileged or impoverished and oppressed, we must confront one simple, inescapable truth: We engage first and foremost with the larger system in which we are immersed as an individual, and the only person in this vast web of interdependence that we truly, completely control is ourselves. For this reason, the work of transforming the injustices of the system we inhabit today must begin with work on the self. Each of us must undertake a personal journey of awakening and transformation. Based on my own journey to this point, I offer the following three key challenges: understanding *ubuntu,* striving to access the potential of one's higher self, and undertaking the hero's journey. Here's an explanation of each of these elements.

Understanding Ubuntu

René Descartes is a central figure in Western math and philosophy. During his lifetime in the seventeenth century, he wrestled mightily with some of the deepest questions of philosophy and life. How do we really know anything exists? How can we really even be sure that *we* exist? Eventually he arrived at what he asserted was a statement of ultimate truth: "*I think, therefore I am.*" If we have the sentience to contemplate our own existence, then we must exist. It's a statement intended to have the power of an axiom in math. It stands as a foundational belief that itself has no deeper proof; we accept it as a given on which the entire philosophical worldview of the West is built.

I am no philosopher, and I most surely was not reading Descartes in my youth and seeking to align my life with his worldview. But in hindsight, I recognize the degree to which this bedrock assumption of Western civilization informed my efforts to understand what is true about race and social change. I have mentioned how, in the early years of my quest, I sought the truth by engaging in solitary reflection. I believed that if I searched my own experience deeply enough, and engaged with race and social change as abstract ideas, I could think and reflect my way to the truth.

I realize now that—metaphorically speaking—I was similar to those White males in their comfortable, air-conditioned basement room. I may have found a spot in a quiet corner to think deep thoughts, but I didn't leave the room . . . and didn't think I had to in my quest for truth. After all, we are all independent individuals, and our capacity to think proves our own existence. Right?

I see now how flawed that philosophy is, and I have encountered an alternative that is far closer to the truth. The philosophy comes from the Zulu tribe in South Africa, and it offers a different assumption about the deepest questions we can ask about reality. How do we know we exist? How do we know anything exists? The Zulu response is the concept *ubuntu*, which translates as "I am because you are; my humanity is tied to yours."

Descartes posits that we are each isolated, independent individuals engaged in abstract thought. *Ubuntu* posits that we only exist in relationship; we are immersed in a vast web of life, and this interdependence is the deepest truth there is to our existence. We cannot possibly understand anything—ourselves, others, the world in which we live—outside of relationship.

I see now that my experience with that fishbowl in the Virginia dormitory was an early moment of awakening to this truth. It is folly to try to understand matters of race and social change in the absence of meaningful encounters with the "other" that illuminate the invisible threads of interconnection that bind us all to each other. The fact is that if we seek to awaken to the truth, then we must begin by confronting the foundational assumption of Western philosophy. We do not exist because we think; we exist because we are related to every other human on the planet through our participation in a vast web of interdependence. Only when we embrace this insight can the journey of awakening begin in earnest.

Striving to Access the Potential of One's Higher Self

The philosophy of *ubuntu* advances that "I am because you are; my humanity is tied to yours." Although this statement may seem so clear and simple that it needs no additional exploration, that's not the case. Who, exactly, is the "I" in this assertion that "I am"? It turns out that this question opens up another frontier of inquiry illuminating the path we each must walk on our journey of awakening.

We have arrived at a question about the nature of human development that has been explored in great depth since ancient times by many cultures across the globe. As a student of human development, this question of how to understand the self is a passion of mine, and I've read widely on the subject. It turns out that the question has produced what appears on the surface to be myriad diverse, seemingly unrelated, conceptual frameworks. In a theme that should now be familiar to readers of this book, however, underneath all that seemingly infinite complexity there is a simplicity and unity that can be found across a vast range of ages and cultures.

From ancient India, we encounter a chakra system positing that each human has seven energy centers arranged in a vertical line from the base of the spine up to the top of the head. The lower three—at the base of the spine, in the groin area, and in the solar plexus—relate to our basic biological needs and hungers, as well as the powers those energies enable us to access in our lives. The next two chakras—at the heart level and throat level—relate to our social energies, expressed through emotions and speech. The final two—at the "third eye" point on the forehead, and the "crown" at the top of the skull—relate to our capacity for transcendence. When we develop ourselves so that we become able to access the energy of those highest chakras, we transcend our basic animal needs as well as our social hungers for belonging and connection to other people, and we can develop our capacity to attend to "the whole"—an experience of connection to something much larger than ourselves and our group.

Over centuries, from the ancient Middle East to medieval Europe, Jewish kabbalist mystics developed their own related model of human development. They called their model the Tree of Life, and it presents ten *seferot*—vessels—each representing different energies that are balanced and interconnected in intricate ways. According to this framework, the bottom four *seferot* represent our basic biological and animal energies, the middle three *seferot* represent our social energies, and the highest three *seferot* represent the energies of transcendence, when we are able to operate beyond our animal needs or social concerns and encounter a divine wholeness that is present in the universe.

Moving on from the esoteric mysticism of the ancients, we can turn our attention to the way modern Western social scientists have grappled with the question of human development. In one of the best-known theories from the world of psychology, Abraham Maslow presents a hierarchy of needs, with basic physiological and safety needs at the bottom, psychological needs for belongingness and esteem in the middle, and self-actualization needs—achieving one's full potential—at the top. In the field of neuroscience, Paul MacLean has presented a triune brain model that suggests that from a biological perspective, there are three distinct regions of the brain. The most primitive is the reptilian brain, responsible for basic emotions such as fear and anger that trigger our fight, flight, or freeze response. Wrapped around our reptilian brain we find the mammalian brain, which handles emotions and social interactions. Wrapped around that, we find the most recently developed region of the brain, the primate region or neocortex, which handles the sort of higher-level thinking and executive functioning found only in primates—and which is particularly evolved in humans.

This is, of course, a quick overview and dramatic simplification of several complex approaches to conceptualizing the development of the self. Once you learn to look for it, though, this kind of underlying symmetry across radically different cultures and eras is hard to overlook. Personally, I find the undeniable similarity across all these ways of thinking about human development to be fascinating and deeply meaningful. Across East and West, from ancient times up through modern psychology and neuroscience, individuals who have turned their attention to this question of the nature of individual development have illuminated the same basic hierarchy of potential that each of us may access in our lives.

The key point here as this: When we embrace the notion of *ubuntu*—"I am because you are; my humanity is tied to yours," we must confront the question of which level of "I" is showing up to participate in this vast web of interdependence. Are we "in the world" as little more than animals, focused mostly on our next meal or our biological drive for sexual release? Are we "in the world" as social creatures focused primarily on our needs for belonging and connection? Or are we "in the world" with a focus on transcendence, seeking to see beyond our small group or limited perspective in an effort to encounter and honor "the whole"?

The relevance to the Separation Exercise research is readily apparent. In those exercises, we encounter a constellation of individuals living in an unjust, hierarchical, segregated social system, and we know that most of them hesitate to question or challenge the status quo because of the pressures of obedience and conformity. Many of them are clearly "in the world" as social beings who are primarily focused on social dynamics of obedience, belonging, and connection, and they are understandably hesitant to take actions that might risk those relationships. A compelling case can be made that individuals such as Eduardo in Exercise 3 are operating in the world in a different way; they are willing to risk relationships with peers and with authority out of a sense of connection to and responsibility for the larger whole—both within and without. After some courageous and creative efforts by these early resisters to the status quo, we see the awakening of a growing circle of individuals who have transcended their narrow focus on their own group and are now conscious of the larger whole in which they are immersed.

Once again, it is reasonable to think about this in terms of one individual's innermost way of being rippling out to influence the way of being of others in the system. A few people with a transcendent focus on the whole can awaken higher levels of consciousness in others. Eventually, we see a majority of individuals in the system seeking to consciously transform the system, with a few small pockets of groups choosing to stay segregated and focused on the social concerns of their own small group.

Here, then, is a key element of the personal call to action I'm presenting. When we strive to access the potential of our highest selves, we accept the challenge of achieving a higher consciousness of the whole that transcends ourselves and our own social group and begin taking action in the world from that higher consciousness. Whether we choose to accept this call to personal awakening on the basis of the claims of ancient systems of wisdom or of modern science is not terribly important. What matters is that we are awake to the existence of higher dimensions of potential and consciousness within ourselves, and we are actively seeking to access those higher dimensions so that we may participate in the great web of inter-dependence from that higher, more noble place.

Of course, this assertion raises an obvious question: Assuming we are willing to accept this call to action, exactly how do we achieve that higher potential within ourselves? What is the path by which we access our own highest selves? With that question, we arrive at the third and final element of this personal call to action: We must undertake the hero's journey.

Undertaking the Hero's Journey

Earlier in this chapter, I briefly mentioned Joseph Campbell. It's time now to take a deep dive into the wisdom he uncovered through his life's work, because it is relevant to our effort to understand how we might respond effectively to the insights we've been exploring in this book. Yet again, we'll find ourselves exploring terrain in which we encounter universal wisdom buried beneath seemingly infinite complexity that is at once timelessly ancient and as current as today's headlines.

As previously stated, Campbell was a comparative mythologist who studied myths and stories told by cultures from all around the world. In his seminal, four-volume work *The Masks of God* (1995), he explores in depth what we know about the mythology of prehistoric people; the Orient (the Far East and India); the Occident (the Middle East, Europe, and the Americas); and the modern day. It is a stunningly comprehensive overview of the stories that we—humankind—have been telling ourselves in our quest to understand our world and our place within it over the course of millennia of human history. Remarkably, Campbell discovered a single, underlying story hidden beneath the diversity and complexity of the stories being told across time and place. He called it the *hero's journey*, and as we'll see, its relevance to the findings of this Separation Exercise research is profound.

Campbell (1972) laid out his insights in his best-known book, *The Hero with a Thousand Faces*, first published in 1949. Before presenting the details of what he calls *the hero's journey*, he offers a perspective on how we must understand and interpret myths. Campbell explains that myths should not be read as mere stories either to be accepted as literal truth or dismissed as childish fantasy. Rather, myths must be understood as *metaphors for the psyche*. They may not be true literally, but they illuminate the inner journey we must undertake if we are to awaken to our own highest potential.

In other words, when a myth speaks of the hero slaying a dragon, it is a mistake to understand this, literally, as a flesh-and-blood person confronting a flesh-and-blood creature. Rather, the hero is a metaphor for the higher potential that exists within each of us, and the dragon is a metaphor for dark human emotions such as greed (hording of gold), anger (breathing fire), and disconnection (living life encased in indestructible armor that allows for no vulnerability). Read in this way, "slaying the dragon" is neither a literal event nor a childish fantasy; rather, it is a metaphor illuminating a journey of personal transformation. If we are to access our own highest potential, then we must confront the dark emotions within ourselves. Read in this way, myths open up to a treasure trove of guidance, wisdom, and insight that is at once timelessly ancient and utterly modern.

In *The Hero with a Thousand Faces*, Campbell illuminates what he calls *the monomyth*—the one myth underlying all the myths of the world. Once again, we need not concern ourselves with the full complexity of his work, which could fill volumes. We need only grasp the idea in its simplest form to illuminate the work we must do when we accept this personal call to action to confront what is true about race and social change.

In its simplest form, the hero's journey has three key stages: Departure, Initiation, and Return. In the Departure stage, we first encounter the hero as an ordinary, unremarkable individual living in an ordinary, uninspiring, or broken world. Perhaps the world is portrayed in drab, colorless or black and white, or as an endless array of identical gray cubicles, or as a world of widespread, mindless obedience and conformity. Then, something significant happens that pulls the hero out of that ordinary world: perhaps she is forced out through tragedy, or he accidentally stumbles on a pathway out, or she intentionally accepts an invitation to undertake a journey. In any case, the hero leaves behind that familiar, ordinary, comfortable world and heads out on an adventure into the unknown.

In the Initiation stage, the hero encounters a series of tests and challenges that push him or her past known limits. In confronting these trials, the hero is compelled to confront his or her own dark emotions such as fear, doubt, guilt, despair, and anger. In doing so, the hero discovers hidden depths of strength, courage, wisdom, skill, and insight that he or she has always possessed but had not known how to access. Over the course or this journey, limitations are transcended, fears are overcome, and veils of illusion are pierced.

In the final stage, Return, the hero returns home (whatever home may mean) in possession of entirely new levels of strength, wisdom, insight, and skill. The hero has undertaken the journey required to access and act on one's highest potential. Significantly, the journey can be said to be truly complete only when he or she finds a way to put the gifts of the journey to use in serving of others. Then, the work of serving others represents the beginning of the next cycle of the journey, which continues ever onwards and upwards over the course of a lifetime.

This, then, is the monomyth underlying the infinite diversity of myths told around the world. We encounter it in the stories of Moses, Jesus, Mohammed, and Buddha. We encounter it in the stories of modern moral exemplars such as Martin Luther King Jr., Mahatma Gandhi, and Malala Yousafzai. We encounter it in the stories we tell ourselves again and again and again in our own age: *Star Wars*, *Lord of the Rings*, *The Matrix*, *The Hunger Games*, *Divergent*, and many, many more.

So what does all of this have to do with the Separation Exercise in particular and the work of transforming systemic racism in general?

In a meaningful sense, this Separation Exercise research suggests nothing less than an existential condition of humankind. Each of us is born into the world as part of some group immersed in a vast, hierarchical, complex social system that, in its fullness, is beyond our ability to fully witness or understand. We come of age with an inevitably limited understanding of this system, believing that what we see around us in our home community is reality and the way that those around us understand the world is the truth. Metaphorically speaking, we are similar to the participants in the early stages of the Separation Exercise, making small talk in our own social group as the minutes tick by. What the Separation Exercise illuminates so clearly is the truth that our comfortable, homogenous little corner of the world is just one part of something far greater—a whole system whose workings we scarcely understand. To remain eternally in the comfort and familiarity of our group is to remain blind and ignorant regarding the larger truths of our existence. And should we choose to step outside of our own group, we are immediately confronted with the darkness and injustice of the whole system, as well as the courage, resilience, and wisdom we encounter in others we meet on our journey of awakening.

If that description of the existential human condition posited by these Separation Exercises reminds you of a few movies that you have watched lately, then you are beginning to grasp the relevance of the timeless wisdom of myth. Since the dawn of human history, the stories that we have been telling to understand ourselves and our world have reflected the existential human condition experienced by participants in the Separation Exercises.

There is another key matter where the lessons of the Separation Exercises and the wisdom of mythology merge: There is a connection between the transformation of the self and the transformation of the system. As we learned through this research, the most powerful force preserving the current status quo in these systems is our own fear that keeps us in a state of passive obedience and conformity. Should we summon the courage to confront that fear, we find ourselves stepping beyond the boundaries of our familiar, comfortable corner of the world and suddenly encountering the vast—sometime overwhelming—realities of the larger system.

This larger truth is never pleasant to understand or easy to confront, and all who choose this path of awakening soon find themselves engaged in a mighty struggle within themselves to confront dark forces with courage and clarity . . . without allowing that darkness to become the ground of their own being. For when that happens—when we allow the cruelty, hate, anger, and dehumanization of the system to turn us intro cruel, hateful, angry, dehumanized souls—then we begin calling forth through our way of being the very same darkness we aspire to transform. Only through confronting that darkness while remaining compassionate, empathic, kind, courageous, and dedicated to serving others can we access the innermost way of being that calls forth positive transformation in the world around us.

In *The Hero with a Thousand Faces*, Joseph Campbell (1972) explains it this way:

> The hero adventures out of the land we know into darkness; there he accomplishes his adventure . . . and his return is described as a coming back out of that yonder zone. Nevertheless—and here is a great key to the understanding of myth and symbol—the two kingdoms are actually one. The realm of the gods is a forgotten dimension of the world we know. And the exploration of that world, either willingly or unwillingly, is the whole sense of the deed of the hero. (p. 217)

According to Campbell, myths tell us that the outer world systems in which we are immersed and our innermost ways of being that are transformed when we undertake the hero's journey are actually one and the same. The notion that outer and inner—the "two kingdoms"—are separate is an illusion that falls away at some point in the journey. When we turn inward to confront dark emotions such as fear, guilt, or anger, we are actually grappling with the emotions that outer-world systems and structures evoke within the self. When we transcend those forces within the self, we find our consciousness of the world in which we are immersed has been transformed. We not only see the world differently but also we begin calling forth and cocreating different structures in the world around us.

Consider the following examples of myths, both ancient and modern:

> Moses lives a life of privilege in the pharaoh's court in Egypt. Aware of his Jewish heritage, he has an awakening one day as he watches an Egyptian soldier beat a Jewish slave. In a fit of anger, he kills the soldier and must flee the life of privilege he has always known. After a mystical experience in the dessert,

he accepts the call to confront the oppressive power structure of his era in an attempt to free the enslaved Jews. With the help of God he succeeds, and spends his days seeking to serve the freed Jewish people as their leader.

Siddhartha Gautama—the Buddha—leaves his life of privilege in a royal palace in search of truth; on his journey he is forced to confront dark energies within himself (lust for sex, craving for power); through overcoming those inner forces, he attains enlightenment and dedicates the rest of his life to serving others through sharing his hard-earned wisdom.

Luke Skywalker is living a dull and uninspiring life on a remote dessert planet, until he discovers he is part of an ancient lineage of warriors. He joins a diverse interplanetary movement dedicated to confronting an empire seeking to dominate and oppress the galaxy; on the way, he must struggle to not let the dark emotions of fear, anger, guilt, and hatred evoked by the journey overwhelm him, lest he become an agent of the dark side himself. He successfully confronts the darkness within and without, and dedicates himself to teaching a new generation of Jedi.

The list of hero's journeys could go on and on and on, and my purpose here is not to present a lesson in religion, literature, or screenwriting. Neither is it to be irreverent or disrespectful. Rather, I seek to once again highlight the remarkable simplicity that exists beneath a diversity of stories told across cultures and times. Once we know what to look for, it becomes very clear that we have been telling ourselves the same story for millennia, and its ubiquity across cultures and endurance across centuries suggests that it must be grounded in some profound understanding of the human condition and some truly universal insight into the process of human transformation.

Significantly, it's a story that resonates powerfully with the understanding of the human experience inherent in these Separation Exercises. For the participants in these exercises, it was possible to choose the path of unquestioning obedience and conformity, engaging only with others who, for the most part, look and think the same way. The alternative was to step out of that comfortable place to confront the reality of the injustices of the larger system. The challenge then is to work for a world that is more fair and just for all, without allowing dark emotions such as anger or fear to become the ground of one's being. Rather, we must harness and direct those emotions productively toward service to others.

Of course, at some point we must move from this discussion of the wisdom of myth to matters far more concrete and practical. Exactly how do we undertake our own personal hero's journey? The answers are simple to state but often not so simple to do:

Step out of your comfort zone. Connect across boundaries. Embrace curiosity and courage over fear and conformity. Dethrone the self from the center of the universe and awaken to a higher consciousness of the self as positioned somewhere in a vast system engaged in the process of developing toward complexity.

This is the inner work. What this may look like in terms of concrete actions in the outer world is far too infinitely variable to pin down here. For some White readers with privilege, the journey may begin with something as simple as striking up a conversation with a person of color; journeys of transformational awakening must begin with this choice—however modest—to build relationships beyond the borders of one's familiar, comfortable social group. Other readers of all backgrounds may already have spent years engaged in learning and activism related to matters of racial justice, and for them "stepping out of the comfort zone" might mean attending a training or educational experience exploring matters of race and social change, participating in a protest against an act of injustice, or perhaps running for political office. The possibilities of specific individual actions are infinite and are inevitably grounded in our own experiences, passions, gifts, history, and sense of mission and calling.

Ultimately, the hero's journey is about intentionally pursuing a deeper awareness and higher consciousness of the inviolable whole that is our nation, and doing what we can to narrow the gap between America's noble values and her painfully imperfect current reality. We must take this journey while holding the sort of paradox that is so central to understanding the workings of whole systems: On the one hand, anything that we do is an almost comically insignificant act in a vast system whose scale and complexity transcends anything we can fully understand. On the other hand, everything we do calls forth and cocreates an entire world at whatever fractal scale of organization that we influence most directly, and whatever actions we take and consciousness we cultivate is connected to every other being in the web of interdependent life on this planet.

Our own personal journey is utterly insignificant. Our own journey can change the world. Both of those statements are true at the same time. Our choice is to either take the journey or live our lives constrained by fear, conformity, and ignorance.

Individual action, however, is not enough. Given the depth of our disconnection from each other, the systemic barriers that keep us apart, and the long and painful history of injustice and trauma influencing our communal life right now, we shouldn't and can't just hope that a critical mass of citizens will self-organize an effective, sustainable, large-scale response to these structural challenges. As a nation, we must make a concerted and systematic effort to make that opportunity to connect across boundaries an essentially universal rite of passage on every America's journey to adulthood. Which brings us to the second element of this dual call to action: a call to dramatically expand participation in national service.

The National Call to Action: Voluntary National Service as a Civic Rite of Passage

When you help, you see life as weak. When you fix, you see life as broken. When you serve, you see life as whole.
                                                    —RACHEL NAOMI REMEN

Let me begin this undertaking on a note of sincere humility. In the pages ahead I will offer an impassioned argument for dramatically expanding opportunities for voluntary national service in this country. Before presenting the reasons why I believe this would represent a powerful and effective response to some of our nation's most pressing challenges, I'll begin by noting that this is in no way the only useful productive, effective approach to creating positive change. To understand the pervasive impact of systems of injustice—and the logic of fractals underlying social dynamics—is to recognize that opportunities to promote racial healing and equality are quite literally everywhere.

Parents can have important conversations in their families; employees can do invaluable work in their organizations, and volunteers and elected officials can do meaningful work in their communities. Artists, businesspeople, students, medical professionals, activists, technology experts, entrepreneurs, writers, comedians, academics, social workers, friends, family, and individuals of every age, race, nationality, creed, gender, sexual orientation, and background can and currently are doing vital work to create change across our nation. In making the case for national service, I do not intend to diminish or dismiss the myriad pathways that caring and compassionate individuals choose in their own quests to bring about greater racial equity and healing.

That being said, I believe that national service is an idea with a unique ability to have an impact on a large scale. As I will argue, it represents a logical next step for a whole system that has evolved to the level of complexity that we find ourselves immersed in in the real world today.

As a way into understanding the full transformational potential of the idea of national service, I invite you to reflect on the following question: *What are your thoughts about high school?* Perhaps the question evokes memories of good friends and joy-filled years of success and popularity. Perhaps it evokes memories of academic frustrations, social awkwardness, and adolescent angst. Perhaps you dropped out; perhaps high school is your current reality. Whatever your thoughts may be, the key point is that all of us have thoughts about high school; it's an essentially universal life experience, and there is near-unanimous agreement that if you don't complete high school—or some equivalent academic experience—you have missed a crucial rite of passage on the journey to adulthood and are almost definitely not going to be fully prepared to compete and thrive in the modern economy.

This was not always the case. Up through the nineteenth century, high schools were rare, and most Americans ended their formal education after seventh grade, when they began working full time in the agrarian economy. At the dawn of the twentieth century, however, two trends inspired a movement to dramatically expand high school education. The first was the transition to the industrial economy and the related demand for a more educated and skilled workforce. The second was a growing unease with the vast social inequalities of the age; this was a moment when a small number of captains of industry had accumulated vast wealth while the majority of Americans were barely getting by. The high school movement sought to promote economic growth and greater economic equality.

In his book *Our Kids: The American Dream in Crisis*, Harvard sociologist Robert D. Putnam (2015) notes that the percentage of young people graduating from high school rose dramatically over the course of the twentieth century, from 6% at the beginning of the century to 80% by 1970 (p. 183). He notes that according to several leading economic analysts of this movement, it was "the seminal force behind both economic growth and socioeconomic equality in America during the twentieth century" (p. 160).

Here, in the early years of the twenty-first century, we confront a surprisingly similar set of challenges, including a new era of vast economic inequality and a growing recognition that America's economic competitiveness in the information economy depends on having an even more highly educated workforce. We're also confronting an era of bitter divisiveness that is corrosive to our sense of shared national purpose and that threatens to destroy the fabric of our civic connectedness.

As I have already said, important work can be done to address these matters in our families, communities, and organizations. But big challenges demand big solutions. Making a year of national service a universal civic rite of passage—as much an integral part of the journey to adulthood as high school is today—can be that big solution. It is a single policy initiative with the potential to renew our democracy, dismantle the legacy of generations of systemic injustice and discrimination, promote racial understanding and reconciliation, develop personal responsibility and an ethic of service, and usher every young American across the threshold of adulthood with a clear sense of one's duties and responsibilities as an American citizen.

The intellectual argument for national service was first laid out by William James in a 1910 essay entitled *The Moral Equivalent of War*. James was a pacifist who believed that in the modern era, war had become so destructive, expensive, and counterproductive that it was clearly something to be avoided at all costs. Yet he recognized that there were elements of the military experience that had value and could be harnessed for peaceful purposes. James believed that "the martial type of character can be bred without war. Strenuous honor and disinterestedness abound everywhere." He argued that the moral equivalent of war would involve engaging young people in a year or more of service focused on civilian challenges; his examples included activities like road-building, tunnel-making, framing skyscrapers and more. Such an experience would serve young people in that they would "get the childishness knocked out of them, and . . . come back into society with healthier sympathies and soberer ideas." Writing back in 1910, he stated, "Individuals, daily more numerous, now feel this civic passion. It is only a question of blowing on the spark until the whole population gets incandescent" (James, 2015).

Today, this is an idea that has already become a reality. Military service remains an option for young men and women eager to serve their country, of course. Over the last several decades, that uniquely courageous path of service has been complemented by civilian service options such as the Peace Corps (an international service program founded in 1961) and VISTA (Volunteers in Service to America—a domestic antipoverty program founded in 1965). More recently, AmeriCorps was founded in 1993 to engage young adults in a wide variety of civilian service experiences, including disaster preparedness and relief, promoting economic opportunity, environmental stewardship, and education. It currently engages approximately 80,000 members a year and will soon graduate its one millionth alumnus.

City Year is a proud member of AmeriCorps, and in my time there I had the opportunity to see the impact national service has on the communities served and on the young people who provide that service. The organization is just one of a vast constellation of organizations that are part of AmeriCorps, but it is of course the organization with which I am most familiar. I describe it's work here as an example of how the institution of national service represents a powerful response to many of the most important challenges of our era.

I have already mentioned that in the twenty-first century it is clear that an advanced degree is increasingly important to thrive in the information economy. In the 2016 presidential campaign, there was a debate about the importance of making higher education more affordable and accessible for all, and I understand the imperative in this economy to have far more high school graduates continue on to college. But there's an angle on this debate that needs to be thoughtfully considered.

Research shows that in many US cities, nearly half of all students who start high school do not graduate, and the vast majority of these students are young people of color (Balfanz, Bridgeland, Fox, DePaoli, Ingram, & Maushard, 2014). Although the reasons for these academic outcomes are complex, there is no debating that the current educational status quo is the legacy of generations of structural discrimination that kept people of color segregated in neighborhoods that provided far fewer resources and opportunity than wealthier White communities.

Research also reveals the interdependent nature of many different systems and structures of inequality (America's Promise, 2016; Sum, Khatiwada, McLaughlin, & Palma, 2009). Young people without a high school degree are a remarkable 63 times more likely to be incarcerated than peers who graduate from a 4-year college. So there is a powerful link between education and incarceration. Compared to peers who graduate high school, they are significantly more likely to live in poverty or be unemployed, and they will earn fully $1 million less over the course of a lifetime than peers with a college degree. So there is a link between educational achievement and economic inequality. High school dropouts are significantly more likely to be in poor health, so there is a link between education and inequality in health outcomes. And all these problematic outcomes represent a significant cost to the nation. The same research notes that every individual high school dropout costs the nation approximate $292,000 in lost tax revenue and social service costs related to health care and incarceration (Sum et al., 2009). Multiply that by the 760,000 individuals currently dropping out every year, and it turns out that these dropouts will cost the nation $2.2 trillion dollars over the course of the next decade.

Imagine what it would mean if we were to find way to provide the right balance of support and challenge that would get those kids on track academically so that they could graduate high school with the skills required to succeed in college. If we could make that happen at scale, we could make some significant progress at addressing systemic inequalities in the areas of education, public health, economics, and criminal justice. If we simply smooth the pathway between the existing institutions of high school and college, however, it's hard to imagine how that would benefit the vast numbers of kids who are failing in our current system. If half of all students in high-needs schools are not graduating from high school, how could we expect them to succeed in college, even if we somehow made that option financially viable?

Here, then, is just one facet of the promise of a vastly expanded national service program. If we were to harness the talent, energy, and idealism of great numbers of young adults and deploy all that human capital strategically to address this kind of critical civic challenge, then we could transform instead of reinforce today's structural inequalities. Universal national service has the potential to be to the twenty-first century what universal high school was to the twentieth: a newly universal civic rite of passage, a great civic equalizer, an engine of positive social change, and a driver of economic growth that renews our democracy at the same moment it enhances our competitiveness on the global scene.

In making this call to expand national service, I add my voice to a robust movement that has been working to make this vision a reality for decades through work at both the grass roots and the grass tops. Currently, the issue is being championed most vocally by an organization called Service Year Alliance. Their vision—which I endorse completely—is as follows:

> Service Year Alliance is working to make a year of paid, full-time service—a service year—a common expectation and opportunity for all young Americans. A service year before, during, or after college—or as a way to get back on track—gives young people the chance to develop their skills, make an impact on the lives of others, and become the active citizens and leaders our nation needs. Expanding service years has the power to revitalize cities, uplift and educate children at risk, and empower communities struggling with poverty. It can unite the most diverse nation in history, binding people of different backgrounds through common cause. Service Year Alliance is asking nonprofits, higher education institutions,

cities and states, companies and foundations, policy-
makers of both parties, and people of all ages to join
the movement. (Service Year Alliance, 2016)

To be clear, the vision here is that this year of service would be voluntary, not mandatory. Although no one would be compelled against his or her will to serve, the vision is that completing a service year would be so widespread, so culturally encouraged, and so socially expected as a responsibility for every American citizen that it would be nearly universal.

National service has a long history reflecting a strong tradition of bipartisan support in the United States, but that history is beyond the scope of what we need to discuss here. The national service move-ment also includes fairly complex constellation of organizations and initiatives, and again an in-depth presentation of those details is not necessary here. For this discussion, it will suffice to present a highly simplified overview of how it all works.

In the United States, our national service efforts are managed by a federal organization called the Corporation for National and Com-munity Service (CNCS). CNCS oversees AmeriCorps, which is essentially a funding stream of federal dollars. Local nonprofits in every state apply for access to those funds in a competitive process in which the programs with the strongest evidence of impact are awarded 3-year grants. Programs must reapply every 3 years, and if they can't demonstrate effect, their funding may be cut and redir-ected to another more impactful program. It's a structure that ensures that the work on the front lines is being managed by local community organizations, and there is a structure of accountability to ensure that these funds flow to only the most effective programs. A small sample of organizations that engage AmeriCorps members includes Youth-Build, Teach for America, Boys and Girls Club, New York City Coalition Against Hunger, Jumpstart, Communities in Schools, Girl Scouts of the USA, Boy Scouts of the USA, and many, many more.

City Year is one of these organizations, and its work has been focused on the education sector. Its approach has been deeply influenced by the research illuminating the scope, scale, and consequences of our current high school drop-out rates in this country. That research has galvanized a vast movement across the education sector, and for the past 9 years City Year has been focused on demonstrating that young adults engaged in national service have a role to play in responding to this challenge. The organization now partners with school districts to identify the high schools with the highest drop-out rates and then places highly diverse teams of 8 to15 AmeriCorps members in the ninth grade at those schools as well as in the elementary and middle schools that feed students into those high schools.

Significantly, City Year AmeriCorps members serve on highly inclusive teams. Privileged young adults from the suburbs work daily as equals alongside young adults from the community being served, and together they spend the year engaged in intense collaboration focused on effectively serving their students. As with military service, this kind of civilian service opens up a rare space in American civic life in which citizens from all walks of life come together as equals, learning from and with each other over the course of an intense and demanding year of service to the nation.

It's a rigorous, strategic, collaborative, research-focused, and data-driven effort to confront a pressing public problem, and it's getting results. A rigorous evaluation conducted by Policy Studies Associates found that when compared with similar schools, City Year schools were twice as likely to see improvements in English scores and three times as likely to improve proficiency in rates in math. (Meredith & Anderson, 2015). Also in 2016, one of the largest randomized control studies in the history of education research found that the approach City Year was taking along with partner organizations produced a "positive and statistically significant impact on the percentage of students with no early warning indicators—students with better than 85 percent attendance, fewer than three days suspended or expelled, and passing grades in both English/language arts and math" (Corrin, Sepanik, Rosen & Shane, 2016).

Not only does it work but also it's cost effective. A team of City Year AmeriCorps members brings an infusion of human capital to a school, allowing the school to provide a new level of support to large numbers of students in a highly cost effective manner. If a school were to hire a professional to provide academic support, another professional to provide school climate support, and yet another to provide after-school support, the estimated annual cost per student would be $2,280. The cost of having a team of City Year corps members provide all these supports is only $687 per student, and because school district dollars are matched with federal dollars (through AmeriCorps) and private sector dollars (through corporate sponsorships of teams), the actual cost to districts or schools is only $152 per student (City Year, 2013).

It's also cost-effective for the nation as a whole. A recent study found that every dollar invested in national service through Ameri-Corps produces nearly four dollars in benefits (Belfield, 2013). This is a sound and wise investment of federal dollars.

Furthermore, national service delivers a dual benefit. The students being served are not the only ones whose lives are improved; the young adults delivering the service also benefit immensely from the experience. According to a rigorous evalua-tion, when compared with peers who did not serve, young adults who completed a City Year were significantly more likely to vote, more likely to volunteer, more likely to manage volunteers, and reported being more comfortable working with diverse peers (Anderson, Laguarda, & Fabiano, 2007). A rigorous study of Ameri-Corps alumni found that after completing a service year, AmeriCorps alumni reported having high career-oriented soft skills including cultural competency and self-efficacy, were more able to solve problems and persevere in the face of challenges, and felt more connected to their community (Cardazone et al., 2015). Clearly, national service has the potential to simultaneously address pressing public challenges while developing a new generation of engaged, informed, effective, responsible civic leaders.

It's important to note that vast numbers of young people are already eager to serve. For the last few years, America has allocated enough money to support roughly 80,000 participants in Ameri-Corps per year. Yet the interest in serving far outpaces the number of slots available. In 2011 and 2012, for example, more than 500,000 young people each year applied to the program, meaning that nearly one million young people who were ready to dedicate a year of their lives to full-time service to the nation were denied the opportunity (Brown, 2012). That's a whole lot of potential to do good on a national scale that is being left untapped.

In this book, we have highlighted the uniqueness of Separation Exercise 3; it was the only activity that produced an emergent, self-organized movement for nonviolent social change. It is important now to recall how that exercise unfolded. After 2 hours of essentially unchanging stasis, the act of a courageous participant served as a tipping point that triggered a process of rapid, dramatic change that resulted in the emergence of that self-organized movement. We must remember, however, how that exercise ended: the system had reached some kind of ambiguous liminal state. A great many participants had come together to challenge the unjust norms . . . but many other participants had not. At the moment that the exercise was brought to a close, the most egregious injustices of the system had been challenged, and the members of the protest movement were gathered together trying to figure out what to do next. The answer was not at all clear.

Here, then, is why I believe it is necessary to end this book with a *dual* call to action. In the twenty-first century, the undertaking of a personal journey of awakening about matters of race and social change is essential, but it is not enough. The systemic and structural injustices that endure today are incredibly complex and have endured for generations. Any serious effort to measurably, meaningfully transform these systemic national challenges will require large-scale and strategic coordination of vast numbers of citizens engaged in long-term and highly collaborative change efforts. Individual efforts are noble and important, but national service has a unique potential to have an impact on a national scale. Imagine if every future politician, police officer, teacher, entrepreneur, businessperson, artist, activist, and parent began his or her adult life by spending a year working alongside diverse peers in a collective effort to address a pressing public problem. How might that kind of universal civic rite of passage transform our civic life?

Final Thoughts on the Dual Call to Action

I recognize that the two dimensions of this dual call to action may seem disjointed and disconnected to many readers. After all, these personal and national calls to action illuminate dramatically different landscapes and issues. Turning the bright light of our attention inward, we encounter the notion of *ubuntu*, suggesting that all beings are connected via invisible webs of spiritual interdependence. We contemplate the possibility of transcending our base, animal selves and striving for the as-yet untapped upper limits of individual self-actualization. We imagine ourselves embarking on a journey of personal transformation inspired by the lives of Moses, Buddha, Jesus, Gandhi, King, and Yousafzai. If the truth is that each of us travels in two worlds, we are invited to consider that the inner world is a place of spirit, myth, heroism, courage, curiosity, and awakening. It is enchanted.

Turning our attention outward to consider the reality of today's civic challenges, we make an abrupt and jarring shift from the enchanted to the prosaic. Here, we encounter a landscape of government agencies and federal budgets, evaluation and measurement, impact and metrics, accountability and return on investment.

We have entered the realm of the visible, tangible, and measurable, and one would be forgiven for believing that this relatively dry and prosaic realm is utterly disconnected from the world of enchantment within.

According to all the insights we've explored here, that would be a mistake.

In *The Social Animal*, *New York Times* columnist David Brooks (2011) offers a book-length argument that a great many efforts to address pressing public problems in recent decades have been hobbled by a problematically simplistic and limited understanding of the human experience. His perspective is very relevant to our discussion here:

> Over the past generations we have seen big policies yield disappointing results. Since 1983, we've reformed the education system again and again, yet more than a quarter of high-school students drop out, even though all rational incentives tell them not to. We've tried to close the gap between White and Black achievement, but have failed. We've spent a generation enrolling more young people in college without understanding why so many don't graduate.
>
> One could go on: We've tried feebly to reduce widening inequality. We've tried to boost economic mobility. We've tried to stem the tide of children raised in single-parent homes. We've tried to reduce the polarization that marks our politics. We've tried to ameliorate the boom-and-bust cycle of our economies. In recent decades, the world has tried to export capitalism to Russia, plant democracy in the Middle East, and boost development in Africa. And the results of these efforts are mostly disappointing.
>
> These failures have been marked by a single feature: Reliance on an overly simplistic view of human nature.

Many of these policies were based on [a] shallow . . . model of human behavior. Many of the policies were proposed by wonks who are comfortable only with traits and correlations that can be measured and quantified. . . . They were executed by officials that have only the most superficial grasp of what is immovable and bent about human beings. So of course they failed. And they will continue to fail unless the new knowledge about our true makeup is integrated more fully into the world of public policy, unless the enchanted story is told along with the prosaic one. (pp. xiv–xv)

Closing Thought

A sentiment regarding the nature of any true voyage of discovery, attributed to the French novelist Marcel Proust (n.d.), has become widely quoted—actually, misquoted—in our day. In its most frequently cited version, the statement reads as follows:

> The real voyage of discovery consists not in seeking new landscapes, but in having new eyes.

It is a simple, powerful articulation of the experience of a journey of awakening in which we remain in the exact same physical location, yet perceive the whole world in which we are immersed in radically new ways. It turns out, however, that this well-known version is actually a simplification of what Proust actually said in his novel *Remembrances of Things Past*. Given how relevant the actual quote is to the quest for insight that is now coming to an end, I share it here as an appropriate concluding thought. Proust states:

> The only true voyage of discovery . . . would be not to visit strange lands but to possess other eyes, to behold the universe through the eyes of another, of a hundred others, to behold the universes each of them beholds, that each of them is. (Robbins, 2011)

With that insight, we bring this book to a close by returning to the same place we began: with three quotes that, I hope, land at least a little bit differently now than they did when we encountered them on the first pages of this journey of discovery:

"Justice is never given; it is exacted and the struggle must be continuous for freedom is never a final fact, but a continuing evolving process to higher and higher levels of human, social, economic, political and religious relationship."

A. Philip Randolph

"Consciousness precedes being, and not the other way around . . . For this reason, the salvation of this human world lies nowhere else than in the human heart, in the human power to reflect, in human meekness and in human responsibility.

Without a global revolution in the sphere of human consciousness, nothing will change for the better . . . and the catastrophe toward which this world is headed—be it ecological, social, demographic or a general breakdown of civilization—will be unavoidable."

VACLAV HAVEL

"I would not have you descend into your own dream.
I would have you be a conscious citizen of this terrible and
beautiful world."

TA-NEHISI COATES

References

Adams, M., Bell, L. A., & Griffin, P. (1997). *Teaching for diversity and social justice.* New York, NY: Routledge.

Alexander, M. (2012). *The new Jim Crow: Mass incarceration in the age of color-blindness.* New York, NY: The New Press.

Alexander, M. (2014, July). How to dismantle the "New Jim Crow." *Sojourners.* Retrieved from https://sojo.net/magazine/july-2014/how-dismantle-new-jim-crow

America's Promise. (2016). *High school graduation facts: Ending the drop out crisis.* Retrieved May 3, 2016, from http://www.americaspromise.org/high-school-graduation-facts-ending-dropout-crisis#Endnote_16

Anderson, L. M., Laguarda, K. G., & Fabiano, L. (2007). *The City Year alumni studies: Summary of findings.* Washington, DC: Policy Studies Associates. Retrieved from http://www.policystudies.com/_policystudies.com/files/City_Year_Alumni_Studies_Summary.pdf

Asch, S. (1951). Effects of group pressure on the modification and distortion of judgments. In S. Guetzkow (Ed.), *Groups, leadership and men.* Pittsburgh, PA: Carnegie.

Balfanz, R., Bridgeland, J., Fox, J. H., DePaoli, J., Ingram, E., & Maushard, M. (2014, April). *Building a grad nation: Progress and challenge in ending the high school dropout epidemic.* Retrieved April 20, 2016, from http://diplomasnow.org/wp-content/uploads/2014/04/BGN-Report-2014_Full.pdf

Bar-Yam, Y. (1997). *Dynamics of complex systems*. Reading, MA: Perseus Books.

Bar-Yam, Y. (2001). *Introducing complex systems*. Cambridge, MA: New England Complex Systems Institute.

Belfield, C. (2013). *The economic value of national service*. Washington, DC: The Aspen Institute.

Bellafante, G. (2015, Jan. 16). The dark side of "broken windows" policing. *New York Times*. Retrieved from http://www.nytimes.com/2015/01/18/nyregion/the-dark-side-of-broken-windows-policing.html

Bond, R., & Smith, P. (1996). Culture and conformity: A meta-analysis of studies using Asch's (1952b, 1956) line judgement task. *Psychological Bulletin, 119* (1), 111–137.

Brafman, O., & Beckstrom, R. (2008). *The starfish and the spider: The unstoppable power of leaderless organizations*. New York, NY: Portfolio.

Brooks, D. (2011). *The social animal: The hidden sources of love, character, and achievement*. New York, NY: Random House.

Campbell, J. (1972). *The hero with a thousand faces*. Princeton, NJ: Princeton University Press. (Originally published in 1949).

Campbell, J. (1995). *The masks of god: Creative mythology*. New York, NY: Arkana Publishing. (Originally published in 1968).

Cardazone, G., Farrar, A., Frazier, R., . . . Willey, J. (2015). *AmeriCorps alumni outcomes: Summary report*. Burlingame, CA: JBS International.

City Year. (2013). *In school and on track: A plan for transformational impact*. [Prospectus] Boston, MA: Author.

Coates, T. (2015). *Between the world and me*. New York, NY: Speigel & Grau.

Corrin, W., Sepanik, S., Rosen, R., & Shane, A. (2016). Addressing early warning indicators interim impact findings from the investing in innovation (i3) evaluation of diplomas now. Retrieved from http://www.mdrc.org/publication/addressing-early-warning-indicators.

Crenshaw, K. (1991). Mapping the margins: Intersectionality, identity politics, and violence against women of color. *Stanford Law Review, 43* (6), 1241–1299.

Dalai Lama. (1999). *Ethics for the new millennium*. New York, NY: Riverhead Books.

Du Bois, W.E.B. (1999). *The souls of Black folks*. New York, NY: W. W. Norton. (Originally published in 1903).

Faulkner, W. (2012). *Requiem for a nun*. New York: Vintage.

Gladwell, M. (2000). *The tipping point: How little things can make a big difference*. New York, NY: Back Bay Books/Little, Brown, & Co.

Gottman, J., & Silver, N. (1999). *The seven principles for making marriage work: A practical guide from the country's foremost relationship expert*. New York, NY: Harmony Books.

Hanh, T. N. (1992). *Peace is every step: The path of mindfulness in everyday life*. New York, NY: Bantam Books.

Harari, Y. N. (2015). *Sapiens: A brief history of humankind*. New York, NY: Harper.

Heifetz, R. (1994). *Leadership without easy answers*. Cambridge, MA: Belknap Press of Harvard University Press.

Irving, D. (2014). *Waking up white, and finding myself in the story of race*. Cambridge, MA: Elephant Room Press.

James, W. (2015). *The moral equivalent of war*. Obscure Press. (Originally published in 1910).

Kahane, A. (2010). *Power and love: A theory and practice of social change*. San Francisco, CA: Berrett-Koehler.

Kellerman, B. (2012). *The end of leadership*. New York, NY: HarperCollins Business.

Keyes, K., Jr. (1982). *The hundredth monkey.* Camarillo, CA: DeVorss & Company.

Khazei, A. (2010). *Big citizenship: How pragmatic idealism can bring out the best in America.* Philadelphia, PA: Perseus Books.

King, M. L., Jr. (1967). *Where do we go from here?* Delivered at the 11th Annual SCLC Convention. Retrieved December 20, 2015, from http://kingencyclopedia .stanford.edu/

Mandela, N. (2013). *Long walk to freedom.* New York, NY: Back Bay Books.

Mandelbrot, B. (2014). *The fractalist: Memoir of a scientific maverick.* New York, NY: Vintage Books.

Milgram, S. (1974). *Obedience to authority.* New York, NY: Harper & Row.

NCCJ. (2016a). National Conference for Community and Justice home page. Retrieved May 3, 2016, from http://www.nccj.org/

NCCJ. (2016b). Programs (ANYTOWN). National Conference for Community and Justice. Retrieved May 3, 2016, from https://nccj.org/programs-anytown

Palmer, P. (2009). *A hidden wholeness: The journey toward an undivided life.* San Francisco, CA: Jossey-Bass.

Palmer, P. (2011). *Healing the heart of democracy: The courage to create a politics worthy of the human spirit.* San Francisco, CA: Jossey-Bass.

Perry, G. (2013). *Behind the shock machine: The untold story of the notorious Milgram psychology experiments.* New York, NY: The New Press.

Proust, M. (n.d.). BrainyQuote.com. Retrieved November 15, 2016, from https:// www.brainyquote.com/quotes/quotes/m/marcelprou107111.html

Putnam, R. (2015). *Our kids: The American dream in crisis.* New York, NY: Simon & Schuster.

Rilke, R. M. (2013). Letter 4. *Letters to a young poet.* New York, NY: Penguin Classics. (Originally published in 1934; written in 1903).

Robbins, H. (2011, April 8). *Familiar (mis)quotations*. Retrieved December 4, 2015, from https://www.insidehighered.com/views/2011/04/08/robbins

Scharmer, O. (2003). *The blind spot of leadership*. Retrieved December 23, 2015, from http://www.ottoscharmer.com/sites/default/files/2003_TheBlindSpot.pdf

Senge, P. M. (1990). *The fifth discipline*. New York, NY: Doubleday Business.

Service Year Alliance. (2016). *What is a service year?* Retrieved from https://serviceyear.org/about/

Sherif, M., Harvey, O. J., White, B. J., Hood, W. R., & Sherif, C. W. (1961). *Intergroup conflict and cooperation: The Robbers Cave Experiment*. Norman, OK: University of Oklahoma Book Exchange.

Sum, A., Khatiwada, I., McLaughlin, J., & Palma, S. (2009). *The consequences of dropping out of high school: Joblessness and jailing for high school dropouts and the high cost for taxpayers*. Boston, MA: Northeastern University Center for Labor Market Studies. Retrieved May 3, 2016 from http://www.northeastern.edu/clms/wp-content/uploads/The_Consequences

Volkan, V. (1998). *Bloodlines: From ethnic pride to ethnic terrorism*. Boulder, CO: Westview Press.

Waldrop, M. (1992). *Complexity: The emerging science at the edge of order and chaos*. New York, NY: Simon and Schuster.

Wheatley, M. J. (1999). *Leadership and the new science: Discovering order in a chaotic world*. San Francisco, CA: Berrett Koehler.

X, M., & Haley, A. (1992). *The autobiography of Malcolm X*. New York, NY: Ballantine Books.

Zakaria, F. (2008). *The post-American world*. New York, NY: W. W. Norton.

Zimbardo, P., Maslach, C., & Haney, C. (2000). Reflections on the Stanford Prison Experiment: Genesis, transformations, consequences. In T. Blass (Ed.), *Obedience to authority: Current perspectives on the Milgram paradigm (Ch. 11)*. Mahwah, NJ: Lawrence Erlbaum Associates.

Appendix A

Research Methodology Overview

The three Camp Anytown Separation Exercises presented here were all observed between the months of June and November 2004. On every site visit, I was accompanied by at least one (and sometimes two) other researchers who were individuals of color, ensuring that there was diversity within the research team observing these exercises. Together, we observed the staff planning meeting that occurred prior to every Separation Exercise (either the evening before or the morning of the activity), the activity itself, as well as the participant debrief session that immediately followed each activity.

Within 3 days of each site visit, each observer wrote up notes from the observation. I then reviewed all the notes and used them to compose a first draft of the narratives that you'll encounter in the pages ahead. All the researchers then reviewed the draft and provided feedback, and we continued to revise the description of events until all researchers agreed that it accurately reflected the events that they observed at each activity.

As you'll see, the narratives are written in the first-person voice ("I walked into the dining hall . . ."); this was a stylistic decision that was agreed on by all researchers, because early attempts to try present the viewpoints of two or three different researchers complicated the narratives considerably. We agreed to write the narratives as though there was only one observer, while using a review process that ensured that the perspectives of all researchers were accurately represented in the narrative.

In addition to in-person observation by multiple researchers, we also distributed a questionnaire that participants filled out at the conclusion of the debrief session following the exercise. The full text of the questionnaire can be found in Appendix B.

In an effort to preserve the confidentiality of all staff members and participants, all names have been changed, and the locations where the exercises occurred are not revealed.

The following table presents the return rates on questionnaires at each session.

	Exercise 1	Exercise 2	Exercise 3
Total Number of Participants	42	46	50
Number of Returned Questionnaires	23	45	48
Return Rates	55%	98%	96%

In analyzing this data, the research team engaged extensively in a methodology that is known as *grounded theory*. In this method research starts by reviewing the raw data and then developing codes based on themes that emerge from the data. The value of grounded theory is that you do not begin with a hypothesis of what you think will happen or construct a preexisting framework before diving into the data; rather, you start by exploring the data and seek to build a theory based on themes and insights that emerge through deep engagement with that data. The goal is a theory that is powerfully grounded in the data—it accurately reflects what was observed because it was developed from scratch using the raw data.

Working separately, each member of the three-person research team reviewed the raw data from each of the questions on the questionnaire and generated a series of codes related to themes we felt emerged from the data. We then worked together to create a master code list that covered the major themes that emerged from this analysis.

Appendix B

Sample Questionnaire

Name:_____

What group were you placed in?_____

*   *   *

1. Tell your story of what happened during this exercise and how events progressed. Be sure to include the important events that occurred over the course of the exercise.

2. What did it feel like being a member of your group? Why?

3. In your opinion, what was the most important group? Why?

4. Why did you not break the exercise earlier than when you did?

5. How did it feel to break the exercise?

Appendix C

Codes Related to Research Question 1: "How do Individuals Understand Their Involvement in Macro-Level Systemic Dynamics?"

No.	Code Title	Description	Example*
1	*Confusion About What Was Happening*	Lack of clarity regarding the purpose and goals of the exercise	"Well when Thomasina and Drake read the groups off I didn't know what was going on . . ."
2	*Awareness of Privilege Differences*	Recognition that groups received different types of treatment during the course of the exercise	"In the morning we were split into groups . . . We ate our meals separately and were served in an order based on the social power of the groups. The groups also served people if they were Black women, swept if they were Hispanic men and were benefited [or] hurt in other ways depending on the gender race religion of the people."

No.	Code Title	Description	Example*
3	*Fear of Punishment*	Unwillingness to challenge the rules for fear of suffering consequences	"I think when the director told us not to bring up our dishes that's when I felt like we had to strictly follow the rules, and that 'reprimand' kind of stuck with me. I really didn't want to get in trouble."
4	*Matter of Fact*	Responses providing a simple, factual review of important events during the exercise	"We were put into certain groups and told to follow each other when we need to go somewhere. Then, we went to a breakfast, and after we were told to go in the field and stand up. During breakfast my group was told to put away everyone's dishes. Eventually, we got tired of standing up in the field and went to the discussion room to go sit down, then to get beverages, then to the cabin, then stayed in the discussion room and played jump rope and danced."
5	*Symbolic/ Systemic Understanding*	Going beyond a simple description of the exercise to interpret larger systemic or symbolic meanings	"I think what happened was that they were trying to make White people rich and like first class. The spanish be maids and Black girls be clean up people too. And I think that they were trying to make Black males have no job."
6	*Faith in the Process*	Refusing to challenge the exercise out of a belief that	"People cried because they couldn't interact with the people they enjoyed being

No.	Code Title	Description	Example*
		the authorities must have a good reason for what they were doing	with. I felt the same but I know it was an activity."
7	*Oblivious*	Apparently unaware that anything unusual was going on	"It was not until the rebellion increased and actually told us what was happening did I begin to realize that the project we were working on was not the objective."
8	*Grapevine Rebellion*	Suggestion that a collection of small acts led up to a major break in the exercise	"Ibrahim came over and told us that he walked out and we should too. Later when we saw the big bunch of freed people we joined too."
9	*Avoidance*	An unwillingness to recognize what is going on	"I stuck with my group trying to stop thinking what was going on."
10	*The Power of One*	An emphasis on the one person or action that led to a break in the exercise	"Karen was not singing so they made her get up and sing and she was crying and someone took a stand and everyone followed."
11	*Emotional Response*	Focus on emotional experience over the course of the exercise	"Everyone ended up together and happy instead of apart and miserable, aggrevated even afterwards though people felt bad and still mad at themselves and others."

No.	Code Title	Description	Example*
12	*Tension Build-up to Break*	Describing the exercise as the slow increase in tension (anger, frustration) that led to a public breaking of the rules	"Soon after awhile people in our group began to notice discrimination when seeing that we were denied certain privileges and given jobs such as picking up trash . . . When the groups were put to sing the ice broke. The groups couldn't take how the leaders were demanding and harsh . . ."

*Text in this column presents direct quotations from participant questionnaires. Here—and in all subsequent cases in which participant quotes are presented—no effort was made to correct spelling or grammatical errors.

Appendix D

Responses to Question 2: "What did it feel like being a member of your group? Why?"

Exercise 1

White Males	"Awkward. I didn't really want the privileges I was given. I felt undeserving."	"Depressing, because I wanted to follow rules."		
White Females	"There are just no words. I really don't know."	"Uncomfortable because we were served/had our tables cleared by the Black woman group. It was also hard to watch the Jewish group and the Black woman group bake in the hot sun."	"I felt very offended because I am not all White. I'm only 25% Italian . . . I felt like they took one look at me and assumed I'm all White."	
Jewish	"It was uncomfortable . . . not being treated fairly. The badge, which was a Holocaust star, made me feel like less of a person. It made me identify with my			

	ancestry and the segregation of my own people in the past."				"I felt downsized. Lower than others. The only other group I felt equal to was the Black females."
Latinos	"Fun because I like this group."	"I felt like I was appreciated for being my race."	"Bad' cause they was making us clean but good' cause it was fun . . . we was just hanging out."	"Fun because we found a fun thing to do."	
Black Females	"I felt like a slave because we had to put away everyone's dishes. I also felt like a child because everyone had to follow me wherever I went."	"It felt good most of the time when they didn't put me down."	"It was cool being in a group of people that I never got to know before."	"They had us pick up everyone's dishes that's when I started thinking like why do they have all Black females picking up dishes?'"	

Black Males	"It felt the same as any other day because that is who I hang out with. We felt like we was the tightest or closest because we spent so much time together."	"At first it felt good . . . because I was with . . . most of my friends. Later on it got boring because we were lonely. We felt privileged because we didn't have to clean like the others."	"Kind of bad because we went last for everything."	"It was true to put me in that group because of the stereotypes and how we act."
Isolates	"I felt alone because there was no group and I was bored as hell."	"It felt depressing because I was isolated from everything and everyone. It felt horrible because all I wanted to do was TALK!"		

Exercise 2

Whites	"It felt like everyone was looking at us because we were White & we had most of the privileges."	"I was ashamed because we received special attention."	"No variety. . . . kinda boring. . . . We weren't expressing any negative reactions such as anger or frustration."	"misplaced. Because my whole life I've lived in a mixed community."
Asians	"Bad . . . Because some of my good friends is not here."	"Comfy and belonged because they are my own race . . . They know what my culture is."	"Even though my group was having fun I felt isolated and lonely."	
Native Americans	"Sad that I wasn't with people I normally talk to; sorry for people who had to clean."	"I didn't really feel anything because . . . we were just talking about our culture . . ."		

American-Born Hispanics	"Angry and frustrated . . . I was separated from my buddies; my group had to pick up trash . . ."	"I was getting to know what descrimination felt like . . . it was pretty exciting."	"Unjust . . . they made [us] do manual labor and clean up. I was frustrated."	"we were treated below and less what the other groups were."	"I felt proud because it was some of my friends and we stuck together."	"It was fun . . . everyone was getting along and when we got mad we all calmed each other down."
Multiracials	"I am proud to be mixed."	". . . because we all had a little bit of everything in us, so its not like we were separated totally."	"It felt cool I mean I got to say what I wasn't to say and my words were heard clear."	"I felt OK because my group was very friendly and playing around."		
Mexican-Born Hispanics	"I was going to do something but I was not sure if to do it."	"I felt proud but bad. I'm very good to communicate with my race. I also felt bad because I saw [isolate] alone."	"I felt mad and sad being a member of the hispanics. The reason is that I now realize what they actually went through years ago . . ."	"It felt very bad because now we understand how it is to be a Mexican who is always bossed around . . ."	". . . After we got out I was thirsty so I went to the drinking fountain but it said it was for the White people only so I got a little madder . . ."	"It felt fun. I just felt like telling the negative people to shut the FUCK up and who cares everyone cleans in life make the best possible about it."

Isolate	"Uneasy and boring. I felt like I was in trouble . . ."			
African Americans	"They were disrepecting us by telling us that we needed to move . . ."	"I felt OK at first . . . but then I was pissed because I didn't like the attitude we was given."	"I didn't feel anything about being in my group I just wanted to know why we were separated by race."	"I liked being in my group because I was comfortable."	"I am very proud to be African-American, so it didn't bother me a lot. I am proud of the goals I have accomplished and the things I have been through."

Exercise 3

White Males	"It was relaxing to just sit and watch TV . . . made me feel guilty and embarrassed to go outside and reunite with friends, not knowing how they would react and judge us."	"It felt comfortable . . . being comfortable allowed us to block out some things we saw but also made us feel guilty."	"Not only did we all know each other, we were constantly isolated from the other groups . . . I was ashamed of my group's special treatment."		
Blonde Females	"It did not feel too bad, because we felt we were doing something meaningful."	"I try hard not to demonstrate the media's version of a woman . . . I plan on using the anger I have now; putting it towards CHANGE."	"We were very confused because our group assignment wasn't that abnormal."	"It felt kind of petty and pathetic that we were sitting around putting on makeup . . ."	"I felt priv-ileged and isolated . . ."
Non-Blonde Female	"I felt like I was being forced to fulfill the role of a woman as my mother always told me not to. But . . . I felt like I was making someone else's job easier . . ."				

Latinos	"Our group was dysfunctional . . . I enjoyed it at times . . . I felt like I didn't want to listen to the authority, but then didn't have the guts to stand up to it."	"It felt great because I have a lot of pride."	"I felt by listening to the adults and they saying good job I was making my people proud but I was wrong."	"It didn't feel any different than what I see everyday because of stereotypes . . ."	"Normal. We all understood each other yet most of the group was against rebelling."
Jewish	"OK. We were not particularly stereotyped or anything."	"I resented being told I am only a Jew because I consider Judaism simply my religion, not who I am . . ."	"Lonely, boring, and without the people I wanted to be with."		
Multiracials	"I felt ashamed because I didn't know much about my family coming here from Panama."	"I was nervous but could relate to everyone there."	"I felt very comfortable . . . [we were] treated neutral, not bad but not the best."		

Isolates	"I loved that I was representing my people but it was not great being alone . . ."	"I hated it being all by myself. I loved it when . . . the revolt came over and tried to bring me over to their side."			
LGBTQQ	"It felt terrible being considered only a lesbian. It felt dehumanizing, degrading, and embarrassing.	"Suffocating. Because I was shut in a tiny closet with four other people. Because all the seriousness and fear and unfairness felt was so overpowering."	"It was sad because some people came over to us and tried to get us to break free and some of our members started to cry."	"Awful—being constantly reprimanded by authority figures feels bad."	

			"It felt very stereotypical. I felt as if they expected manners and discipline. For us to be smart and silent."	
Asians	"I don't really know how I felt . . . I felt kind of 'dissed' that I was in a 'typical' Asian group with mainly Chinese and Viet."	"I felt annoyed. I didn't want to be segregated from other people . . . I knew it was wrong."	"I felt like I wanted to scream because I couldn't look anywhere or move around and I felt so confused."	
South Asian/ Middle Eastern	"Not terrible because personnally I have never been a victim of terrorist stereotypes."	"I don't like being separated, but I thought it was something done for a reason . . ."	"I felt like they expected us to know everything about terrorism, which I obviously don't. I also didn't know why I was in the group I was in . . . I am also latina & multiracial . . ."	

Privileged Blacks	"It felt weird. We were all Black but then again I felt connected to them."	"It felt normal . . . our group wasn't really affected or yelled at."	"I felt angry and ignored."	"I felt insulted because the topic we had to write about made me feel like I couldn't make it to college without affirmative action."	
Black Males	"I felt fine, because I know everyone in my group."	"It felt good because we were trying to make a stand against all the advisors and co-directors."	"I felt the authority was being abused . . . [B]lacks have been oppressed for so many years that it felt like we all immediately understood our situation."	"I felt important because I had a job to hold just like everyone else in the group."	"I felt trapped and it reminded me of Jim Crow and the sixties. Because we were so oppressed."

Appendix E

Responses to Question 4: "Why did you not break this exercise earlier than when you did?"

Exercise 1

Code	Example	%	No.
Fear of consequences	"I had a sort of fear or dislike of punishment for breaking the rules."	48	11
Confused about exercise	"I honestly didn't know what we were doing."	9	2
No one else was breaking	"We didn't 'break' the exercise because everyone or nobody did anything."	9	2
Waiting to be saved	"Because I thought Thomasina was going to come and 'rescue us.'"	9	2
(No answer)	—	9	2
Other	"Because some delegates were to pressure to make some decisions."	4	1
Tired of following rules	"I wanted to follow directions . . . but I got tired of standing and waiting so long."	4	1
I did break	"I did break the exercise."	4	1
Trusted authority	"I was given a rule and I followed it because I didn't think it was going to lead me in the wrong direction."	4	1

Exercise 2

Code	Example	%	No.
Fear of consequences	"I was scared about what was going to happen to me."	63	29
Confused about exercise	"Because I thought it was just an activity."	9	4
Needed help	"Until people started speaking up, I honestly didn't know how to."	4	2
(No answer)	—	4	2
Let others talk me out of it	"Honestly, I really wanted to break it, but I let the people around me talk me out of it and now I feel like crap for letting someone else have that power over me."	4	2
Not strong enough	"I was not strong enough to break it. I felt so bad because I thought I was too weak to."	2	1
Build up to anger, courage	"I guess it took me a long time to build up enough anger and guts to do so."	2	1
See what happens	"I wanted to get the full effect of what has happened, and what is still happening."	2	1
Didn't care	"The reason I didn't break it sooner is because I didn't think much of it."	2	1
Fake	"I did not break the exercise because I knew that it was not real."	2	1
Unaware	"I didn't experience in my opinion the full exercise because my group was inside cleaning."	2	1
Didn't want to be rude	"I didn't want to be rude or profane to anyone."	2	1

Exercise 3

Code	Example	%	No.
Fear of consequences	"I was scared of getting in trouble."	28	15
Confused about nature of exercise	"I was not sure if the exercise was real or fake."	17	9
Unaware of what was happening	"I didn't know any movement was going on. We were kind of secluded and didn't know what was going on outside of where we were."	9	5
Other	"My group broke very early we couldn't break too much earlier."	6	3
Didn't want to be a follower	"When the revolution began I didn't want to be a follower of something I didn't agree with wholeheartedly."	6	3
Afraid of leaving group	"I wanted to be with my Latino group but help ourselves at the same time."	6	3
Wanted to see what would happen	"Wanted to see how it shaped out."	4	2
No one else was breaking	"Because I was waiting on others and it was not great thing that I did."	4	2
(No answer)	—	4	2
Needed help	"Because I needed help."	4	2
Not unified enough	"We couldn't break because we were not organized or unified enough."	4	2
Knew it was fake	"Knew it was an exercise & FAKE."	2	1
Didn't think we would be accepted	"We didn't think our movements would be as valued by the group since we didn't receive any hardships."	2	1
Didn't care	"Because I really didn't care."	2	1

| Thought it would be wrong | "I thought it would be wrong to do it especially when a whole movement wasn't started yet." | 2 | 1 |
| Not sure | "I have no idea. I am still thinking about that." | 2 | 1 |

Appendix F

Quantitative Attention Distribution Charts by Exercise

Exercise 1

	White Males	White Females	Asians	Jewish	Latinos	Black Females	Black Males	Isolates	All	None	Unspecified
White Males	3						1				1
White Females			1	1		1					
Jewish							1				
Latinos	1				1	1	1			1	1
Black Females	1						1			1	1
Black Males	2				1	1					1
Isolates	1					1					1
Total	8	0	1	1	2	4	4	0	0	2	5

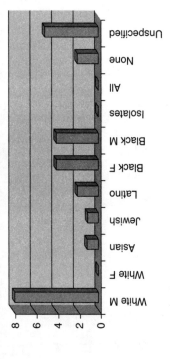

Exercise 2

	Whites	Asians	Native American	American-Born Hispanics	Multiracials	Mexican-Born Hispanics	Isolates	African Americans	All	Unspecified	Other
Whites		2				2	1	1	2		
Asians		1				1	1	1	1		
Native Americans		1					1		1		
American-Born Hispanics	1	1		1		2	2		1		
Multiracials					1		1	1	3		
Mexican-Born Hispanics	3	1		1		3	3		7	1	1
Isolates	1						1				
African Americans	1					1	1		1		1
Total	6	6	0	2	1	9	11	3	16	1	2

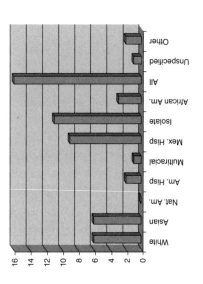

Exercise 3

	Blonde Females	Non-Blonde Females	White Males	Latinos	Jewish	Multiracials	Isolates	LGBTQQ	Asians	South Asian/Middle Easterners	Privileged Blacks	Black Males	All	None	Rebels	Unspecified	Other
Blonde Females				1				1				2	2		2		
Non-Blonde Females	1							1									1
White Males			1					1				1		2			
Latinos	1			1								4	3				
Jewish								1				2	1		1		
Multiracials	1			2								2	1				
Isolates												1	1				
LGBTQQ			1					1			1	2	1	1	2		
Asians								1								1	
South Asian/Middle Easterners				1				1				1			1		

Privileged Blacks				2							2		1	1	2	1	1
Black Males			1	3	1			2					2	1	1		
Total	3	0	3	10	2	0	0	6	0	0	2	17	10	4	8	2	1

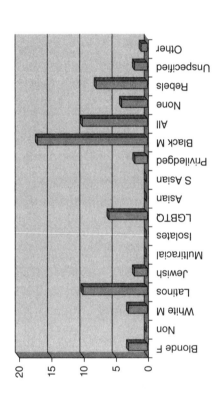

Appendix G

Qualitative Data Related to Question 3: "In your opinion, what was the most important group? Why?"

Exercise 1

			"they didn't clean, they had a lot of space for them like two bathrooms and the water fountain and the soda machine."
White	"they were treated better than other groups."	"because of the way they were treated."	"They supposedly was better and you can look at the history books."
	"they made us feel like shit."	"they got all the privileges and they got to do everything they wanted."	
Asians	"without them, no one would have had enough courage to stand up and break the rules."	"they were told they were not good enough to sing."	
Native Americans			
American-Born Hispanics			
Multiracials	"Our culture group was really cool and down to earth. We were similar in race also our thoughts and actions."		

Mexican-Born Hispanics	"[they] did all the dirty work."	"they were forced to work just like their ancestors did."	"they had to work hard they did good and were getting yelled at like bitches."	"they were the only ones working and doing something."
Isolates	"it was profound to see one person isolated and treated badly alone."	"he was the only one by himself and that cause people to feel for him."	"It showed that people still have emotions even people that don't show it."	"The group with only one person in it was most important."
	"Even though some people might look fine on their own, they might be in real pain and not be able to show it."	"this individual was important because although the groups were separated they wanted to associate with him."	"there are people like that but you don't actually notice because they are not your friends."	
African Americans	"[they] were the last to eat."	"they suffer so much and did so much."	"they went through stuff like this more than others."	
All	"Every group was reacting differently, yet all the same all at once."	"All the groups were important because without them the exercise would not have been as effective."	"It looked to me that no group standed out more than any other they all were the same."	"we should all be happy we can be with each other."

"we are all one, we were all important in this life-changing lesson."	"we were all treated importantly because we all have our views on life."	"All groups are important because once a person threw down his bandana, they all did as well."	"I love my friends very much and not being allowed to talk to them really hurt."

Exercise 2

White Males	"they were all treated like kings got their food given to them and didn't do anything. Which I think is just wrong."	"[They] had the most privilege."	"They got to go to breakfast first and had their food set up already."	"The White group was favored and was most important because their food was prepared . . ."
	"Because they are so set on obeying the rules and having things given to them and my group have to fight for the stuff we do here."	"People set their table for breakfast."	"It was as if they were masters, and everyone else were slaves."	"[They] had the most freedom."

	White Females			
Asians	"People sometimes forget them . . . Asians are not bad people . . . they are nice."			
Jewish	"It was hard to watch the Jewish group . . . sit in the hot sun . . ."			
Latinos	"they were the only people that cleaned."	"they did the most cleaning."		
Black Females	"Both the African-American groups were the most important because those participating in those groups broke the segregation barriers . . ."	"they were the only people that cleaned."	"[they] cleaned up after [the White males]."	"they did the most cleaning."
Black Males	"They have become go-getters from years of internalization and they were able to help somewhat break up the group."	"We had the most people."		
Isolates				
All				

None	"No group was important. Not even mine because we should be together."	"there are no other important groups . . . I was only thinking about our group and getting out of the sun . . ."	
Other	"Others, because they are people I know."		

Exercise 3

White Males	"they got all the privileges. they represented a group who benefited from oppression."	"the single group that was treated fairly was the White male and was the least likely to revolt due to the special treatment we received."	"they literally got to sit and relax basically throughout the whole exercise."	"[they] were treated with more respect."
Blonde Females	"they had to serve the 'better' groups."	"the latinos, Blacks, and women, because they had the impact of creating a diversified front."		
Non-Blonde Females				

Latinos	"[they] were necessary in organizing [the revolution]."	"they tried to assemble a successful march with powerful songs."	"they helped me realize I was right when I said I wanted to rebel."	"We were the ones who got the worst stereotypes."
Jewish	"they were the first 'non-colored' group to join the movement."			
Multiracials				
Isolates				
LGBTQQ	"they are a group that is constantly oppressed . . ."	"[they] were so heinously treated that they inspired others to stick up for them and rebel."	"[they] were locked in a closet."	"Their being put in a closet was the thing that inspired most people to feel what was happening was wrong."
	"they are some of the biggest groups of people that been isolated in society."			
Asians				

South Asian/ Middle Easterners				
Privileged Blacks				
Black Males	"[they] started the revolution."	"[they] were forced to march."	"they were the ones who made us realize what we were being forced to do."	"they started to rebel."
	"they broke the exercise."	"they started the revolution."	"they had to 'step' to entertain."	"tried to assemble a successful march with powerful songs."
Rebels	"they brought a lot of people together."	"we were the ones that changed the course of the exercise by rebelling."	"the first ones to walk out. They started the domino reaction."	"they understand oppression from their history and were the first to recognize it."
	"they abolished my ignorance."	"The Black group, the latino group, and the Jewish group. I felt that all of us were able to unite similar to the Civil Rights movement."		

All	"All groups were important . . . they had different levels of oppression just like in society."	"they were all stereotyped an then worked through it."	"They were all important because they all showed the oppression and although we know it is wrong we still choose to not help one another."	"we are all the same no matter what."
	"Everyone was extremely important because the exercise was about community."	"They were all important because we all had to stop listening to the staff."		
None	"Not only did our group fail to break out but no other groups even attempted to contact us."	"no group was better than the next."		

Other	"the groups with the most number of people because they had the most influence."	"because we spend most of our time off to ourselves we never saw too much of any group."	"he's important because he was the first to say that this exercise of oppression was bullshit."	"I think the enforcers/authority figures were most important . . . they proved how little effort it takes for someone to agree and comply with oppression both of themselves and others."

Acknowledgments

This book has had two lives: It came into the world first as a doctoral dissertation, and then over a decade later it was reborn as the significantly revised version you now hold in your hands. Over the course of the decade and a half it took to take this work from a grad student's research proposal to a rewritten and publishable manuscript, a whole lot of people provided support and guidance along the way.

Michael Nakkula was the chair of my doctoral committee back in grad school, and he was a source of tremendous wisdom and support throughout this process. He provided crucial guidance with the theory and practice of qualitative methodology along with invaluable emotional support and professional guidance over those exciting but challenging years. Robert Selman, the second member of my committee, began to push my thinking on these ideas as the instructor of my very first course as a doctoral student at the Harvard Graduate School of Education. As a student and TA for his courses over the years, I had the opportunity to reflect deeply on issues of perspective taking, moral development, and social dynamics. I am grateful for his guidance, patience, and encouragement. The third and final member of my committee, Hugh O'Doherty, has played a role that can appropriately be called spiritual guide on my journey. He modeled courage and compassion in confronting some of the great challenges of our age. I hope those qualities have inspired this work to some degree, and I am grateful for all the time we were able to work together.

In addition to my committee members, three other professors played a major role in the development of these ideas. My encounter with the adaptive leadership model developed by Ronald Heifetz was a revelation. His ideas about leadership, authority, and systemic change inform this study in fundamental ways. Carol Gilligan's work on moral development and relational psychology were also extremely influential. Her ideas inform this study in less direct but equally fundamental ways. I am grateful to have been able to work with both of them during my studies. Finally, Yaneer Bar-Yam introduced me to the dynamics of complex systems. I am grateful to have had the chance to study with him personally.

This research wouldn't have been possible without the support of many professionals connected with the National Conference for Community and Justice. They have requested confidentiality, so I will not mention their specific names here, but the research could not have happened without the consent of the national organization and local program directors. I am grateful for their willingness to let us in. Also, this pilot study could not have been conducted without the support of the staff members and participants at the exercises we visited.

Dumisani Nyoni and Derria Byrd were ideal research assistants. They both brought wisdom and experience to the task, and they tolerated some trying circumstances in the name of research. I particularly appreciate the time they arrived by rental car at 3 AM, only to catch three hours of sleep on uncomfortable bunk beds before waking at 6 AM to begin observation of the exercise. That, truly, was above and beyond the call of duty! They provided thoughtful analyses of the data, and I appreciate the hours they put into coding and discussion of the work in progress. I should also add they are both idealistic and powerful individuals doing great things in the world, and it was an inspiration to work with them on this project.

My summers were spent out of the classroom, but those experiences were frequently as important to the development of these ideas as my time in school. Thanks to the staff members and participants of Genesis at Brandeis University in 1999 and 2000. Thanks also to my coleaders and participants on the American Jewish World Service International Jewish College Corps program to Honduras and Ukraine in 2002, and the IJCC trip to Ghana and Ukraine in 2003. Our conversations while digging ditches, lugging bricks, and pouring concrete are as much a part of this research as my academic papers and classroom discussion over the past six years.

Just a few months after completing my doctorate, I had the remarkable good fortune to land a job at City Year. I may have left academia at that point, but the learning that happened in my time there was every bit as important as my studies in the classrooms of Harvard. I'm grateful to Michael Brown and Alan Khazei for launching what is undeniably a great American institution, and to Andy Munoz, who hired me to work in the research department he ran at City Year. I'm grateful to Stephanie Wu, who gave me the freedom to innovate with some new practices related to leadership development and allowed the experiments to continue even when initial efforts were, shall we say, underwhelming. I'm grateful to a vast number of City Year corps and staff members who pushed my thinking, challenged my assumptions, and inspired me on a daily basis. And I offer special thanks to Charlie Rose, who was an invaluable guide, mentor, and champion during my time there. He is true social justice warrior, a wholehearted leader of leaders, and among the most woke and spiritually evolved individuals I've been blessed to meet.

When I finally got around to revising my dissertation for publication as a book, a host of friends and colleagues agreed to read my drafts and provide invaluable feedback. Thanks to Angel Acosta, Ejaj Ahmad, Yoni Bock, Alice Chen, Ora Grodsky, Hubie Jones, Metta McGarvey, Roberta Oster Sachs, Gary and

Jill Rabideau, Charlie Rose, my sister Michal Klau-Stevens, and my twin brother, Nathan Klau, for their time, effort, and thoughtful comments.

Thanks also to Susan Komives for very generously recommending me to her colleagues at Jossey-Bass. It's been a pleasure working with Alison Knowles and Connor O'Brien at Jossey-Bass; they have proven to be able guides over the course of this process of getting my first book out into the world.

A great deal of credit for this book also goes to my amazing parents, David and Barbara Klau, and my awesome siblings—Daniel Klau, Deborah Ordan, Michal Klau-Stevens, and Nathan Klau—as well as their wonderful spouses and many beloved offspring. The truth is that this book is really just the continuation of decades of memorable and formative discussions around the Klau dinner table. It's a discussion that began decades ago with the seven of us and over the years grew to include today's vastly expanded multigenerational, highly opinionated, extremely verbal family. I know I'm not the only one of us who looks forward to this discussion continuing on for many, many more years to come!

Finally, I offer a special prayer of gratitude for my remarkable wife, Beverly, who in so many ways both direct and indirect made this book possible. Thanks for the constant support and encouragement, the thoughtful and constructive feedback, the rock-solid emotional strength and boundless ability to manage our family and home in ways that gave me the space to get this done. Quite simply, I couldn't do any of this without you, Bev.

This book is dedicated to my endlessly amazing, entertaining, and inspiring kids, Bernie and Sadie. May it contribute in some small way to improving the world they and their generation will inherit in the years ahead.

Index

Civil rights movement (1960s);
People of color
Blind men and the elephant meta-
phor, 22–23
"Blind spot" of leadership, 198–199
Bloodlines (Volkan), 242
Blue eyes/brown eyes exercise (1968):
description and outcomes of, 49–52;
epiphanies and increased empathy
outcomes of the, 175; intergroup
level of analysis of, 52–55, 70–71,
164; origins and purpose of, 48.
See also Elliot, Jane
Bond, R., 42
Bosnia-Herzegovina civil war, 242
Boy Scouts of the USA, 291
Boys and Girls Club, 291
Brafman, Ori, 93–94
Bridgeland, J., 288
A Brief History of Humankind (Har-
ari), 87
Brinsley, Ismaaiyl, 261
"Broken windows" theory of crime
reduction, 59n.1
Brooks, David, 296–297
Brown, Michael, 3, 33, 34, 261
Buddha (Siddhartha Gautama), 282,
295
Butterfly effect, 61–62

C
Call to action. *See* Dual call to action
Camp Anytown program: description
of the, 5, 25; expertise of those
running the, 29–30; higher consciousness and deeper understanding
outcomes of the, 30; history and
philosophy of NCCJ and, 29–30,
112–113; important insights on
social change learned at, 6–9;
Separation Exercise experience
at the, 5–9, 10, 25–28, 30–31.
See also National Conference for
Community and Justice (NCCJ);
Separation Exercise (Camp Anytown)

Campbell, Joseph: comparative
mythologist work by, 270;
The Hero with a Thousand Faces
by, 277–278, 281; insights into the
hero's journey by, 276–284; on in-
ternal awareness and outer participation, 269
Canada: mistreatment of indigenous
peoples by, 246; Truth and Recon-
ciliation (2008) to acknowledge and
change treatment of indigenous
peoples, 247
Cardazone, G., 293
Carson, Johnny, 51
Carter, Jimmy, 242
Castile, Philando, 3, 35
Category I systems: description of, 73;
none of the Separation Exercises
as, 181
Category II systems: description of, 73;
Thomasina and Drake's System
(Exercise 1) as a, 180
Category III systems: description
of, 73–74; none of the Separation
Exercises as, 181
Category IV systems: description
of, 74; John and Susan's System
(Exercise 3) as, 181
Cell walls, 63
Cellular automata tool: emergence of
stable patterns in simulations
using, 68fig–69fig; insights into nat-
ure of complex systems using
the, 70–72; model of panic simu-
lated using the, 67fig
Chakra system (India), 273
Challenger explosion, 242
Chavez, Cesar, 101, 108
China: Great Leap Forward, 107–108;
Olympic Games held in, 102
"Chosen traumas," 242–243
City Year: description and focus of
the, 32–33; education focus
of, 292–293; volunteer national
service opportunities through,
288

of one's higher, 273–276; *ubuntu* philosophy of, 272–273, 275, 295; understanding the system and context of the, 263–267

Self-organization: cellular automata tool for simulation of, 66–70; complex systems characteristic of, 65–72; evidence of system-level, 65–66; flocks of bird formation example of, 66, 70

Seneca Falls Convention (1848), 97

Senge, Peter, 207–208, 249–252

Separation Exercise (Camp Anytown): as civil rights movement petri dish, 6, 28; description of the, 5–6, 25–28, 111, 294; developing a complex methodology for study of, 31–32, 113–114; higher consciousness and deeper understanding outcomes of the, 30; interpersonal and intergroup level of analysis of, 10; metaphor hero's journey and mythical wisdom of the, 279–280, 282–283; Palmer's hidden wholeness theme illuminating the research on, 204–206; potential of individual power to transform system of, 248; processing session to reflect on individual experiences, 160–161; realizing the potential to learn from this, 28; receiving IRB approval for doctoral research using the, 29–32; relevance to the "real world" and social change insights, 6–9, 13, 30–31, 275–276; "time collapse" phenomenon observed during, 244; weighing ethical concerns of the, 30–31. *See also* Camp Anytown program; Human behavior experiments; Simulations; Staff members

Separation Exercise intergroup level of analysis: asking what group were most important question for, 164–165; Exercise 3 "rebels" led

by Eduardo, 135–140, 172–173, 192, 197, 201, 275; qualitative attention distribution for Exercises 2 and 3, 172–173; qualitative attention distribution grid for Exercise 1, 168–173; quantitative attention distribution for all exercises, 165–168; special attention in Exercise 2 on Asians, 134, 172. *See also* Intergroup level of analysis

Separation Exercise interpersonal level of analysis: differences between those who did and did not break exercise, 159; Exercise 1—Thomasina and Drake's System, 147–151, 163t; Exercise 2—Connie and Laurie's System, 151, 163t–164; Exercise 3—John and Susan's System, 152 t–153, 163t; exploring connection between individual and systemic change, 153–156; exploring individual agency, 161–164; findings on power of conformity, 156; frustration regarding their identified race/ethnicity finding, 150; guilt and shame evoked by hierarchical privilege, 151–152; lesson on possibility of overcoming fear, 160; memories evoked of a historical trauma finding of, 151; processing session to reflection on experiences, 160–161; questionnaire given to participants used for, 144–145; reports on experience of LGBTQ participant, 152t–153; responses to how it felt to break the exercise, 157–161; responses to question about not breaking exercise earlier, 154–156; revelations on pain experienced by isolates, 149t, 152; sample questionnaire responses by participants, 145–147; understanding self in the system, 264. *See also* Interpersonal level of analysis